RELIGIONS
IN THE
MODERN WORLD

FOR JUNIOR CERTIFICATE

Shuna Hutchinson-Edgar

Gill & Macmillan

Gill & Macmillan
Hume Avenue
Park West
Dublin 12

www.gillmacmillan.ie

© Shuna Hutchinson-Edgar

978 07171 5278 0

The paper used in this book is made from the wood pulp of managed forests.
For every tree felled, at least one tree is planted, thereby renewing natural resources.

For permission to reproduce photographs, the author and publisher gratefully acknowledge the following:

© Alamy: 3T, 3C, 4T, 4B, 6, 7T, 7B, 12, 21R, 21L, 24R, 25, 26L, 28, 29, 31T, 31B, 33, 37, 43TR, 43BL, 43BR, 43CR, 45, 46T, 46B, 55, 66L, 66CL, 66CR, 71T, 72T, 81T, 82T, 82B, 87T, 87B, 88, 89, 90T, 90B, 91T, 91B, 93T, 93CT, 93CB, 93B, 100, 101, 110B, 111T, 111B, 112, 115, 117, 118T, 118B, 119T, 120, 123, 124, 135, 139, 140, 141, 146T, 148, 149, 150, 151T, 151CR, 151L, 151CR, 151BR, 152, 153B, 155T, 163, 168T, 168B, 169L, 170T, 170BL, 173, 174TL, 174CLT, 174CLB, 174BR, 174BL, 181T, 183, 185B, 187, 192CR, 193T, 193BL, 194, 201L, 201R, 202TL, 202TR, 202BL, 202BR, 204T, 207T, 207B, 211T, 211B, 212, 213T, 213B, 214T, 214B, 217T, 220, 221, 225, 227B, 234L, 234C, 239T, 239B, 240, 241, 243, 243, 245B, 246B, 247B, 254, 256, 257L, 257R, 259TL, 259TR, 259B, 262L, 262R, 263B, 266, 267T, 267B, 268T, 268B, 272B, 273CL, 273C, 273B, 276T, 276B, 277TL, 277TCL, 277TC, 277TCR, 277BCR, 277BR, 278B, 279R, 280T, 280C, 280B, 284T, 284B, 285T, 285C, 285B, 286, 287T, 299, 300B, 302B, 304T, 307, 315, 316B, 317, 318C, 319T, 319L, 319CL, 319CR, 319R, 325L, 325R, 330T, 332L, 332R, 334R, 338, 339L, 339C, 339R, 340, 345B; © Bridgeman: 70, 80R, 83T, 84, 102, 181B; © Collins: 7B, 35, 51T, 59T, 164T, 164B, 185T, 260, 308TL; © Corbis: 36B, 59, 119B, 304BL, 323; © Getty Images: 3B, 14, 24L, 26R, 34T, 42, 43TL, 48, 51B, 54, 56, 57B, 66R, 72B, 77, 81B, 99, 110T, 114, 136, 142T, 142B, 146B, 151CL, 152BR, 153T, 154, 167, 170BR, 171, 174TR, 174CR, 175T, 178, 184, 196R, 204B, 216T, 228, 229, 234R, 238, 244C, 244R, 245T, 246T, 247T, 253, 255, 257C, 259TC, 263T, 265T, 265B, 272T, 273TL, 273TC, 273TR, 274, 277BL, 277BCL, 277BC, 287BL, 287BR, 288, 290, 296, 300T, 301B, 308CR, 314L, 314C, 314R, 316T, 318L, 318R, 319BR, 331, 334L, 335; © Imagefile: 22, 71B, 113, 169R, 172, 175B, 216B, 227T, 277TR; © Inpho: 16T, 16B; © Irish Times: 308B, 345T; © Kobal: 137L; © Mary Evans Picture Library: 59B, 80L; © Moviestore Collection: 137R; © National Library of Ireland: 196L; © Photocall Ireland: 13, 164CR, 249, 302T; © Press Association: 301; © Rex Features: 152T, 217B, 304BR, 308TR, 330B; © Shutterstock: 309CL, 310CTR; © Sportsfile: 244L; © Superstock: 125; © Topfoto: 34B, 198; Courtesy of Christopher Moriarty: 38; Courtesy of Corrymeela Community: 47TL, 47TR; Courtesy of Dublin City Library & Archive: 155B; Courtesy of Scouting Ireland: 279L; Courtesy of State Examination Commission: 10, 53T, 53B, 106T, 106B, 177, 218, 223, 251, 270, 282, 305, 341; Courtesy of The United Dioceses of Dublin and Glendalough (Church of Ireland): 50; Courtesy of Wikimedia: 20TR, 36T, 152L, 309TR, 309TL, 309CR, 309BR, 310TR, 310TL, 310CTL, 310CBR, 310CBL, 310BR, 310BL.

The author and publisher have made every effort to trace all copyright holders, but if any has been inadvertently overlooked we would be pleased to make the necessary arrangement at the first opportunity.

Contents

Note: The chapters marked with ✸ are for Higher Level only.

Note: The chapters marked with H are for Higher Level only.

Section

a

Communities

of Faith

This section of the syllabus aims:

- To explore the nature and pattern of human communities.
- To identify the characteristics of communities of faith/churches.
- To examine these characteristics as they occur in communities of faith/churches in local, national and international examples.

Community

Key Concepts

community, role, co-operation, sharing/share, communication, community breakdown

What is a community?

A community is a group of people with something in common. Most people belong to many communities. The smallest community most people belong to is their family.

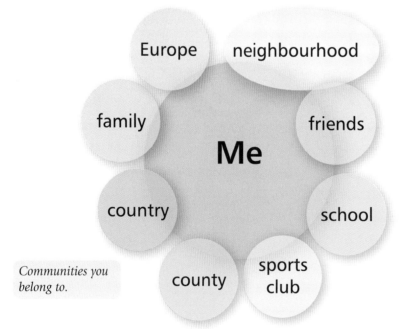

Communities you belong to.

Glossary

Community
A group of people having a particular characteristic in common.

In every community people have different roles, parts to play or jobs to do. Think of your school: it is a community, as all the people in it have membership of this school in common.

Glossary

Role
The function or part played by a person in a particular situation.

What roles are there in a school?

- Teachers
- Students
- Principal
- Year heads
- Form teachers
- Tutors
- Caretaker
- Cleaners
- Others.

The people in a school community
have a variety of different roles: to lead, to listen, to provide
things, to organise, to communicate, to administer etc.
Each role needs to be carried out or the community doesn't work.
Being able to work well with others is called co-operation.

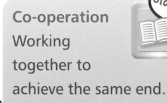

Co-operation
Working
together to
achieve the same end.

Glossary

Discuss

How important is co-operation in
a school community?

Other communities people belong to include:

- Sports clubs
- Friends
- Music groups
- Drama clubs
- Religions
- Neighbourhoods
- Charities
- Political groups.

Over
to You

Write a page on any community you
belong to, describing three roles
and how important co-operation is
to make it work.

The benefits of living, working and sharing in communities

It is clear that not only humans live in communities: when you look at nature you can see many examples of animals, insects, fish and birds living in communities. Take the bee, for example: honeybee hives have long provided humans with honey and beeswax. All honeybees are social and co-operative insects. A hive's inhabitants are generally divided into three types: the queen, drones and workers. These three roles need to be fulfilled or the colony will not work.

In the frozen Antarctic, the emperor penguin must co-operate with others in the colony for survival. In temperatures of minus 60°C, the penguins huddle together to escape wind and conserve warmth. Individuals take turns moving to the group's protected and relatively warm interior. Once a penguin has warmed a bit, it will move to the edge of the group so that others can enjoy protection from the icy elements. Emperor penguins not only spend the winter on the ice, they also breed during this harsh season.

Did you know? At sea, emperor penguins can dive to 1,850 feet (565 metres) — deeper than any other bird — and stay under for more than 20 minutes. David Attenborough's *Life* series is very useful for looking at animal communities.

Over to You In groups or pairs, research two examples from nature where creatures live in communities and show what benefits they get from being in a community instead of being solitary.

For humans there are many benefits to living in communities. They are important in many different ways: it is easier to share resources and to organise transport, schools, hospitals etc. Communities work on the basis of people being able to share – whether that is objects, ideas, resources or talents. Communities may be local, national or international. In your school community, teachers share their knowledge. Within the government, people share ideas about how to run the country. In the European community, people share citizenship – they all belong to the EU. In the international community, World Health Organization doctors and scientists share their skills to help the world's citizens.

Sharing
Having part of something with others.
A share
A person's part or contribution to something.

Glossary

Discuss What roles are there in the family community and what is shared by its members?

Further benefits for people living in a community

Not only are communities important in providing for people's physical needs, living in a community with others is very important in providing for people's emotional and spiritual needs. Abraham Maslow, a psychologist in the twentieth century, came up with a list (hierarchy) of people's needs. As well as having physical needs such as the need for food, water, shelter etc., Maslow listed other needs that people have.

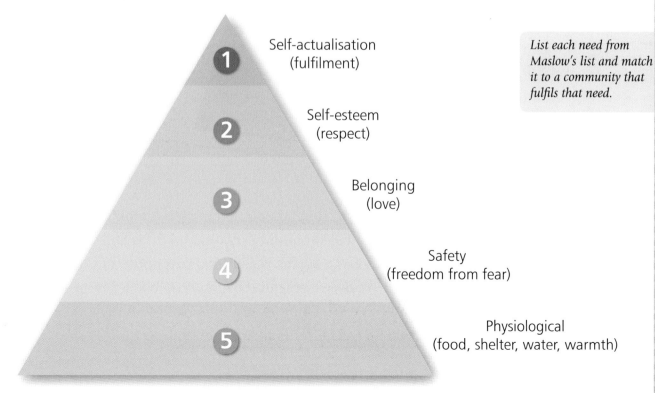

1. Self-actualisation (fulfilment)
2. Self-esteem (respect)
3. Belonging (love)
4. Safety (freedom from fear)
5. Physiological (food, shelter, water, warmth)

List each need from Maslow's list and match it to a community that fulfils that need.

Problems in communities

Mostly communities encounter difficulties or problems when:

- People don't carry out their roles.
- There is a problem with co-operation.
- There is a lack of communication.
- People argue about what is happening.
- There is poor leadership.

Communication

Communication basically refers to the way people share information or ideas. Good communication is vital for a community to work. If people who are trying to achieve something fail to communicate properly, then it is likely they will fail to achieve much.

We communicate in a number of ways in the twenty-first century – talking, texting, emailing, writing, phoning, television, Facebook, Skype etc.

The fact that we can communicate easily does not mean that there are no communication problems. Think about a time you received a message too late or misunderstood a message. Friends often fall out over a mix-up in communication: 'I never said that' or 'That's not what I meant'. The same can happen in communities. If people don't know what

Write out which of these three you last used and for what purpose.

their role is meant to be, don't mention if there is a problem, and don't communicate, the community falls apart. This is known as community breakdown. Conflict is a normal part of life and there are ways of dealing with disagreements. Getting people to agree again is often difficult but worthwhile. A person in charge of this sort of process needs certain skills to do this.

Communication | Glossary
Imparting or exchanging information by speaking, writing or using some other medium.

Community breakdown | Glossary
When a community fails to work and is no longer achieving its aims or is not benefiting its members.

Possessing a skill means having the ability to do something well. For example, some people can be skilled in communicating, organising or problem solving, while others do well at encouraging others. Members having and using different skills helps a community.

When does conflict or disagreement arise in communities? What sort of skills would a person need to deal with conflict in a community?

Leaders

One of the most important roles in any community is the leader. A leader guides and takes charge of a group of people. A good leader or a bad leader influences most people in a community. Leaders have different styles of leading: some lead by example, some are good communicators, some challenge people and some are persuasive. Many leaders use more than one style.

Religion and community

So, what has all this to do with religion? Well, you may have already noticed that religions are types of communities. People of the same religion have belief, faith and outlook on life in common. You may not always agree with everything or have much else in common with some of the others in your religion, but you are still part of the same community as others in that religion.

In what area of life did these people lead? How did they become leaders?

Examples of religious communities

There are literally hundreds of religions worldwide: the big ones are Christianity, Islam, Judaism, Hinduism, Sikhism and Buddhism. Within each of these, there are also many branches or groups.

There are many other religions too. Some of these religions have millions of members worldwide. Have you ever heard of the following?

Religion	Members
Baha'i	6 million
Zoroastrianism	190,000
Candomblé	2 million
Unitarianism	800,000
Jainism	4.2 million

What is religion?

It is extremely difficult to define religion in a sentence or even a paragraph. Religion is about many different things and means different things to different people. Some religions involve a belief in a God or Gods; others have no definite belief in a God. Some involve teachings that followers have to believe; other religions are more of a way of life.

Religion is about many things. The following list of words is just a beginning – you should add your own ideas to it.

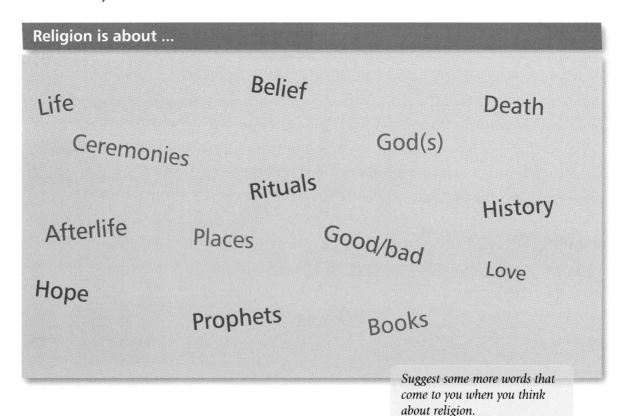

Religion is about ...

Life Belief Death

Ceremonies God(s)

Rituals

History

Afterlife Places Good/bad

Love

Hope

Prophets Books

Suggest some more words that come to you when you think about religion.

Copy the words down and add some of your own ideas. When you have finished, in your own words try to write an answer to the question, 'What is Religion?'

Religion has been around as long as there have been people in the world. For many people, it is of ultimate importance to their life and death. It provides a way of viewing their place in the world. It gives a sense of order to the world and a reason for existence. Throughout the world, religion is expressed in a variety of ways. Studying the phenomenon of religion involves looking at the particular ways it is practised, and understanding the ideas behind the actions, words and ways of life which are part of the different religions in our world today.

Key Terms

community, role, co-operation, sharing/share, communication, community breakdown

Chapter Questions

1. What is a community?
2. Name three roles in any community to which you belong.
3. Define co-operation.
4. Who was Abraham Maslow?
5. What human needs did Maslow list?
6. What problems do most communities deal with?
7. What is the role of a leader of a community?

Exam Practice

Ordinary Level 2008: Short question
A community is a group of people who share something in common: true or false.

Exam Practice

Higher or Ordinary Level 2007: Picture question

Pick **one** thing from the photograph that shows this religious sister is serving the needs of others.

Name **one** example of a community.

Suggest **two** reasons why people need to be part of a community.

Mini-Project

Write about any community you belong to using the following headings:

- Name of the community
- Leader
- Roles
- Aims of the community
- Your role
- Co-operation
- Communication
- Problems.

Communities at Work

2

Key Concepts

commitment, service, vision, leadership

As we have seen, all people belong to a variety of communities: from family to friends, school, neighbourhood, youth clubs, sports clubs, country and the world. Community means people sharing something in common. This might be a common aim or the pursuit of a common interest. Communities are essential in helping people to fulfil their needs. This might be by providing food and shelter, or by helping people to achieve their full potential and to feel confident, worthwhile, safe and loved.

Classwork

List as many different local, national and international organisations as you can think of. Choose three from the list and answer the following:

1. What is each organisation trying to do?
2. Do any have similarities?
3. How do they benefit individuals?
4. How do they benefit the wider world?
5. Identify three roles within each organisation.

Participation and commitment

Every community organisation requires people to take part. Participation can be in many different ways, from turning up to train for a football team to helping organise a fundraiser for the club. Without people's involvement and participation, an

Commitment
Dedication to a person, cause or activity.

organisation will not be able to work. When people become involved, they make a commitment – they undertake to do something in that organisation. Some people become very involved and show great commitment or dedication to help the community they are a member of.

Over to You

How do people show they are committed to something?

James Cameron, the movie director, made the films *Titanic* and *Avatar*. Here he talks about the commitment that is necessary to make such big productions. He also acknowledges the need for others to participate. The community he is leading is made up of actors, producers, technicians, engineers, writers etc. There are many roles in any community and it is important for everyone to play their part.

'You have to have made the commitment within yourself to do whatever it takes to get the job done and to try to inspire other people to do it, because obviously the first rule is you can't do it by yourself.'

James Cameron

Serving the community

In many organisations, people involved serve others and the community. When someone fulfils their role in a community, they are serving that community. To serve others is to do something for the benefit of other people or the wider community. Some organisations are set up with the idea of serving others as their main aim.

Service
The action of helping or doing work for someone.

Discuss service as 'doing something for others'. What do you do for others? How do you help friends, family, people in class, school, sports clubs etc.? Would you like to work for others in the future?

A community serving others: Dublin Simon Community

The Dublin Simon Community was set up in 1969 by a group of Trinity College and UCD students who started providing soup and sandwiches to people sleeping rough in Dublin city centre.

Since then the community has grown and now its work is to prevent and address homelessness in Dublin. Services include: the Rough Sleeper Team who engage with those sleeping rough on the streets; emergency accommodation; specialist health, addiction treatment and learning services; help for people to make the transition from homelessness to support in their own homes.

The mission of the Simon Community is to provide high-quality services to homeless people to end long-term homelessness. Their vision is that everyone who is homeless, or at risk of being homeless, has the support they need to access and maintain a home of their own.

The Dublin Simon Community has values of respect and integrity. They believe in giving people a sense of belonging, and of being fair and equal in their dealings with people.

How is the homeless person in the picture being shown respect?

Vision

Like the Simon Community, many organisations that are active in communities have a vision. This is the goal or aim of the organisation; it is what they hope to achieve.

1. How and when was the Simon Community formed?
2. What is the aim of the organisation?
3. How does the organisation try to achieve its aim?
4. What would the organisation like to see happening in the future?
5. Find out more about the work of the Simon Community and give a presentation to another class on the work of their volunteers.

Glossary

Vision
To see. In this sense, having a plan for the future, imagining what it could be like and what it is you are working towards.

One Irish organisation that is active at a local, national and even international level is the GAA. The community of the GAA has a clear vision to serve the community, and has a dedicated and committed membership. The GAA is led by an elected president and there are many other roles in this widespread Irish community.

How important is Croke Park to the members of the GAA?

Profile of a community: the GAA

Founded in 1884 in Thurles, County Tipperary, the Gaelic Athletics Association (GAA) was set up for 'the preservation and cultivation of national pastimes'. As such, it is a cultural and sporting association. With over 2,300 clubs, the GAA is a very active community at all levels of Irish society. Members are encouraged to have a strong sense of community at local or club level, while also being members of a larger national community.

GAA values

The values of the GAA – that which is important to the association – are to help people of all abilities to reach their full potential, to provide the best facilities and playing experience for members, and to enrich the lives of individuals, their families and their community. The GAA aims to foster a sense of identity, to encourage respect both on and off the field, and to promote the value of teamwork. This value is most evident in their slogan: 'Ní neart go cur le chéile'. (There is no strength without working together.)

The GAA aims to be inclusive and to serve all its members. It also encourages service as it is a volunteer-led organisation. To volunteer is to offer freely to undertake a task or to work for an organisation without being paid.

How important is teamwork in any organisation?

GAA mission and vision

The mission of the GAA – what it wants to do – is to promote Gaelic games, culture and lifelong participation. The vision of the association is: *'... that everybody has the opportunity to be welcomed, to take part in games and culture, to participate fully, to grow, develop and to be inspired to keep a lifelong engagement with the association.'*

GAA structure and leadership

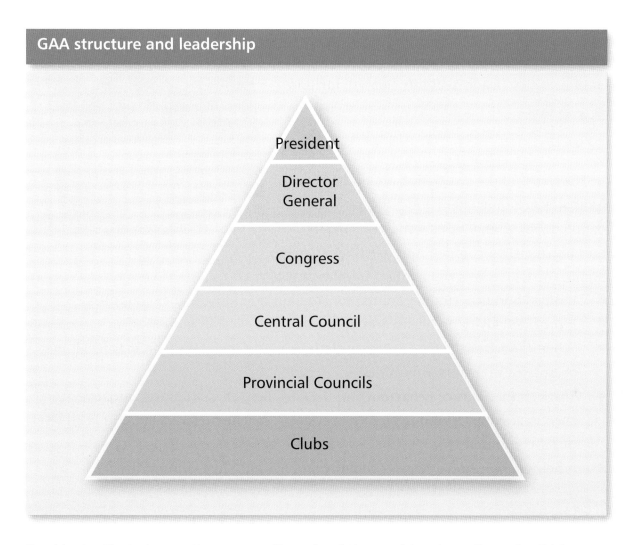

President – Elected every three years. The role of the president is to direct the GAA, develop policy, appoint committees and act as ambassador for the association.

Director General – Responsible for the day-to-day running of the association. The president and director general work together.

Congress – An Annual General Meeting is held with representatives from all subsections of the association. It elects the president and oversees changes to rules.

Central Council – The governing body.

Provincial Councils – Govern the provinces.

Clubs – Train and foster players, organise community-based activities and provide the facilities for social interaction among members.

As we have seen, the leader of the GAA is democratically elected every three years. The person who gets the honour of leading this community will have to have the support of a majority of the members. They will usually have worked their way up the association from the grassroots level of the clubs. The skills of the leader will vary but will include being able to communicate, listen, make decisions, direct, encourage and inspire.

Leadership

Glossary

The action of leading a group of people or an organisation, and having the ability to do this.

What qualities do you think a president most needs?

The sports of the association are hurling, football (including ladies' football), camogie, handball and rounders. As well as organising training, matches, competitions, facilities and club events, the GAA serves its members in other ways:

- It offers bursaries (money grants) for students attending higher education.
- It provides advice on health and injuries.
- Schemes such as the GAA Social Initiative support members who may feel lonely or isolated in their communities.
- Through the Code of Behaviour and the Give Respect Get Respect initiative, it encourages respect among players, spectators, coaches, referees etc. and at all levels of the community.
- It helps people find a sense of identity and place in their community.

Did you know?

The social initiative of the GAA was set up when former president Mary McAleese and her husband Dr Martin McAleese observed a lack of participation of older men at community functions. A forum was set up to look into this problem and this initiative emerged as a result.

Over to You

Draw a jersey with your county colours in your copy.

Which of the needs from Maslow's Hierarchy of Needs (see Chapter 1) is fulfilled by wearing your club or county colours?

The GAA – looking to the future

The 'Inclusion and Integration Strategy', launched in 2009, was set up to make the association a welcoming environment for everyone. The vision to be achieved by 2016 is as follows: *'We have an outstanding reputation for attracting and retaining members in all our sports from all sections of the community. We welcome people of all nationalities, ethnicities, religions, ages and abilities into our sports and we make it easy for everybody to take part.'*

1. When and why was the GAA founded?
2. In what way is the GAA a community?
3. Who is the leader of the GAA?
4. Identify three roles in the GAA.
5. Explain how the GAA helps people in the community.
6. What does it mean to volunteer?
7. What is the GAA's vision?
8. How did the social initiative come about?
9. In what ways does the GAA try to be inclusive?
10. List three ways the GAA serves its members.

Key Terms

commitment, service, vision, leadership

Chapter Questions

1. Why is participation so important for any community?
2. Explain what it means to be committed to something.
3. Describe what it means to serve the needs of others.
4. What does it mean to have a vision?
5. Why was the Dublin Simon Community set up?
6. Do you think communities benefit from having a vision?
7. What is the role of a leader of a community?

Exam Practice

Higher Level 2007: Section 4, question 1

Giving direction is one way a person can lead a community. Outline what is involved in **two** other ways of leading a community that could be used by a leader.

Explain how the way in which a community is led can have an effect on its members.

Being a leader is one role a person can have within a community. Describe another role a person can have within a community.

Mini-Project

Read the mission statement of the Society of St Vincent de Paul (SVP) and in your own words explain what it means.

Find out the about:

1. The origins of the SVP
2. The work of the SVP

The founder of the SVP, Frederic Ozanam, instructed his followers that their work for those in need must be 'of love, of kindness', giving of their time, their talents and themselves. Do you think the society still tries to follow that instruction? Why? You can find some information on the website *www.svp.ie*.

Communities of Faith

3

Key Concepts

denomination, religion, sacred text, polytheism, monotheism, revelation, founder, preaching, gospel, church, faith/belief, identity, inspiring vision, vocation, mission, religious commitment

Ireland today is very different from what Ireland was like fifty years ago. Decades of emigration, immigration, changes in attitudes and our links with the outside world have contributed to a diverse religious landscape. While Christianity, based on the teachings of Jesus Christ, is still the religion practised by more Irish people than any other, there is now a wide range of religious beliefs in Ireland.

Within Christianity, there are many subgroups, known as denominations.

Outside of Christianity, thousands of Irish citizens belong to a variety of other religions. Many other people do not belong to any religious group. Some people are atheists, while others choose not be members of any particular community of faith.

The five big world religions – Hinduism, Judaism, Buddhism, Christianity and Islam – all have members in Ireland.

- What are these five religions about?
- Where and when did they start?
- Who founded them?

Let's look at each in turn, beginning with the oldest, Hinduism, and ending with the newest, Islam.

Glossary

Denomination
A recognised branch of the Christian Church.

Glossary

Religion
A particular system of faith and worship.

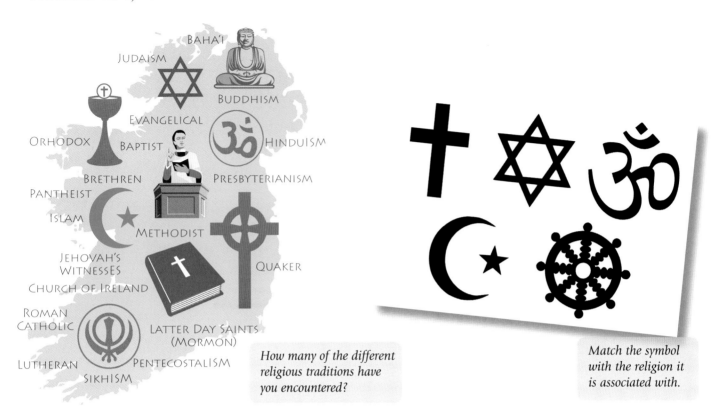

BAHA'I
JUDAISM
BUDDHISM
EVANGELICAL
ORHODOX   BAPTIST   HINDUISM
BRETHREN   PRESBYTERIANISM
PANTHEIST
ISLAM
METHODIST
JEHOVAH'S
WITNESSES   QUAKER
CHURCH OF IRELAND
ROMAN
CATHOLIC
LATTER DAY SAINTS
(MORMON)
LUTHERAN   PENTECOSTALISM
SIKHISM

How many of the different religious traditions have you encountered?

Match the symbol with the religion it is associated with.

Hinduism

Hinduism is an ancient religion. It is very much associated with the subcontinent of India. Hinduism is a way of life, a way of seeing the world and understanding an individual's role or purpose in it. Hinduism originated around the Indus Valley, near the River Indus in modern Pakistan.

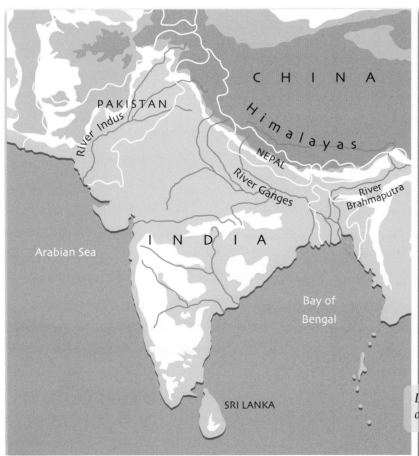

Locate India and Pakistan on a map of the world.

Did you know?

The River Indus rises in the Himalayan Mountains and flows nearly 3,000 kilometres to the Arabian Sea. In the Sanskrit language of ancient India, the Indus was called the Sindhu. This is where the word Hindu comes from.

Hinduism is in fact so ancient that no one knows who founded it. It is said to have been started by a group of unknown wise men or *rishis*.

The origins of Hinduism go back to approximately 2,500 BCE during a period, known as the Indus Valley Civilisation, or the Vedic period when the sacred writings known as the Vedas were composed and then followed. The language of this period was Sanskrit, which remains the language of Hinduism.

Hindus have many, many Gods, but they believe that one universal God, Brahman, exists in all life. They also believe in reincarnation – the belief that when a person dies their soul is reborn into a new life in this world. Each life cycle depends upon one's behaviour in a previous life. The ultimate goal in life is to break this cycle of birth, death and rebirth and achieve *Moksha* or union with God.

Many of the Gods have been written about in the sacred texts of Hinduism. The writings are divided into those that were received direct from the Gods (*Shruti*) and those that are 'remembered' or passed down through the generations (*Smriti*). The main Hindu texts are the Vedas and their supplements (books based on the Vedas). *Veda* is a Sanskrit word meaning 'knowledge'.

Sacred texts
The texts that various religious traditions consider to be sacred or of central importance to that religion.

Glossary

What is the purpose of a sacred text for any religion?

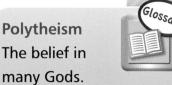

How does this image of God compare with your image of God?

Polytheism
The belief in many Gods.

Glossary

Mahatma Gandhi was a holy man and politician, and is probably the best known Indian and Hindu of the twentieth century. He helped negotiate independence for India, but was bitterly disappointed by the partition of his country. He was assassinated in 1948.

'You must be the change you want to see in the world.'

Mohandas K. Gandhi (known as the Mahatma or 'Great Soul')

What do you think Gandhi meant?

1. Where does Hinduism come from?
2. Who founded it?
3. What is Sanskrit?
4. Name a Hindu sacred text.
5. What does polytheism mean?
6. Explain one of the following: Moksha, Shruti, Smriti.
7. Who was Mahatma Gandhi?

Judaism

The oldest monotheistic faith in the world, Judaism is said to have exerted more influence on the world than any other religion. It is closely related to Christianity and Islam.

Founding story – Abraham

Abraham (originally Abram) started the belief in one God. From Ur and later Haran in Mesopotamia, known as modern-day Iraq, Abraham received a revelation from God that he should move to a Promised Land. God had chosen him to be the father of a great nation.

Monotheism
The belief in one God.

Revelation
When God or Gods make something known to a person or people.

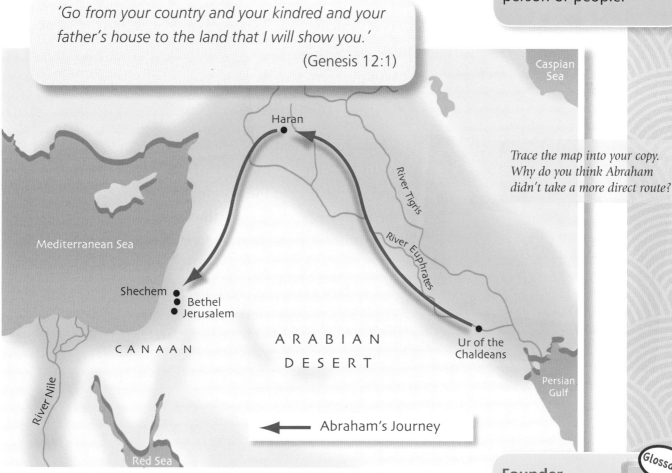

> 'Go from your country and your kindred and your father's house to the land that I will show you.'
>
> (Genesis 12:1)

Trace the map into your copy. Why do you think Abraham didn't take a more direct route?

← Abraham's Journey

The land promised to Abraham was Canaan and is roughly where the modern state of Israel is today. Abraham had started what is central to Judaism – a covenant or agreement between the people and God. Abraham, his son Isaac and grandson Jacob are considered the founding fathers or Patriarchs of Judaism.

Founder
The person who starts a movement or institution, including a religion.

23

Moses

The covenant (agreement) continued throughout the generations from Abraham to Moses. Moses is hugely important in Judaism and it could be said that Moses began the central practices and ideas of the Jewish religion. It is Moses who encounters God, receives God's name, brings the people out of slavery in Egypt and receives the Torah or law. This is not law in the modern sense but rather teaching, instruction or guidance. The most famous part of the law is the Ten Commandments.

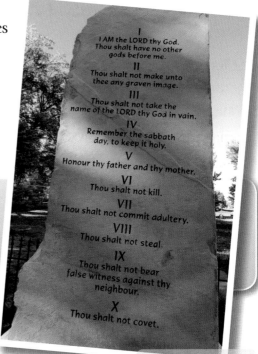

 Did you know?

There are actually 613 commandments covering many aspects of life, including law, family, personal hygiene and diet.

Judaism is based on the belief in God's revelation to the people through the prophets. A prophet is someone who brings a message from God to the people. The story of that revelation is told in the sacred texts of Judaism: the Torah (law), *Nevi'im* (prophets) and *Ketuvim* (writings), also known as the *Tanakh*.

Do you know any of the Ten Commandments?

A synagogue is a Jewish place of worship. Why do you think it would be important to keep a copy of the Torah in a synagogue?

 Over to You

1. What does monotheism mean?
2. Who made the covenant with God?
3. Where is the Promised Land?
4. Where did Moses bring the people out of slavery from?
5. What does Torah mean?
6. How many commandments are there?
7. What is the name of the sacred writings of Judaism?

Buddhism

Buddhism began in the sixth century BCE in the northeast of India and is based on the idea of an individual's need to achieve enlightenment.

Buddha – the Enlightened One

The founder of Buddhism was Prince Siddhartha Gautama. He was born into a very wealthy family and he grew up with all that privilege could bestow. He married, had a son, and was protected from all unpleasantness. The prince, however, was not at peace and in his twenties left the palace for the first time. On this journey, he saw for the first time many signs of suffering: he encountered a sick man, an old man and a dead body. He also saw a holy man, who despite having very few possessions seemed happy. These sights completely shook him and he soon left the palace for good, in search of a deeper meaning to life.

His first course was to try asceticism – a life of hardship as practised by many Hindu holy men. He decided this achieved nothing except making him feel unwell, so he advocated a middle way: neither luxury nor poverty. While meditating for seven days under a Bodhi tree, Siddhartha achieved enlightenment, known as *Nirvana*, becoming the Buddha or 'enlightened one'.

Enlightenment is a state of spiritual knowledge or insight. For Buddhists enlightenment is their goal and it breaks the cycle of rebirth, which each person has to go through. To be enlightened is to have overcome suffering by knowing the answer to what life is about.

The Mahabodhi Temple, a Buddhist temple in Bodh Gaya, is said to be the site of the Buddha's enlightenment. It is now a pilgrimage site for Buddhists.

Does this temple have any similar features to any other places of religious significance?

Classwork

Locate Bodh Gaya on a map.

The teachings of the founder, the Buddha, are central to Buddhism. The idea of a soul, rebirth and the ability to find an answer to life's suffering are all part of this religion. Most followers of Buddhism do not worship the Buddha, though some do. They try to follow his example to try to reach personal enlightenment. The question of whether or not there is a God is not definitively answered in Buddhism.

The spiritual leader of Tibetan Buddhism is known as the Dalai Lama. The current Dalai Lama is the fourteenth leader and lives in exile outside Tibet.

The Buddha's main teachings are summed up in the 'four noble truths', which refer to suffering and how to overcome it. The way to overcome suffering is to follow the 'noble eightfold path'. One of the main symbols of Buddhism is an eight-spoked or *dharma* wheel.

In your opinion, why do many religions have statues?

The sacred texts of Buddhism are the writings of the Buddha. First his teachings were passed on by word of mouth and then eventually written down. These are known as the Pali Canon or the Three Baskets. Pali is the ancient language they were written in. The Three Baskets are so called because they are divided into three sections and it is said they were stored in baskets when they were originally written down.

The main branches of Buddhism are *Theravada*, *Mahayana* and Tibetan.

What is the name of these texts?

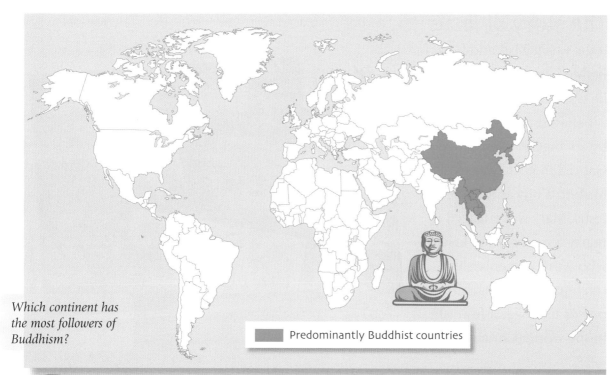

Which continent has the most followers of Buddhism?

Predominantly Buddhist countries

Over to You

1. Where did Buddhism originate?
2. Who was Siddhartha Gautama?
3. What does *Nirvana* mean?
4. Where is the Buddha said to have reached enlightenment?
5. What is the name of the main sacred text of Buddhism?
6. What title is given to the spiritual leader of Tibetan Buddhism?
7. Name two branches of Buddhism.

LEBANON

SYRIA

Sea of Galilee

Mediterranean Sea

Nazareth

River Jordan

West Bank

Jerusalem

Bethleham

Gaza Strip

Dead Sea

ISRAEL

JORDAN

EGYPT

Gulf of Aqaba

SAUDI ARABIA

Christianity

Christians, like Jews, believe in one God. This religion is based on the teachings of Jesus of Nazareth, who lived in Israel around 2,000 years ago. Most Christians see Jesus as the Messiah, God's anointed or chosen one. Another title given to him is the Son of God.

The story of Jesus

Jesus was Jewish and born in Bethlehem in Judea. Before he was born his mother Mary is believed to have been told by an angel of God called Gabriel that she was to give birth to a boy and name him Jesus. Mary was engaged to marry a man named Joseph, who was a carpenter. The celebration of Jesus' birth is one of the biggest festivals in the world: Christmas.

What parts of the story of Jesus' birth are shown in the cards?

Did you know? When he was a baby, Jesus' family had to flee and spent time as refugees in Egypt. His parents only returned home with him after King Herod's death.

Jesus grew up in Nazareth in Galilee in the north of Israel. As an adult, Jesus was baptised and became a teacher who taught people about God and God's kingdom. He is also believed to have performed miracles. Jesus was a very inspiring teacher and large crowds gathered to hear him speak. He had a small group of close followers, known as disciples.

Discuss How do people show love of God?

'"Love the Lord your God with all your heart and with all your soul and with all your mind." This is the first and greatest commandment. And the second is like it, "Love your neighbour as yourself."'

(Matthew 22:37–39)

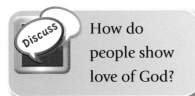

Glossary

Preaching
Publicly proclaiming or teaching a religious message.

At this time the Romans ruled Israel and Jesus became known to them as a troublemaker. The Romans convicted Jesus of treason (for acting against the government) and he was executed. After his death his followers believed he had been resurrected, i.e. he had been raised from the dead. The disciples continued his teaching and despite

Why is Constantine important for the history of Christianity?

serious persecution the religion spread across the Roman world for the next three hundred years.

In 313 CE, shortly after the Roman Emperor Constantine became Christian, the persecution of Christians ended.

The writings of Christianity are put together in the Bible. The Bible includes many of the Jewish sacred texts in the Old Testament, as well as the writings of early Christian leaders in the New Testament. The most important section of the Bible for Christians is the Gospels, meaning 'good news', which are found in the New Testament and are regularly used in Christian worship. The Gospels are four accounts of the life and teachings of Jesus: Matthew, Mark, Luke and John.

Christians believe in life after death and that they will be judged for how they lived their life. According to the Christian teaching of the Trinity, God is Three in One: the Father, Son and Holy Spirit.

Christianity is the most widespread religion in the world with over two billion followers. Christians are divided into many branches or denominations. The main traditions within the religion are Roman Catholic, Orthodox and Protestant. Most Christians worship in a church.

Gospel *Glossary*
Literally means 'good news'; refers to the accounts of the life and teachings of Jesus found in the New Testament part of the Bible.

Church *Glossary*
A building used for public Christian worship, where Christians pray and worship God. Church can also mean a particular Christian denomination with its own leaders and teachings, e.g. the Roman Catholic Church or the Church of Ireland.

Over to You

1. When and where did Christianity begin?
2. What does Messiah mean?
3. When do Christians celebrate Jesus' birth?
4. What were Jesus' followers known as?
5. Why was Jesus executed?
6. Where do Christians read about Jesus' life?
7. How many Christians are there in the world today?

Islam

This is the last of the three 'Abrahamic' faiths. Like Jews and Christians, the followers of Islam, known as Muslims, believe in one God. The word Islam means peace through submission to Allah (God). A Muslim is one who submits to Allah's will.

Founding story

Islam was founded in a town called Mecca in Saudi Arabia. A man named Mohammad was born there in 570 CE. As a child he was orphaned and was brought up by his uncle. As a young man he worked for a widow named Khadijah, and they fell in love and were married. Mohammad was highly respected as a trader and was nicknamed 'the trustworthy'. He was unhappy with the treatment of people in the town of Mecca, especially the pilgrims, who flocked to a building known as the Ka'ba. They went there to worship the many gods whose statues were built there.

Where on the map was Mohammad born?

In 610, while spending time in a cave in Mount Hira outside Mecca, Mohammad is believed to have had his first revelation from Allah, in which an angel of Allah told him that he was to be Allah's prophet (messenger). From then on, Mohammad tried to preach the message that there is only one God, Allah. He was forced to flee Mecca in 622 and went to the town of Medina. This journey is called the *Hijrah* (migration) and the event was so important for Islam that 622 is the year in which the Islamic calendar begins. In 630 Mohammad returned to Mecca with his followers and took over the town. He removed the idols from the Ka'ba and rededicated it to Allah.

Throughout his life he continued to receive revelations from Allah. The words that he heard were recorded and are the words of the sacred text of Islam: the Qur'an. Mohammad died in 632 CE.

For Muslims Mohammad is 'the seal of the prophets'. He is the final prophet and his message is the final message from God.

Did you know?

In Islam, Jesus, Moses and Abraham are respected as prophets of God.

Whose words are recorded in the Qur'an?

One of Mohammad's most famous speeches concerns the direction in which prayers should be offered to God: 'We have seen you turning your face towards heaven. We shall surely turn you in a direction that shall satisfy you. So turn your face towards the Sacred Mosque (built by Abraham); wherever you are, turn your faces to it.'

The Ka'ba is the house of God, believed by Muslims to have been built by Abraham (Ibrahim) and his son Ishmael (Ismail). This is the direction in which all Muslims pray every day.

Muslims believe in life after death and that at death people will be judged. There are two main groups within Islam: *Sunni* and *Shi'a*.

Why is this building so important to Muslims?

Over to You

1. What does *Islam* mean?
2. Who did Mohammad marry?
3. Where did Mohammad receive his first revelation from Allah?
4. What is the Hijrah?
5. What is the name of the sacred text for Muslims?
6. What is the Ka'ba?
7. Which are the three Abrahamic faiths?

Revision

Copy out and complete the following chart for all five major world religions in your copy book.

Name of religion	Drawing of the symbol	Founder	Belief about God	Place of origin	Date of origin	Name of sacred text

Faith
Complete trust or confidence in someone or something; a strong belief in the teachings of a particular religion and commitment to following them.

Glossary

Belief
Something one accepts as true or real, a religious conviction. To believe is to have faith.

Glossary

Identity
The characteristics that determine who a person is.

Glossary

Belonging to communities of faith in Ireland today

People who belong to the different communities of faith share that faith or belief with others in that community. To have faith in something is to be committed to it. The inspiring vision of the founders of each of the major world religions has led millions of people to put their trust in that idea of the world, to share that faith in a God or Gods or meaning of life.

To believe in something means to accept it as true. It is important to the person who holds that belief. While people in the different communities of faith do not necessarily agree on everything or believe the exact same details about the world, life or afterlife, what they share is an overall understanding of what is important in life. In this way they find a shared identity with others in their faith community.

What is identity?

Our identity is who we are, what we are about, and what makes a person individual and unique. It is about our role in the communities we live in, our personality, thoughts, ideas, interests and relationships.

WHO AM I?

Classwork

Draw the outline of your hand on a piece of paper. Inside the outline, write words that describe you. Are you a sister, brother, son, daughter? Are you sporty, musical or clever? Do you like football, tennis, rugby, hurling or dancing? The hands can be cut out and displayed.

An inspiring vision – Martin Luther King Junior

When Martin Luther King Jr said, 'I have a dream', he was talking about a vision he had for the United States and even the rest of the world. A vision is seeing the way things could be. King had an 'inspiring vision', a way of seeing the world as a place where people would be treated equally, regardless of race, colour or belief. King's vision was inspiring because when others heard it, it became their own; they campaigned to spread the message and to bring about King's vision.

Born in 1929, Martin Luther King Jr became a Baptist minister in 1948. In 1955 he was inspired to join the civil rights movement after Rosa Parks, an African American woman, refused to give up her seat on the bus to a white person. He made his famous speech on 28 August 1963 at the Lincoln Memorial in Washington to a crowd of 250,000 civil rights supporters, after a march to Washington for jobs and freedom. Martin Luther King Jr was awarded the Nobel Peace Prize in 1964. He was assassinated in 1964 in Memphis, Tennessee.

'I have a dream that my four little children will one day live in a nation where they will not be judged by the colour of their skin but by the content of their character.'

Martin Luther King Jr

Discuss What did Martin Luther King Jr mean by 'content of their character'?

In 2008 Barack Obama was elected as the 44th president of the United States and was inaugurated in 2009. For many, he is the 'American dream' of King's vision. In 2011 when he visited Ireland, the Taoiseach Enda Kenny introduced Obama to the crowd in a rousing speech, echoing these words, 'the American Dream'.

Did you know? On the day before he was assassinated, Martin Luther King Jr made another famous speech, in which he famously said, 'I have seen the promised land.' He ended the speech with the following words: 'I'm happy tonight, I'm not worried about anything, I'm not fearing any man.'

An inspiring vision
Glossary
Something that enables people to see the possibility of things being different and motivates them to work to achieve it.

Why do you think Barack Obama is regarded as the American Dream?

An inspiring vision is a view of the way the world could be. In many ways the beginnings of most religions start with an inspiring vision. For Jews, it is the inspiring vision of Abraham and the belief in one God with whom the people can have a special covenantal relationship. For Christians, it is the vision of the kingdom of God as outlined by Jesus. Buddhists have the Buddha's vision of an individual's ability to achieve a state of enlightenment or Nirvana. For Muslims, inspiration is in the teachings of Mohammad as written in the Qur'an, the vision of people worshipping and submitting to the will of Allah.

The inspiring visions of the major world religions have motivated millions of people. These people have then had their own inspiring visions, informed by the teachings of their faith. In this way many small communities of faith and organisations or movements have been founded. The Society of St Vincent de Paul began when Frederic Ozanam wanted to live out the message of the Gospels by helping the impoverished of Paris. He said, 'Let us go to the poor'. The vision he had inspired many others and today the society is at work in many countries, including Ireland. Its members wish to serve others.

What was it that motivated Frederic Ozanam?

Vocation
Glossary
A feeling of strong suitability for a particular occupation. In religion, it refers to the idea of having a calling to do something, to serve a community of faith in some special way.

They have made a commitment to help the society fulfil its mission. Their vocation or calling is to serve others.

For many communities of faith, there is a desire to spread its message and encourage others to share that vision. This is sometimes referred to as the mission of the community.

To examine this further, we shall look at two communities of faith in Ireland today and examine their inspiring vision, the motivation of members to serve others, the roles within each community, the mission of each community and the impact they have on individuals and the wider community.

The Islamic community in Ireland

The Islamic community in Ireland now numbers approximately 50,000 people. The followers of Islam, known as Muslims, are generally divided into two groups: Sunni and Shi'a. This goes back all the way to the time of the Prophet Mohammad himself and relates to the decision about who should be his successor. All Muslims share their beliefs about God and the Prophet Mohammad. They hold that the Qur'an is the word of Allah and his final message to the people. Interpretation can of course vary and there are a number of different schools of thought within Islam.

Within the Shi'a community, there is a clear system of clergy. The leader of a mosque or Islamic centre is known as an *imam*. The title *mullah* is generally used to refer to a Muslim man who is educated in Islamic theology and sacred law, while the highest level, which literally means 'sign of God', *Ayatollah*, is given to those who have reached a very high level of learning.

The imam, for Sunni Muslims, is the one who leads Islamic worship and prayers. There is usually a director of an Islamic centre, such as the one in Clonskeagh in Dublin, and most communities would also have a *shura*, a committee of volunteers to act as a legislative body, making decisions for the community and managing its affairs.

The community is very important to Muslims and meets regularly throughout the year for ceremonies, celebrations and lectures. The imam serves the community by leading prayer and by carrying out rituals at birth, marriage and death. Practical and social needs are looked after by drawing on individuals in the community who have the resources

How important do you think it is for the Muslim community to have a mosque in Dublin?

that are needed. In this way many people help to serve the needs of the community. Private individuals will build a mosque where the need arises. They will usually dedicate it in their family name.

There are two mosques in Dublin, one on the South Circular Road and the other in Clonskeagh, which are both Sunni. Both are centres of Islam and offer services from weddings to funerals, as well as providing education, translation, food, library facilities, sports facilities and shops.

Would you know from the outside that this was an Islamic centre? Why/why not?

The Shi'a community centre in Dublin is the Ahlul Bayt Islamic Centre in Milltown. It aims to serve the social, cultural and spiritual needs of the entire Shi'a Muslim population of Ireland. It has a full-time resident imam and is open every day for prayers.

The mission statement of the Islamic Cultural Centre of Ireland is the following:

● *Invite (all) to the way of your Lord with wisdom and beautiful preaching. (Holy Qur'an, Chapter Al Nahl, Verse No. 125)*

● *I only desire (your) betterment to the best of my power. (Holy Qur'an, Chapter Houd, Verse No. 88)*

Its vision is 'To preserve the strength and commitment of the Muslim community in Ireland and enable it to carry out its duties in introducing Islam and its cultural virtues as well as playing a positive and constructive role (both groups and individuals) in various spheres of the Irish society's life.'

What difficulties might Muslims face in Ireland?

Muslims, of course, are a part of the wider Irish community, working, studying and socialising in all walks of life. They are also involved in interfaith groups such as the Three Faiths Forum, a meeting that takes place regularly with representatives from the Jewish, Christian and Islamic communities. They have a shared prayer, an aim to educate and are a peace-led group. They also participate in the Dublin Inter-Religious Council and took part in a meeting with representatives from all 32 counties on the future of faith in Ireland. A Muslim Council of Ireland is currently being formed.

Over to You

1. What are the two main branches of Islam called?
2. Name three roles within an Islamic community.
3. What is the duty of the imam?
4. What is a shura?
5. List at least three services the different Islamic centres provide for the community.
6. Do you think there is much evidence that Muslims want to serve the community? Explain your answer.
7. What is the Three Faiths Forum?

A Christian community in Ireland today – The Religious Society of Friends

The Religious Society of Friends, also known as Quakers, believe in God the Father, in Jesus Christ and in the Holy Spirit. They are a Christian community with approximately 1,600 members in Ireland today.

This Christian church started in the 1600s in England. The founder George Fox (1624–1691) had become disillusioned with the religious life of his time and wanted a renewal of Christianity based on the teachings of Jesus. He wanted to live out that message in a simple way. The first Irish meeting of the Society of Friends took place in 1654 in the home of William Edmundson in Armagh.

In what century did George Fox live?

Members of the Society of Friends are known as Friends or Quakers. As well as their belief in God, they share the belief that there is 'that of God or the light of Christ' in every person. Unlike most other Christian communities, Quakers do not have any sacraments such as Baptism or the Eucharist. They also have no written creed or statement of faith. The Bible is central to the community and they believe anyone can receive an insight from God.

Quakers value honesty, equality and integrity, and want to make the teachings of Jesus relevant to everyday life. The emphasis they place on equality is seen in the full role that women have had for over 340 years within the community. Quakers are pacifists. They do not believe in fighting or war in any circumstances. They believe that war does not match Christ's teachings.

The most important part of the community is the Meeting, which takes place every Sunday in a Quaker meeting house. They worship and pray together in quiet, depending on God and seeking God's will. Anyone can speak or pray, read from the Bible or some other writing. Spoken ministry or talking at meetings is something anyone can do. Service of any kind, whether caring for others, helping to make tea, cleaning the meeting house or organising things are all a type of ministry. Attenders are people who worship and work with the community but have not yet joined.

Roles in the community

Elders are Quakers who focus on the spiritual life of the community at meetings. They shake hands with each other to start a meeting and look after weddings and funerals. Elders are appointed at the quarterly meetings. Overseers have the role of looking after the care of members, such as visiting a Friend who is unwell or a Friend who is leaving school.

Would you know this was a building for worship? Why?

Some meetings are held for worship; others are held for business and in order to make decisions. A clerk has the role of introducing items to consider and recording decisions. Decisions may be on religious matters, tasks that need to be done, such as repairs to the meeting house, or events that need to be organised. When there is an important decision to be made and it is a very large meeting, an assistant clerk and treasurer may also be present.

In Ireland there are 29 local meetings for groups of Quakers around the country, three quarterly meetings for the different provinces and one yearly meeting for the whole community. The central office for the Religious Society of Friends in Ireland is in Quaker House, Dublin 16.

Serving the community

In 1812 Quakers founded Bloomfield Care Centre in Dublin to provide care for the elderly. It helps elderly people who are active and those who need full-time nursing care.

Quakers have also been involved with helping to educate young people. In Ireland today there are four Quaker schools. These are Newtown School, Waterford; Drogheda Grammar School; the Friends School, Lisburn; and Rathgar Junior School.

 Did you know? Two well-known Irish companies, Jacob's biscuits and Bewley's coffee and tea merchants, started out as Quaker businesses.

Along with the St Vincent de Paul, a group of Dublin Quakers have also worked to help the families of people in prison. One part of this work was to have a new visitor centre built for Mountjoy Prison.

 Over to You

1. When and why was the Religious Society of Friends started?
2. What are members of the society known as?
3. Write out two beliefs of the Society of Friends.
4. How is Quaker worship carried out?
5. List three roles found in the Quaker community.
6. How do Quakers serve the community?
7. Do you think George Fox, the founder of the Society of Friends, had a vision? What was it? Does the community still have that vision in your opinion?

Challenges for communities of faith in the modern world

All religious communities today are faced with challenges. These challenges have changed over time and are very often to do with the times people are living in. The following are just some of the problems religious communities face in the twenty-first century.

Time: People live fast-paced lives, with commitments to work, school, hobbies, family and friends. They often don't have time to pay much attention to their religious community. Shops are open all week, matches are played at weekends, and when people are not busy they just want time to rest and relax, and don't see religion as a way to do so.

Religious commitment
The dedication a person shows to their religion.

Commitment: Making a commitment to anything is difficult and, as seen above, people can have many commitments already. Involvement in a religious community does have different levels of commitment, but it can be hard to get people to fill the various roles in any community.

Distractions: People are constantly bombarded by the media with information on so many different things that religion can get put to the side. People who want to get involved in community issues, such as homelessness, the environment or equality, find other ways of doing so.

Image: How people are viewed by society if they try to be committed to their community of faith can be quite negative. Nowadays people can be ridiculed or criticised by others for showing their religious faith publicly. The image that many people have of some of the different communities of faith is not positive and can put others off being associated with them.

Money: All religious communities face financial issues. Running places of worship and providing services costs money. Raising money can be difficult for any organisation. People cannot always afford to contribute.

Relevance: All communities of faith need to consider how relevant they are for the people who belong to them. If they are not relevant, then people will not want to be involved. They need to be able to share their message or vision with a new generation all the time. They have to adapt to a constantly changing world.

Discuss

What do you think is the biggest challenge faced by communities of faith in today's world? How can these challenges be overcome?

Key Terms

denomination, religion, sacred text, polytheism, monotheism, revelation, founder, preaching, gospel, church, faith/belief, identity, inspiring vision, vocation, mission, religious commitment

Chapter Questions

1. All Irish people belong to the same religious community: true or false?
2. Name the five major world religions.
3. Choose five words from the key terms and in your own words explain them.

4. What is an inspiring vision?
5. Name any sacred text and the religion with which it is associated.
6. What does it mean to say a person has a strong sense of identity?
7. What challenges do religions face in the modern world?

Exam Practice

Higher Level 2004: Section 5, question 1
Discuss the effect that an inspiring vision can have on a community of faith.

Ordinary Level 2006: Section 4, question 1
Name **one** community of faith you have studied that works *either* locally *or* nationally.
Outline the work done by the community of faith you have named above.
Explain **one** way in which the needs of people are being served in the work done by a community of faith.

Higher Level 2008: Section 4, question 1
In religious traditions what does the term 'vocation' mean?
Outline **two** ways in which people live out their vocation in a community of faith you have studied.
Describe **two** things that inspire the religious commitment of members in a community of faith you have studied.

Higher Level 2011: Section 5, question 1
Imagine that you are writing a piece for a school magazine about the way in which a community of faith is organised. Outline what you would write about the organisation of a community of faith under the following headings:
i. Communication   ii. Vision

Test Yourself
eTest.ie

Mini-Project

Research the inspiring vision of one of the following:
Oscar Romero, William Wilberforce, John Wesley, Mother Teresa, Mahatma Gandhi, Hillel, Muhammad Ali Jinnah.

Relationships between Communities of Faith

4

Key Concepts

tolerance, sectarianism, ecumenism, interfaith dialogue, religious conflict

Differences

All people are different, whether it is the language they speak, the colour of their eyes, hair and skin, their height and weight, where they live, what they like or dislike, what football team they support, what car they drive or what music they listen to. People are different.

How many differences can you see? What do they all have in common?

Within the many communities of faith, people share a common belief or view of the world, but even then there are many differences. What can be said of one person cannot necessarily be said of another. Sometimes it is a person's religious belief that marks them out as different. In Ireland more people identify themselves as Christian than as members of any other major world religion. Therefore, if a person is a Hindu, Muslim, Buddhist or Jew, they may be sometimes seen as 'different' by other Irish people.

Religious difference exists all over the world and it can also be related to other cultural differences. Sometimes it affects what a person wears and eats, their day of rest and even their names. Why do you think the Irish weekend is Saturday and Sunday?

What religious observations are going on in these two pictures?

Classwork

Survey names in your school community and see where they originate.

The fact that all people are different is good; the world would be a boring place if everyone was the same. Religion has found expression in many different ways around the world and when people travel they can encounter different places of worship: mosques, churches, synagogues, temples etc. They can experience other religious festivals, rituals and ways of life.

Do you know the location of any of these places?

> **Tolerance**
> A fair, objective and respectful attitude toward opinions and practices that differ from one's own.

It is important for people to acknowledge that while their views or beliefs are important to them, it is the same for other people too.

Being open to listen to and understand another person's viewpoint or religious beliefs and to respect that difference, though you may not agree with it, is to be tolerant. Tolerance is very important in religion. When it does not exist, lack of tolerance can lead to conflict and mistreatment of individuals and communities.

> **Discuss**
> How can you show people that you understand that their religious beliefs are important to them?

Sectarianism and discrimination

Even within each of the various world religions, there are different branches whose members sometimes mistrust and dislike one another. When hatred arises between people because of membership of a different group within the same religion, this is known as sectarianism.

> **Sectarianism**
> Hatred of someone because they belong to a different group (sect) of a religion.

There are many different reasons why sectarianism occurs. Very often, underlying sectarianism is fear, ignorance and misinformation.

Sectarianism is a serious problem where it occurs. While to some people it may appear acceptable to tell a joke about members of a different faith community, this can be a stepping stone to further mistreatment of an individual or group. When people are not treated equally or fairly because of their religious beliefs, this is called discrimination. This can become very harmful to the person and in turn the community.

Discrimination involves treating people differently. One reason people have been discriminated against is because they are members of a different denomination or religion.

How are people discriminated against?

- They are not allowed to do certain things.
- They are not allowed to go to certain places.
- They are not allowed to have certain jobs.
- They are treated differently.

According to the United Nations Declaration of Human Rights (adopted in December 1948), Article 18: 'Everyone has the right to freedom of thought, conscience and religion; this right includes freedom to change his religion or belief, and freedom, either alone or in community with others and in public or private, to manifest his religion or belief in teaching, practice, worship and observance.'

What ideas come to mind when you see the symbol of the United Nations?

In other words, people have the right to practise their religion, change their religion and profess their religion. A person should not be discriminated against for this. Even in societies that do not widely discriminate and where the government upholds the United Nations Declaration, people may still experience sectarianism or discrimination in the way that some other people behave towards them.

The role of ignorance and misinformation

Ignorance or not knowing about a religion can lead people to have the wrong impression or ideas about that religion. Some people deliberately pass on the wrong information about a religion and this can be accepted by other people who then become misinformed.

Nowadays in Ireland, Europe and the world, as there are so many different religious traditions, it is important to have the correct understanding of a wide range of beliefs. It gives people the ability to challenge false information and leads to a better understanding and acceptance of all. This in turn leads to a more tolerant society.

Over to You

1. What is tolerance?
2. Give examples of how people are different.
3. How can you see religious difference?
4. What is sectarianism?
5. What does the United Nations say about religious freedom?
6. What is discrimination? Give an example.
7. How would education help stop religious discrimination?

When sectarianism becomes a serious problem

Over many decades, Northern Ireland had problems with sectarianism. It was a society where people had become clearly defined according to their membership of either the Roman Catholic Church or one of the Protestant Churches. While these different communities of faith are Christian, they are different denominations or sects of the Christian community.

What do these images mean? How would seeing these images on a regular, daily basis affect you?

History, politics and cultural traditions combined with this religious difference to divide the community further. When the Irish Free State was founded in 1922, Northern Ireland was separated and it emerged as a community deeply divided along these sectarian lines.

Images from the troubled history of Northern Ireland show this divide.

While many individuals were not themselves sectarian, they were living in a community that was being dominated by a sectarian outlook. This led to violence, discrimination and bitterness. Religious difference was not the only cause or reason for community breakdown in Northern Ireland or for all the problems that emerged there, but it was certainly used to fuel hatred. Thus, while some individuals and groups worked towards bringing the two communities together, it was not only essential but appropriate for the religious communities to make a greater effort to encourage understanding and respect between Christians in the community.

Overcoming sectarianism

An example of an organisation working for peace and understanding is the Corrymeela Community. The Corrymeela Community was founded in 1965 to promote reconciliation and peace-building through healing social, religious and political divisions in Northern Ireland. Its vision is to create a Christian community of reconciliation and peace where people of diverse backgrounds can come and meet each other. The work it carries out is about encouraging interaction and building positive relationships between all sorts of people.

Programmes run by the Corrymeela Community	
Community work	– To deal with intercommunity relations.
Schools work	– To address community relationships and citizenship.
Family work	– To provide respite and development.
Church work	– To help people encounter different traditions.
Youth work	– Especially with marginalised young people.

Corrymeela has an international reputation for work on reconciliation. Many members have become active in a variety of peace activities and in conflict transformation. The community currently has 150 members and approximately 5,000 visitors each year.

Contrast the images on the previous page with the ones here and discuss the difference. What message are these images giving? What do they mean? How do they make you feel?

Ecumenism

The attempt to encourage understanding and respect between Christians from different denominations is known as ecumenism. Christians belong to the same religion but have different traditions, ways of doing things, leadership and viewpoints.

Ecumenism at work in the community involves:

- Sharing places of worship.
- Attending joint services.
- Meeting together for prayer and/or education.
- Joint involvement in community projects and work.
- Sharing resources.

Glossary

Ecumenism
Initiatives aimed at greater Christian unity or co-operation.

Why is this a picture of ecumenism?

The World Council of Churches and ecumenism

The World Council of Churches (WCC) was set up in an effort to bring about church unity worldwide. It was established in 1948 in war-torn Amsterdam, where it held its first assembly. At that first meeting 147 churches sent delegates and the closing message from the assembly stated: 'We intend to stay together.' The second assembly took place in 1954 in Illinois in the United States during the Cold War, when there was a good deal of tension between the Americans and the Soviet Union. The American President ensured that all delegates would be allowed to attend.

What issues would have concerned people in 1948?

Since then the Council has expanded and today there are 349 different churches, denominations or fellowships in the Council, representing 560 million Christians and 110 different territories or countries. Its aim is to deepen the fellowship of different churches, but not to make them all the same. Member churches are from a range of Protestant traditions including Anglican, Presbyterian, Methodist, Baptist and independent churches. Most Orthodox churches are also members. The Roman Catholic Church is not a full member of the Council but works closely with it and sends representatives to meetings.

Over to You

1. When was the WCC established?
2. How many churches sent delegates to that first meeting?
3. Where did the second assembly meet?
4. How many churches are members of the WCC today?
5. What is the aim of the WCC? Do you think it should try to make all Christian Churches the same? Why/Why not?

The WCC has created a worldwide ecumenical movement. It encourages the sharing of resources and helps Churches to work together, enriching the experience of individual members of the different Churches and helping relationships between them. It established an annual week of prayer for Christian unity and develops a theme for this each year. The Council also encourages Churches to participate in struggles for justice and peace. It has a programme to combat racism and member Churches have added a voice to defend human rights wherever they may be threatened. The Council sees the importance of inter-religious dialogue and encourages member Churches to promote respect and acceptance in the modern world.

 Discuss Should a religious organisation work on issues such as justice, peace and racism?

Interfaith dialogue

When people from different religions come together to talk about their beliefs and experiences in a meaningful way which aims to improve understanding of each other, this is referred to as interfaith dialogue.

Not only does it help to prevent conflict, violence or hatred, knowing about different religions can enrich a person's own life. It also gives a person the opportunity to explore other beliefs and ideas.

The Roman Catholic Second Vatican Council's Declaration on the Relation of the Church to Non-Christian Religions states: *'The Church, therefore, urges her sons to enter with prudence and charity into discussions and collaboration with members of other religions. Let Christians, while witnessing to their faith and way of life, acknowledge, preserve and encourage the spiritual and moral truths found among non-Christians, also their social life and culture.'*

Examples of interfaith dialogue

In the world and in Ireland, there are a number of organisations, groups and individuals that aim to increase understanding among the different religions. The following are actively involved in doing so in Ireland:

- Irish Council of Christians and Jews
- Three Faiths Forum of Ireland
- Dublin Inter-Religious Council.

The *Irish Council of Christians and Jews* is part of an umbrella organisation known as the International Council of Christians and Jews. It has 38 dialogue organisations worldwide and is intended

Glossary

Interfaith dialogue
Members of different religions talking to each other in an attempt to gain a better understanding of each other's religions.

to improve relations and understanding between these two major world religions. In Ireland, the council has had a branch since 1981 and also established a branch in Northern Ireland in 1996. The *Three Faiths Forum of Ireland* is an interfaith meeting for Christians, Muslims and Jews and was inaugurated in Dublin in 1999.

The *Dublin Inter-Religious Council* (DIRC) was inaugurated in December 2010, in an event jointly hosted by the Roman Catholic Archbishop Diarmuid Martin and the Church of Ireland Archbishop John Neill. Representatives from the Religious Society of Friends, Hindu, Islam, Baha'i, Buddhist, Methodist, Jewish, Lutheran and Romanian Orthodox faiths attended the first meeting. The DIRC aims to promote the sharing of knowledge among faith communities in Dublin and to help build a peaceful and just society. The Council wants to create an opportunity for different faith traditions to discuss issues of common interest and concern, and to promote respect for unique traditions and differences of belief. Its vision is to inspire peace, justice and harmony.

Representatives of different faiths in the DIRC.

Over to You

1. Name three organisations working to increase understanding between the different faiths in Ireland today.
2. What is the International Council of Christians and Jews?
3. When did the Three Faiths Forum begin in Dublin?
4. Which three faiths does it represent?
5. What are the aims of the Dublin Inter-Religious Council?
6. Name four religions that were represented at its inauguration.

Religious conflict

To prevent further religious conflict, some groups not only try to promote interfaith dialogue but are led by an agenda for peace. One such community is the Glencree Centre for Peace and Reconciliation.

Looking forward

Unfortunately, intolerance will probably always be a problem. Leaders need to be inspiring, communities need to work together and trust needs to be encouraged. Conflict will arise, but how it is dealt with will be at the centre of ensuring a peaceful future for everyone. Learning from the past helps us when looking to the future.

When Queen Elizabeth II and President Mary McAleese spoke at the first state banquet for the visit of a head of state from the United Kingdom, they expressed the sentiment 'to bow to the past but not be bound by it'.

The Middle East is a region with difficulties that are partly caused by religious and political differences. These differences can be exploited by some groups and can come into conflict with Western culture. This is an area that will require sensitive and able leadership to bring about a peaceful solution.

Key Terms

tolerance, sectarianism, ecumenism, interfaith dialogue, religious conflict

Chapter Questions

1. In your own words describe tolerance.
2. How do people behave if they are (i) tolerant and (ii) intolerant?
3. What is sectarianism?
4. What causes people to have a sectarian attitude?
5. Define ecumenism.
6. What things can ecumenical groups do?
7. What leads to religious conflict?
8. What is the purpose of interfaith dialogue?

Exam Practice

Ordinary Level 2006: Short question 9

A key part of interfaith dialogue is the sharing of ideas between _____

_____.

Higher Level 2006: Short question 4

In religious traditions sectarianism means _____

_____.

Higher Level 2011: Section 4, question 1

In religious traditions the term 'ecumenism' refers to _____

_____.

Describe **one** example of ecumenism that you have studied.

Explain **two** reasons why ecumenism is important for members of a community of faith.

Within a religious organisation or denomination the term 'community breakdown' refers to _____.

Outline **two** ways in which community breakdown could be prevented within a religious organisation/denomination.

Ordinary Level 2007: Section 4, question 1

Hatred of another person because of his/her religion is: Ecumenism/Humanism/Sectarianism.

Describe **one** example of people being in conflict because of their religion.

Describe **one** example of people working to build respect for the beliefs of others.

Give **two** reasons why people work to build respect for the beliefs of others.

Higher Level 2005: Section 4, question 1

'Archbishop Eames calls for "determined effort" to end sectarianism' (*Irish Times*, December 2004)

What is sectarianism?

Outline **one** example of sectarianism.

Identify **two** effects that sectarianism can have on a community of faith.

What is ecumenism?

Briefly outline **one** example of ecumenism.

Give **two** reasons why people work for ecumenism.

Higher and Ordinary Level 2008: Picture question

This is a photograph of religious leaders at an ecumenical service.

Pick **one** thing from the photograph that shows this is an example of ecumenism.

Give **one** other example of ecumenism.

State **two** reasons why people work for ecumenism.

Higher and Ordinary Level 2011: Picture question

This is a photograph of people gathering for interfaith dialogue.

Pick **one** thing from this photograph that suggests it is an example of an interfaith gathering.

Give **one** other example of interfaith dialogue.

State **two** reasons why the members of a community of faith take part in interfaith dialogue.

Test Yourself
eTest.ie

Mini-Project

Outline the work done by the Glencree Centre in Ireland today.

You can find information on the website *www.glencree.ie*.

Organisation and Leadership in Communities of Faith

5

This is a higher level only section of the syllabus.

Key Concepts

leadership, authority, ministry, service, hierarchy

As we have already seen, communities – whether they are sports clubs, schools, places or communities of faith – have within them a variety of roles. One of the keys to a community working well is that people carry out their roles and co-operate with others. A very important role in any community is that of the leader.

Who is the boss in school?

Leaders in the different world religions

The organisation of the many world religions is different and the titles of leaders have different meanings.

Judaism

Rabbi: Means 'my master'. A rabbi is a religious teacher and interpreter of the Torah. He or she is a minister to the community, a preacher and a leader of the synagogue. Some Jewish communities have women rabbis.

Islam

Imam: Means 'model' or 'example'. In Islam, it refers to a type of leader. The title can be used for the leader of ritual prayer in the local community. The imam is a scholar of the Qur'an and therefore respected. An imam can also be the leader of a particular school of thought. For Shi'a Muslims, an imam is a person with unique spiritual authority, knowledge and charisma.

Mujtahid: A teacher who, on the basis of his own learning or authority, is allowed to give a ruling or a legal decision. In Shi'a Islam, mujtahids have great authority.

Hinduism, Buddhism, Sikhism

Guru: Means 'teacher'. In the Sikh religion, it refers to the ten teachers who ruled the community, from Guru Nanak to Guru Gobindh Singh. In Hinduism or Buddhism, the term can be used for a religious teacher who helps his followers awaken their own spirituality. Hindus also have temple priests.

Christianity

Clergy: A general term for ordained or specially authorised leaders in many Churches. Roman Catholic clergy are usually called priests, but the Church of Ireland also ordains priests, though they are often referred to using other titles. Only men can become clergy in the Roman Catholic Church, though both women and men can become clergy in most of the Protestant Churches in Ireland. Clergy lead services, take care of the spiritual needs of the members of the community and look after the running of the parish.

What does guru mean?

Priest: Someone ordained in the Church with the authority to perform priestly functions, including mediating between God and human beings. Priests perform certain rituals, such as celebrating the Eucharist or Mass.

Minister: A lay or ordained Christian with permission to carry out spiritual functions, ministries or services in the Church. The word is often used in the Protestant Churches as a general term for a member of the clergy.

Moderator: A minister in the Presbyterian Church who has been appointed to the role of presiding over meetings that govern the life of the Church.

Pastor: Literally means 'shepherd'. In some Christian communities, such as Baptists or Evangelical Christian Churches, this title is used for the person who leads services of worship. A pastor is a person who exercises spiritual guidance.

Patriarch: Literally means 'father figure'. This is the term used for the figurehead of the Orthodox Church, e.g. the Patriarch of Constantinople.

Who lives in Vatican City?

Bishop: A clergyman (or woman, in some Protestant denominations) who is in charge of a diocese. They are allowed to ordain priests and can carry out the ceremony of confirmation. An archbishop is in charge of an archdiocese.

Pope: The Bishop of Rome and head of the Roman Catholic Church. This Church regards the Pope as the direct successor of Peter, Jesus' disciple. The Pope leads the largest Christian denomination in the world. The Pope issues teachings or doctrines and pronouncements on matters of faith.

Did you know?

Vatican City is the smallest country in the world.

Leadership
Taking charge of a community or organisation, leading the members, making decisions for the community and accepting responsibility for it.

Chairperson: A person who chairs meetings and is responsible for a committee or group. Some Protestant Churches, e.g. Methodists, have a chairperson who leads an annual meeting that makes decisions regarding the community and who will represent the community at national events.

Leadership

To be a good leader one needs to have good leadership skills. While people have different styles of leadership or become leaders in different ways, it is important that a leader has the respect of the people in the community that they lead. The leader can have a great influence on others in the community.

What do leaders need to be able to do?

- Listen
- Communicate
- Organise
- Believe in the community and their role within it
- Have passion and enthusiasm for what they are doing
- Influence others
- Make decisions
- Be persuasive
- Be inclusive.

Over to You

Show how three of the above would help a leader to carry out his/her role.

Leadership is not always in the hands of one person. Some communities have more than one leader. In communities of faith, there are a variety of styles and ways of leading. With leadership comes great responsibility. People look to the leader for advice, direction, knowledge, inspiration and to make decisions for the good of the community.

A word often used when talking about leaders or individuals and groups with a leadership role is authority.

A person or group with authority has:

- The power to make decisions and direct people.
- The right to do things.
- Responsibility to get things done.
- The power to influence people because they respect their knowledge or official role.
- Trust from people because of their knowledge.

In some communities of faith, the leader is a source of authority, guidance and direction. They are looked to for instruction and wisdom. In other communities of faith, the leader's role has less authority and the job is more as spokesperson for the community.

In order to lead and to be able to get things done, a leader needs to have authority and the power to carry out the role in an effective way. This role, in many communities of faith, is in ministry and serving others.

Vocation

The role of most local religious leaders as head of a community of faith, whether they are priests, clergymen or women, rabbis, imam or gurus, is to serve. Their vocation is a calling to serve; in serving God they must serve the community. Their job is to look after the spiritual life of the members of their community. In practice this means

> **Glossary**
>
> **Authority**
> The power to make decisions, to influence others and to have control. This word can also refer to a reliable source of information or evidence, or a person or group with recognised knowledge about something.

> **Glossary**
>
> **Ministry**
> Performing a role of service to others in a religious community.

> **Glossary**
>
> **Service**
> To serve others. In religion, service can mean serving others and thereby serving God.

conducting rituals, teaching, giving practical help and advice, and maintaining a place of worship.

Organisation and leadership in the communities of faith in Ireland

Christianity is *one* religion with *many branches* and the various types of Christian Church have different organisational structures and leaders. Let us look at some of the main ones in Ireland today.

Hierarchy
Glossary
Organises people or groups into ranks, one above the other.

The Roman Catholic Church in Ireland has archdioceses, dioceses and parishes. The archdioceses are led by an archbishop. The four archdioceses are Armagh, Dublin, Tuam and Cashel. Each archdiocese is divided into dioceses led by a bishop. In turn, each diocese is made up of parishes led by priests. The Pope in Rome leads the Roman Catholic Church worldwide and is considered 'Christ's representative on earth'. He is helped by cardinals. Catholics in their parishes have a role too. They partake in worship and some take on other roles, e.g. serving the wafers during Eucharist, reading, singing in the choir, looking after the church collections or helping to decorate the church.

In this way, the Roman Catholic Church has the following organisational hierarchy.

The hierarchy of the Roman Catholic Church

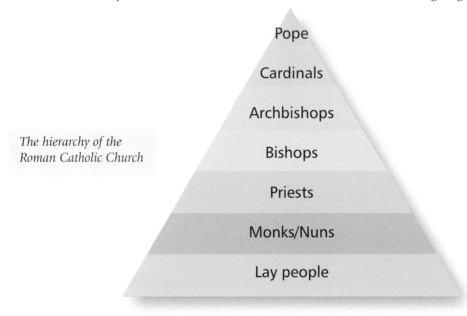

Pope

Cardinals

Archbishops

Bishops

Priests

Monks/Nuns

Lay people

The Church of Ireland, a reformed or Protestant church, is episcopal, meaning that it has bishops. The archbishops of Armagh and Dublin lead this Church. There are also dioceses led by bishops and parishes led by clergymen and women. Again, the ordinary members can be involved in many ways in the parish: reading, singing, teaching, helping with the running of the parish etc. The Synod is the governing body of the Church of Ireland, made up of representatives of the clergy, of the ordinary people of each diocese and the House of Bishops.

Archbishops

The hierarchy of the Church of Ireland

Bishops

Clergymen and women

Lay people

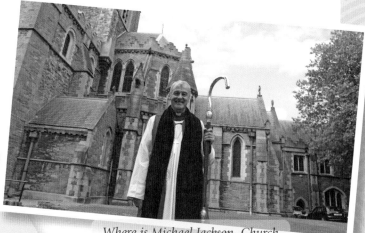

Where is Michael Jackson, Church of Ireland Archbishop of Dublin and Glendalough, standing?

Did you know?

The Quakers are famous in Ireland for the huge amount of charitable work they carried out during the Famine in the nineteenth century.

The Society of Friends or Quaker community is unusual in that there is no official leadership role in this branch of Christianity. They have a weekly 'silent' meeting, where anyone can contribute a thought, prayer or reading on which to reflect. The Quakers have an annual meeting where they make decisions by consensus on organisational issues and other issues that are of concern to the community. In this way, the Quakers have no hierarchical structure within the community and, therefore, no one person is more important than another, emphasising the equality of all. Quakers are also highly regarded for being pacifists, believing that killing is never justified.

During which time in Irish history did the Quakers set up soup kitchens?

Key Terms

leadership, authority, ministry, service, hierarchy

Chapter Questions

1. What is the name given to the leader of the following religious communities: Hindu, Jewish, Buddhist, Christian and Islam?
2. What is the role of a leader in any community?
3. What does it mean to have authority?
4. How is ministry connected to service?
5. Draw a diagram of the hierarchy of the Roman Catholic Church.
6. What does it mean to say that the Church of Ireland is episcopal?
7. Write three facts about the Quaker community.

Exam Practice

Higher Level 2006: Short question
Moderator is the title of a leader associated with the Presbyterian Church: true or false?

Higher Level 2006: Short question
In religious traditions ministry means _____.

Higher Level 2007: Short question
The title 'Rabbi' is most associated with a leader in which of the following world religions? Buddhism/Hinduism/Judaism

Higher Level 2007: Short question
In religious traditions to have 'authority' means _____.

Higher Level 2008: Short question
'Patriarch' is the title given to a leader today in which one of the following Christian denominations?
Anglican/Presbyterian/Russian Orthodox

Higher Level 2009: Short question

In religious traditions the term 'vocation' means a calling to _____.

Higher Level 2008: Section 5, Question 1

Outline the way in which leadership within a community of faith involves –
i. Authority   ii. Service.

Mini-Project

Research the role of a religious leader in a community of faith in Ireland today.

Useful Websites for Section A: Communities of Faith

For this section of the course, the aims are to look at the nature and pattern of human communities, to identify the characteristics of communities of faith/churches and to examine these characteristics as they occur in communities of faith/churches in local, national and international examples.

To find out more about many of the different religious communities in the world today, and to find basic information on these, the following website is very useful:

www.bbc.co.uk/religion/religions

To find out more on the Simon Community or St Vincent de Paul:

www.dubsimon.ie

www.svp.ie

For religious communities in Ireland today the following websites are very useful:

www.hindu.ie

www.jewishireland.org

www.dublinbuddhistcentre.org

www.buddhism.ie

www.catholicireland.net

www.ireland.anglican.org

www.islamireland.ie

www.islaminireland.ie

For information on groups working on inter-religious dialogue or ecumenism:

www.oikoumene.org

www.corrymeela.org

www.threefaithsforum.org

www.glencree.ie

For more information on the structure, organisation and leadership of some Christian communities in Ireland:

www.dublindiocese.ie

www.quakers-in-ireland.ie

www.catholicbishops.ie

www.presbyterianireland.org

www.irishmethodist.org

The following short video clips available on the internet are useful for discussing relationships between communities of faith:

Corrymeela Promo 2009

On the Road to Busan: The Assemblies of the World Council of Churches

The Three Faiths Forum (various clips)

Section

Foundations of Religion – Christianity

This section of the syllabus aims:

- To explore the context into which Jesus was born.
- To identify the Gospels as the main source of knowledge about Jesus.
- To examine the meaning of the life, death and resurrection of Jesus for his followers, then and now.

The Context

6

Key Concepts

the Holy Land, the Roman Empire, ancient Judaism, messianic expectation

Looking at the beginnings of Christianity requires us to go back over 2,000 years ago to a small region in the eastern Mediterranean. The foundations of the world's largest religion are set in a very different time, place and religious understanding than exist today.

Many people are aware that Christianity is based on the teachings of a person known as Jesus, but how much is known about Jesus and where does the information come from?

There are no historical pictures of Jesus, only people's images of him, which can very much depend on the perspective of the person. Discuss how one person's image may be very different from that of another person. Why is this so? Is it important?

Here are some facts about Jesus:

- Jesus was Jewish.
- He was born sometime between 4 and 6 BCE.
- He lived most of his life in Galilee, a northern province in Israel.
- He was executed by the Romans in the city of Jerusalem during the rule of the local governor, Pontius Pilate.

Did you know?

BCE refers to year before year 1 and means before the common era.
CE refers to year after year 1 and means the common era.

To look at the beginnings of Christianity is really a historical study because before looking at the story of Jesus, we need to understand the historical setting for the story.

The Holy Land

Jesus was born and lived in what is modern-day Israel. This was an area in the ancient world that was constantly under foreign domination. In the centuries before Jesus, it had been taken over many times: by the Assyrians, Babylonians, Persians, Greeks and finally the Romans. The reason empires wanted to take over the area was because of its location – it is at the crossroads of three continents: Europe, Asia and Africa, and, therefore, is a valuable trade route and strategic controlling point.

The area had different names over the centuries, including Canaan, Judea, Palestine and Israel. At the time of Jesus, the area was divided into different provinces by the ruling Romans, who designated governors to rule each one.

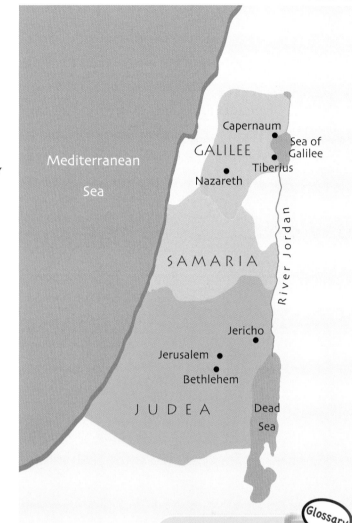

On the map of the Holy Land, note the names of:
1. The three provinces: Galilee, Samaria and Judea.
2. The towns: Jerusalem, Bethlehem and Nazareth. (These towns are associated with the life of Jesus.)
3. The geographical features: the Dead Sea, River Jordan and Sea of Galilee.

Draw the map into your copy book. Make sure to give it a title and to label it fully.

Glossary

The Holy Land
The area around the country currently called Israel. It has had various names and rulers throughout history, once known as Canaan and sometimes Palestine. This area is the Promised Land in Judaism and it is the country Jesus lived and died in.

Why the 'Holy Land'?

There are two reasons why this area is known as the Holy Land. First, the Jewish community saw this area as the Promised Land, the land Abraham was sent to and promised to his descendants as part of the covenant or agreement between their people and God. At the time of Jesus and for more than a thousand years before, the Jewish religion was associated with living in and sometimes ruling this country. Second, Jesus was born and lived there. For Christians, Jesus is the founder of their religion and so the area is significant for Christianity too.

Jesus the Galilean

Jesus was a Jew. He was born in Bethlehem, brought up in Nazareth and died in Jerusalem. His father Joseph was a carpenter. Many of the places on the map feature in the story of earliest Christianity. As well as towns, Israel was made up of small rural communities and many people made a living from farming and fishing. Since Jesus lived most of his life in the northern province of Galilee, he lived among people from this rural area. This also influenced his ideas, and his method and style of teaching.

> 'And he came to Nazareth where he was brought up; and he went to the synagogue, as his custom was, on the Sabbath day.'
>
> (Luke 4:16)

1. Where did Jesus come from?
2. What are the different names of the country he came from?
3. Why did powerful empires want to take over this region?
4. Who ruled it at the time of Jesus?
5. Name the three provinces of Israel at the time of Jesus.
6. How did many ordinary people make their living?
7. How did this country come to be known as the 'Holy Land'?

The Roman Empire

Jesus lived in Palestine/Israel during the reigns of the Roman Emperors Augustus and Tiberius. At this time the Roman Empire ruled this area. It stretched across the Mediterranean from Egypt to Spain and reached as far north as Britain. The Romans were able to take over all this land because they had a very strong army and they were a highly developed civilisation. When possible they appointed local rulers to rule on their behalf, or they sent their own governors. The two main concerns of the Romans were maintaining law and order – keeping the peace – and making sure people paid their taxes to Rome.

Research one of the following: Augustus, Tiberius or Herod. Find out when he reigned, how he came to power and when and how he died. Make up a quiz for others to do.

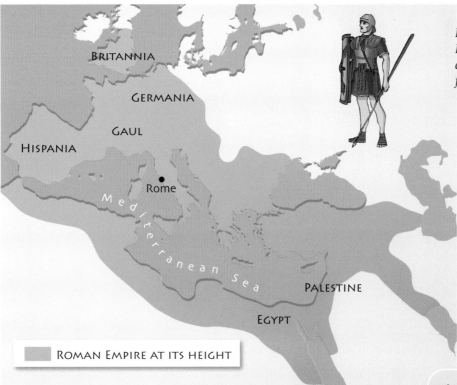

Discuss which parts of the Empire would have been considered most important, from a Roman viewpoint.

ROMAN EMPIRE AT ITS HEIGHT

The Roman Empire

Glossary

An extensive group of countries that were ruled by the Emperor, who had supreme political power. It was established by Augustus in 27 BCE.

What impression of Roman rule do these images give people?

Roman rule

The Romans ruled in two ways: through directly appointed Roman governors (e.g. Pontius Pilate) or local rulers (e.g. King Herod). Herod, known as 'Herod the Great', was king at the time of Jesus' birth. After his death, Herod's three sons ruled over the three provinces of Israel.

What information can be deduced from ancient coins?

The Romans kept the peace through threat. The people were made to fear the Romans, who maintained a visible presence of strength and carried out severe punishments (e.g. crucifixion) for wrongdoing. They used force to keep the people down as they were worried about revolution spreading throughout the empire. Remember, Israel was an important strategic location in the empire. They needed a large amount of money to fund such a huge empire therefore; the Romans made the people pay taxes. This was money that many people could not afford. As a result, the people hated the tax collectors.

 Did you know? Crucifixion was a particularly painful form of execution only carried out on non-Romans. It brought about the person's death through slow suffocation.

 Discuss
1. What were the Romans' main concerns in an area like Israel?
2. Who did they appoint to rule?
3. How did they keep the people down?
4. Was it fair to hate the tax collectors?

Ancient Judaism

Today Judaism is one of the five major world religions. While there is a small Jewish community in Ireland, there are much larger Jewish communities in other countries, especially Britain, America and Israel. When we look back to the time of Jesus, Judaism was the religion of most people (apart from the Romans) who lived in Israel/Palestine and, of course, Jesus himself was a Jew. It is fundamental when trying to understand

Christianity and its beginnings to understand this religion also. Judaism today is somewhat different from ancient Judaism, so it is necessary to look back to Judaism as it was then.

Judaism in the first century AD

The three central aspects of ancient Judaism were *temple*, *Torah* and *land*. This was the focus of the religion.

Land

We have seen that the land of Israel was believed to be the 'Promised Land', but while most people living there at the time of Jesus were Jews, it was ruled by the Romans. Up to this time, the Jews had had a turbulent history as far as the land was concerned, having been exiled from it during the rule of the Babylonians, as well as having it constantly taken over by foreign invaders. The land was a deeply important part of the religion and they strongly wished to return to a time, like that of King David, when they had their own kingdom of Israel.

How hospitable is the land, in your opinion? Why was it so important to the people?

Temple

The Temple in Jerusalem was the centre of Jewish life at this time. The Temple was somewhere people went to worship God. People from far and wide went there during festivals. One of the main rituals carried out at the Temple was to make sacrifices to God. It was at the heart of the everyday life of the community. The time of Jesus is known as the Second Temple Period because the first Temple had been destroyed by

Why did the Second Temple get the name 'Herod's Temple'?

> **Glossary**
>
> **Ancient Judaism**
> The religion of Judaism, based on a belief in one God, as it was practised in the ancient world, including the time of Jesus. It centred on the idea of an agreement, known as the covenant, between the people and God.

the Babylonians and a new Temple was built to replace it. King Herod was heavily involved in the reconstruction of this Temple and so many refer to it as 'Herod's Temple'.

The Temple had separate areas for different people. The centre was known as the 'Holy of Holies'. It was a room only entered once a year on the Day of Atonement (*Yom Kippur*). There was a Court of Gentiles where non-Jews could go, a Court of Women and a Court of the Israelites. Temple Priests and Levites looked after the rituals that took place in the Temple. The Temple was a huge building complex with a market place. In the outer courtyard, the tables of the money changers were set up. This was necessary because the people had to use special Temple coins, not Roman ones, to buy animals for sacrifice. They also bought the animals for sacrifice here.

Why do you think people didn't use these for buying animals for sacrifice in the Temple?

Torah

The Jewish instruction or law, known as the Torah, was another central aspect of Judaism at this time. It is made up of a number of texts found in the *Tanakh*, the sacred writings of Judaism. For Christians, these are in the first five books of what Christians call the Old Testament. The law covers all aspects of life: what to eat and wear, who to marry, business dealings and how to worship. Following the law was the most important part of a Jewish person's life. It was their side of the covenant (agreement) with God.

Do you know what language is written on these?

Over to You

1. What was the main belief of ancient Judaism?
2. What were the three central aspects of ancient Judaism?
3. Describe Herod's Temple. Draw a diagram of it.
4. What are the Jewish sacred writings called?
5. What is the Torah?

Groups in Judaism

At this time, most ordinary people were busy working as farmers, fishermen and craftspeople and, while they were Jewish, they did not belong to any particular religious group. Their main concern was feeding themselves and their families. Others, however, did belong to specific groups within Judaism at that time. These were the Pharisees, Sadducees, Essenes and Zealots.

> *Pharisees* emphasised the need to follow the law (Torah).
> *Sadducees* emphasised the Temple and its traditional rituals.
> *Essenes* lived separate from society in monastery-like communities in the desert.
> *Zealots* violently opposed Roman rule. (There is little evidence of Zealots existing as a distinct group until about 30 years after Jesus' death.)

Two of these groups are mentioned in writings about Jesus. These are the Pharisees and Sadducees. Jesus is often seen to be arguing with the Pharisees over interpretation of the Jewish law or Torah.

> *'For the Pharisees and all the Jews do not eat unless they wash their hands, observing the tradition of the elders.'*
>
> (Mark 7:3)

What aspect of Judaism is noted in this extract? Which group is specifically mentioned?

There were also Jewish rabbis or teachers and there were synagogues where people gathered for worship. Very few people could read or write. In many areas, fewer than ten per cent were literate. Some people worked as scribes – writers or professional copyists; there were different types of work for these people in the towns and villages of Israel. The leaders, whether political or religious, had the advantage of education and, therefore, had considerable power over the ordinary people.

Jewish religious rulers

The main group in charge of Judaism at that time was the *Sanhedrin* or ruling council, which looked after the religious matters of the community. It was made up of seventy elders and presided over by the High Priest. At the time of Jesus' death, the High Priest was named Caiaphas. The Sanhedrin had limited power and was only able to deal with religious matters. It acted as a court of law within Judaism and kept a Temple guard to look after activities in the Temple compound. The Sanhedrin could not give the death penalty. Most power was in the hands of the Romans.

1. What was the main concern for ordinary people living in Israel during the Roman period?
2. Describe the concerns of the four main groups in Judaism at this time.
3. Define these terms: synagogue, rabbi and scribe.
4. What was the name of the Jewish ruling council?
5. What power did it have?
6. Who headed it?
7. Who had most power at this time?

Roman–Jewish tensions

- Romans believed in many gods.
- They saw the Emperor as a kind of god.
- Jews have only one God and would never see the Emperor as a god.
- Jewish people resented foreign rulers and paying taxes to them.

Messianic expectation

Glossary

Messianic expectation
The belief that God would send the people a 'chosen' or 'anointed' one to help them and that this Messiah would restore the Kingdom of Israel. The Messiah would be descended from King David and would begin a new age.

Faced with Roman rule and oppression, many Jews looked to God to send a messiah (saviour) to help them. Their image of a messiah was one who would lead a revolt against the Romans and restore a Kingdom of Israel. The idea of a messiah went back to earlier times. The word itself is a Hebrew word meaning 'anointed one'. It refers to kings, priests and prophets of Old Testament times who were chosen by God as leaders, and were anointed with oil as a sign of being chosen. The idea of a messiah, a chosen one who would help save the people, had its origins in times of difficulty.

The experience of the exile to Babylon in 587 BCE also plays an important part in understanding the Judaism of this time. Jews were fearful of another exile and they reacted in different ways. For the Pharisees, following the law would protect them; for others, defending their homeland was of key importance; and for others again, the longing for a messiah gave them hope.

Discuss the idea of a messiah and why it had become popular during Roman rule. What type of person would the people expect the messiah to be? Describe this person.

Summary

Jesus lived in Palestine/Israel during the first century when the area was part of the Roman Empire. The Romans ruled with a mix of direct rulers and local rulers ruling on their behalf. They were content as long as taxes were paid and peace was maintained.

This was also the time of the Second Temple. The Temple in Jerusalem was at the heart of the Jewish religion. People went there for celebrations and to make sacrifices. Judaism was the religion of the majority of the population and there were several distinct groups within Judaism. The central concerns of Judaism were Temple, Torah and the land of Israel. Many people hoped for a messiah who would free them.

Key Terms

the Holy Land, the Roman Empire, ancient Judaism, messianic expectation

Chapter Questions

1. Where did Christianity begin?
2. When did Jesus live?
3. What religion was Jesus?
4. Who ruled the area he lived in?
5. How did they rule?
6. Who were the leaders of Judaism at that time?
7. Why did people want God to send a messiah?

Exam Practice

Ordinary Level 2010: Short question
A town in Palestine associated with the birth of Jesus is:
Bethlehem/Cana/Jericho.

Ordinary Level 2009: Short question
The people who held political power in Palestine at the time of Jesus were the:
Assyrians/Egyptians/Romans.

Higher Level 2007: Short question
Galilee was a province in Palestine at the time of Jesus:
true or false?

Higher Level 2011: Short question
The Roman Governor in Palestine at the time of Jesus was:
Peter/Philip/Pilate.

Higher Level 2009: Section 5, question 2
Describe life in Palestine at the time of Jesus, referring to each of the following:
i.   The political structures.
ii.   The religious structures.

Mini-Project

Create a poster project of Israel in the Roman period. Include maps, place names, rulers, livelihoods and religion.

Evidence about Jesus

7

Key Concepts

evidence, gospel, evangelist, witness, oral and written tradition, Q document, synoptic

Christianity – origins and sources

Most of our information about Jesus and early Christianity comes from the Bible. There are some sections in the Bible that deal specifically with this information, while other parts of the Bible are from much earlier times. There are also other sources that mention Jesus and the early Christians.

Evidence
The available body of facts or information.

Glossary

Did you know?

In the Greek version of the Old Testament there are books known as the *Apocrypha*. These books are accepted as part of the Bible by the Roman Catholic Church, but Protestant Churches do not include them because they are not in the original Hebrew version.

The Bible

The Bible is not one book! Most people think that if they pick up a Bible they have one book in their hand, but that simply isn't the case. They have, in fact, at the very least sixty-six books. The Bible is a complicated collection of texts written over a period of approximately 1,000 years. The word itself comes from the Greek word *biblia*, meaning 'books'.

Discuss why all the books that make up the Bible might have been put together into one volume.

One Bible – two parts

The first part of the Bible is the Jewish sacred writings, the *Tanakh*, known by Christians as the Old Testament. This is a collection of thirty-nine books which is a mixture of laws, poetry, history, stories and proverbs. It was written in Hebrew between approximately 850 BCE and 150 BCE. It tells the story of the Jewish people and their relationship based on the covenant (agreement) with God. The first five books are very important in Judaism as they contain the Jewish laws or instruction known as the Torah. This has at its heart the Ten Commandments. Christians too take the Ten Commandments very seriously.

The second part of the Bible, known as the New Testament, is where most of the information on Jesus and the early Christians is found. This was written over sixty years from approximately 50 CE to 110 CE.

Testament means covenant or agreement. What do you think Christians meant when they labelled the two parts 'old' and 'new'? What has changed?

1. What does evidence mean?
2. Write out the names of all the books of the Bible.
3. Divide them into two lists: the Old and New Testaments.
4. What does the word 'bible' mean?
5. When was the Old Testament written?
6. What is it about?
7. Where is most of the information about Jesus written?

The New Testament

When trying to find out about early Christianity, this is the part of the Bible of most concern. It is divided into four types of writing:

1. The Gospels
2. The Acts of the Apostles
3. The Letters
4. The Book of Revelation

What is each section about?

The Gospels are the basic stories of the life of Jesus. There are four gospels in the Bible: Matthew, Mark, Luke and John. The Acts of the Apostles tells the story of the spread of Christianity from Jerusalem to Rome after Jesus' death. The Letters, also known as the Epistles, are from early Christian leaders, giving advice to new Christian communities. Finally, coming from a time of persecution, the Book of Revelation, also called the Apocalypse, describes the cosmic battle of good versus evil.

THE NEW TESTAMENT

GOSPELS

ACTS OF THE APOSTLES

LETTERS

REVELATION

The Gospels

*   The word gospel means 'good news'.
*   There are four gospels – Mark, Matthew, Luke and John.
*   Each was written by a different author and so each has its own viewpoint.
*   Each was written for a different group of early Christians.
*   The writers are known as the evangelists or those who tell the good news.

Why did the evangelists write the Gospels?

1. People who had seen or heard Jesus were getting old and wanted to preserve the stories about him. These people were the witnesses to the events described in the Gospels.

Glossary

Gospel
The record of Christ's life and teaching in the first four books of the New Testament.

Glossary

Evangelist
'Proclaimer of the Good News'; another word for a writer of the Gospels.

Glossary

Witness
Have knowledge of something from observation or experience.

2. They wanted to explain Christian teaching. Christianity was a new religion (something that is hard to imagine today). An explanation and record of what Christianity was about was needed. It was important to clear up any misunderstandings about this religion.

3. The early Christians wanted writings for use in worship. As with most religions, sacred texts and writings were used to practise the religion. Without these, it would be difficult to participate in the new religion.

Over to You

1. What types of writing make up the New Testament?
2. What does the word 'gospel' mean?
3. Who are the evangelists?
4. Why did the evangelists want to write the Gospels?
5. What does 'witness' mean?

While the writers wrote to preserve the story of Jesus, each had other reasons to tell the story in a meaningful way for his individual community, making each gospel different.

Mark (approx. 64 CE): Mark wrote to encourage persecuted Christians. The theme of suffering is very significant in this Gospel. This suggests that the writer is giving comfort to an early Christian community. The idea of people suffering for their faith can be seen in Mark 8:34.

What form of persecution is the Roman emperor Nero watching?

Who was Mark writing for?

'He called the crowd with his disciples, and said to them, "If any want to become my followers, let them deny themselves and take up their cross."'

(Mark 8:34)

Matthew (approx. 80 CE): Matthew wrote for Jewish Christians. Most of the first Christians were Jews and therefore they had a Jewish understanding of God and religion. This gospel is full of references to the Jewish scriptures and presents many Jewish ideas in a new light. An example of this is in Matthew 9:36.

'When he saw the crowds, he had compassion for them, because they were harassed and helpless, like sheep without a shepherd.' (Matthew 9.36) This is a reference to a passage in the Book of Numbers in the Old Testament, which says: '... who shall go out before them and come in before them, who shall lead them out and bring them in, so that the congregation of the Lord may not be like a sheep without a shepherd.'

Which group of early Christians did Matthew write his gospel for?

Along with his gospel, what other book did Luke write?

Luke (approx. 80 CE): Luke wrote both his own gospel and the Acts of the Apostles. Luke was a doctor, and tells the story from Jesus' birth to the time when Christianity reached Rome. At the beginning of his gospel, he wrote a dedication to a person called Theophilus, which explains that he wanted to tell the story 'so that you will know the full truth about everything which you have been taught'. The two parts of his writing, the gospel and Acts, are connected, and links between the life of Jesus and the on-going life of the Christian community are made clear. This is especially so in the way he writes about the work of the Holy Spirit.

Which famous Irish manuscript is this portrait of Saint John from?

John (approx. 90 CE): John was trying to explain to Christians that Jesus was the Messiah. Writing after the other evangelists, John sometimes gives further information that makes the life of Jesus more understandable (e.g. John mentions that some of Jesus' disciples had been followers of John the Baptist).

The evangelists were people of faith who wanted to put the story of Jesus on record. Each gospel is different but also similar to the others. Sometimes the faith of the writer comes through: towards the end of his gospel, John says that he wrote it so 'that you may come to believe that Jesus is the Messiah, "the Son of God" and that through believing you may have life in his name'.

Christians see the Bible as inspired by God. The Gospels are not like modern biographies. They aim to set out the meaning and importance of Jesus' life, focusing on what was seen as important by the authors: Jesus' teachings, actions and death. They are more like ancient biographies, such as *The Lives of the Twelve Caesars* or *The Lives of the Eminent Philosophers*.

What information would you expect a biography to contain?

From oral to written tradition

Information about Jesus' life began as oral tradition, told by word of mouth. Remember that in the ancient world only about ten per cent of the population could read and write. Therefore they recounted the evidence they had about Jesus as stories. These were then written down to become written tradition.

Oral tradition
Teachings of Jesus passed on by word of mouth.
Written tradition
Teachings of Jesus that came to be written down, such as the Gospels, which were later included in the Bible.

How were they written?

The Gospels were first written in Greek, the official language of the eastern part of the Roman Empire. A few words also appear in Aramaic, the language of the ordinary people. They would have been written on papyrus. This is a plant that is cut into thin strips and placed in layers, one across the other. When dried out, this forms sheets like paper on which to write. The writers would have written with a stylus, a kind of pen made from reeds. They used ink made from minerals or vegetable substances.

The oldest surviving New Testament writing is kept in the John Rylands Library, Manchester. The biggest collection of New Testament writings from before the fourth century is in the Chester Beatty Library, Dublin. The oldest complete copy of the New Testament is *Codex Sinaiticus*, found in the British Library in London.

Part of St John's Gospel in the Codex Sinaiticus. What do you notice about the words?

Order of writing

The two-source hypothesis (theory) is as follows:

1. Jesus lived around 4 BCE-30 CE. The events of his life, therefore, take place during this time.

2. After his death, a number of his sayings were collected into a document known as the 'Q source'.

3. In around 64 CE, Mark wrote his gospel, telling for the first time in writing the story of Jesus' life and death.

4. Thus, there are two early sources: Mark and Q.

5. When Matthew and Luke wrote their gospels, they used the Q collection of sayings and Mark's gospel. Both Matthew and Luke also had their own material – stories about Jesus not found anywhere else. These became additional written sources for information about Jesus.

6. John's gospel was written later. At this stage the story is known and John does not want to re-tell the events but concentrates on explaining what it all means.

> **Glossary**
>
> **Q document**
> An early collection of the sayings of Jesus.

> **Glossary**
>
> **Synoptic**
> The gospels of Matthew, Mark, and Luke, which describe events from a similar point of view, by contrast with that of John.

Synoptic gospels

This word is used for three gospels – Mark, Matthew and Luke. It comes from the Greek word for 'seeing together' and refers to the fact that they are similar in content. John's gospel is not one of the Synoptic Gospels. It was the last to be written and is very symbolic. As noted, John was trying to explain who Jesus is for Christians, not just telling the story of his life.

 Did you know? There are many more gospels than the ones found in the Bible. Others that never made it into the Bible, such as the gospels of Thomas, Judas and Mary, have been discovered.

Symbols for the Gospels

Tradition has different symbols for the different gospels. The symbols are sometimes found in churches or as illustrations on texts. They are as follows:

- Mark is a lion.
- Matthew is a man.
- Luke is an ox.
- John is an eagle.

Match the symbol with the gospel that it represents.

 Over to You

1. Why are the gospels different accounts of the life of Jesus?
2. Why are they not like modern biographies?
3. What is the meaning of oral tradition?
4. Explain these words (i) Q document (ii) synoptic.
5. Which gospel was written first?
6. Which gospel was written last?
7. Draw the symbol for each of the gospels.

Non-biblical sources about Jesus

1. Josephus was a Jewish historian and leader from the first century. He wrote a lot of books about Jewish history. Josephus also mentioned Jesus and his 'wonderful deeds'.
2. Tacitus was a Roman writer from the first century. He wrote about a man named Jesus who was put to death by the Romans during the rule of Pontius Pilate.
3. Pliny, a Roman leader and writer.

So, in general, there is considerable evidence for the existence of Jesus and his death, but much more of what was written about him is a matter of faith for most people. It is often difficult with a modern viewpoint and a modern understanding of the world to accept things written 2,000 years ago. Much of what is written needs to be understood in the original context in which it was written to make sense, and then it needs to be made relevant for a new age.

Documents of faith

Many people also take much of what is written in the Bible as pointing to important truths or having a moral message, but fewer people nowadays interpret what is written in a literal way. For example, the creation stories are now mostly understood as having an important message without being a literal account of the beginning of the world. For many people, accepting scientific and modern understandings of the world, using historical study and gaining more knowledge does not negate or discredit what it says in the Bible. This sort of knowledge helps Christians to understand the sacred writings and helps them to appreciate better the message they believe in.

Key Terms

evidence, gospel, evangelist, oral and written tradition, Q document, synoptic

Chapter Questions

True or false?

1. The Bible is one book.
2. The first gospel to be written was Mark.
3. John is a synoptic gospel.
4. The Jewish historian Josephus wrote about Jesus.
5. The word gospel means 'good news'.
6. The Gospels contain only historical facts.
7. The symbol for John's gospel is an eagle.
8. The Q document was a collection of the sayings of Jesus.

Exam Practice

Higher Level 2004: Section 5, question 2
Imagine you have been asked to give a talk explaining the stages involved in the development of the Gospels from the oral tradition to the written word. Outline the talk you would give, making reference to the importance of the Gospels in the Christian community of faith.

Mini-Project

Research one of the Gospels. Find out about its background, when it was written, the author and content. Present your findings to the class.

The Person and Preaching of Jesus

8

Key Concepts

kingdom of God, parable, miracle, table fellowship, discipleship, mission, vocation

Let us now look at the story of Jesus from his birth to his adult life as a teacher. In the process we can learn what Jesus was teaching and what his mission was. Along the way, try to note names of places, people and events.

The birth story

Most people are familiar with the story of Jesus' birth as this is told every year during Christmas. It is told through readings in church, nativity plays, children's books, on the television and in the crib, which is found in churches, in people's homes and often in public places like shopping centres. The basic story is that Mary and Joseph have to go to Bethlehem for a census. Mary is about to have a baby. They can't find anywhere to stay so they are given a stable to sleep in, and during the night the baby Jesus is born. Other people involved are the shepherds who are told by an angel to visit the baby, and the wise men who follow a star and find the baby just below where the star has come to rest. The wise men bring three presents: gold, frankincense and myrrh.

How much has Bethlehem changed?

Have you ever seen a crib like this one? Where?

What is significant in the story?

First, the parents, Mary and Joseph, have to go to Bethlehem for a census. A census is a count of all the people; this was carried out by the Romans for the purpose of finding out who had to pay tax. So it is clear that Jesus, even before he is born, is affected by Roman rule. Why Bethlehem? They go there because it is where Joseph's family was originally from. Joseph is significant too because he is said to be from the 'line of King David', which for the Jewish people was a sign he was from good ancestry. Also, the prophecy predicted that a messiah would come from King David's descendants.

Second, Jesus and his parents are *poor* and have nowhere to stay. This isn't what you would expect of the birth of a powerful leader. It takes place in a stable. One of the main themes of the Gospels is that of *inclusiveness*. All are welcome, no one is less or more important. In this story Jesus is identified with the less well off: he is not rich or powerful. As an adult, his followers, like him, are very often not rich or powerful either. The *shepherds* also indicate a lowly aspect to the story. They are ordinary, not rich or important, and yet they are witnesses to the most important event in the story of the beginning of Christianity.

Third, the *wise men* or Magi are important in the story both because of who they are and what they bring. Unlike anyone else in this story, they are not Jewish. Their role, therefore, is to reinforce the idea that Jesus is for everyone: poor or rich, Jewish

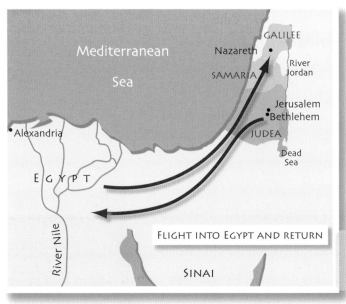

FLIGHT INTO EGYPT AND RETURN

What do we call someone who is forced to flee their own country?

or non-Jewish. The presents that they bring are hugely significant too: *gold for a king, frankincense for a religious leader,* and *myrrh as a sign of suffering and death.* Epiphany, or the twelfth day of Christmas, commemorates the visit of the wise men.

It is interesting that none of the gospels tells the complete story of Jesus' birth. Luke mentions the shepherds and Matthew wrote about the wise men. Mark and John don't tell the story at all. Luke wanted to emphasise the lowliness of Jesus' birth. Matthew, while writing for Jewish Christians, was keen to emphasise that Jesus was not only a messiah for the Jews but for everyone. In both accounts, the story plays an important part in setting the scene for Jesus' life and teaching. The Romans, too, loom large in the background. They determine where the story takes place: in Bethlehem. When King Herod hears from the wise men that they were following a star to lead them to the king, he carries out a mass execution of baby boys in the area. Mary and Joseph, having been warned in a dream, flee to Egypt to save Jesus' life. From there they go back to Nazareth in Galilee, where Jesus grows up.

The story from his childhood on

In the Gospels, the next time the reader sees Jesus he is about twelve years old and travelling with his parents to Jerusalem. Here he talks to religious experts in the Temple in a way that seems beyond his years (Luke 2:41–51). His parents go to find him. They ask him what he is doing there and he answers mysteriously that he should be in 'his father's house'. This story is a pointer to the reader that there is something very significant about who Jesus is. It leads to questions that the writer will try to answer in the events that follow.

Why might Jesus and his family have visited the Temple?

Jesus' baptism

The next event in Jesus' life, as told in the Gospels, is his baptism. Nowadays, baptism is very much associated with Christianity. The very least this story shows is that baptism predates Christianity. Baptism seems to have been practised by some Jews as a way of ritual cleansing, in order to maintain religious purity. It was sometimes used for the admission of Gentiles (non-Jews) into Judaism. John the Baptist was baptising people with water and calling on them to repent (to say 'sorry') for their sins. John is sometimes referred to in Christianity as the 'Herald of the Messiah'; in other words, the one who announces the coming of the Messiah. His words echo Old Testament writings about a voice that would announce that the Messiah was about to arrive.

In your opinion, does the artist portray John well?

John the Baptist

John is famous for baptising Jesus and for his death at the order of Herod. John may have been an Essene and was certainly non-conformist in his views. His open criticism of Herod led to his brutal death. He had his own disciples and may have taught some of Jesus' followers, perhaps even Jesus himself. He is described in the Gospels as living in the desert, on a diet of locusts and wild honey, wearing camel skin, sandals and a leather belt. He carried out baptism as a sign of a change of heart, washing away sin and preparing for the Messiah.

Did you know? John the Baptist was executed by the ruler of Galilee and Peraea (Transjordan), Herod Antipas, who was King Herod's son. He was beheaded for criticising Herod's marriage to his brother's wife.

The word 'baptism' comes from a Greek word which means 'to dip'. When John baptised people, he was preparing them for God's judgment. John also talked about how the one who would come after him would baptise with the Holy Spirit. When Jesus asks to be baptised, John is, to begin with, reluctant to do so. He believes Jesus has a special relationship with God and, therefore, thinks he has no need to repent. He also feels unworthy to carry out Jesus' baptism. Jesus insists, 'In this way we shall do what God requires.' (Matthew 3:15)

Why does Jesus want to be baptised?

What are the names of the two seas linked by the River Jordan?

It becomes clear through Jesus' teaching that he sees a messiah as having a close relationship and identity with the ordinary people. He doesn't see his special relationship with God as a reason to be separated from them. Jesus wants to identify closely with people who are willing to make a big change in their lives to bring themselves closer to God.

Significant points in the story

As Jesus is baptised, two very significant things occur:

1. Jesus hears the words: 'You are my own dear Son. I am pleased with you.'

2. A dove appears. This represents the Holy Spirit descending on Jesus at the moment of his baptism. This indicates the presence of God.

For Christians, Jesus' baptism is a very significant story. It is his first step, as an adult, on his journey to the cross. The words that identify him as God's son are later echoed by the centurion at his death, who says, 'Truly this was God's son.'

With what do you associate the dove? Have you ever seen it on a card?

Jesus faces temptation in the desert

Having been baptised by John, Jesus heads into the wilderness to prepare for his mission. Significantly, Jesus spends forty days there. This was a number that indicated preparation in the Old Testament. For example, following the Jewish people's escape from Egypt in Exodus, they spent forty years in the wilderness before entering the Promised Land.

In each of the cases when Jesus is tempted by Satan – the personification of the opposite of God or goodness – he rejects the temptation, not with new ideas but with references to the Old Testament book of Deuteronomy.

The three temptations and how Jesus resisted them

1. Turn a stone to bread to have something to eat: 'One does not live by bread alone, but by every word that comes from the mouth of God.' Deuteronomy 8:3

2. Show off God's power by jumping from the top of the temple: 'Do not put the Lord your God to the test.' Deuteronomy 6:16

3. Worship Satan and receive worldly power and greatness: 'Worship the Lord your God and serve only him.' Deuteronomy 6:13

This passage shows that Jesus was to face temptation throughout his life. It indicates what sort of temptations he would face, and they do occur again: when he faces death, the temptation

What sort of landscape is this?

to run away and to test God recurs. Christians believe him to be a messiah who serves and suffers. The fact that he knew his Jewish scripture shows his Jewish religious understanding and his knowledge of what is right in a person's relationship with God.

The teaching, preaching and actions of Jesus

Jesus the teacher

It is clear that Jesus was a teacher. He is called Rabbi, which means 'my master' or 'my teacher', by his followers. He preaches to thousands and discusses religious matters with the experts of the day. But he was a different type of teacher from many at that time and he was very conscious of the idea that 'actions speak louder than words'. Jesus' teaching was not only in what he said but also in what he did.

What did Jesus want to teach?

The main theme of Jesus' teaching was the *kingdom of God*.

The kingdom of God is an 'ideal kingdom' that could be brought about 'on earth' as 'in heaven' by people. He taught about it in two ways:

1. In *words* through preaching and telling parables.
2. In *actions* through the miracles, behaviour towards others, discipleship and table fellowship.

> **Glossary**
>
> **The kingdom of God**
> An ideal order of things where God's will is done. It is not just one place; it exists where God is obeyed. Jesus announces that it is already present in him and where people have God in their hearts. It is seen in his preaching as he explains how people should behave towards each other in order to bring about the kingdom of God.

Parables

A parable is a type of story with a hidden meaning. Parables work like fables; they are stories with an underlying lesson. Some of the most famous fables are those by Aesop, such as 'The tortoise and the hare' or 'The boy who cried wolf'. On the surface they are just simple stories, but underlying them is an important lesson. Parables are similar to fables. On the surface they seem like very simple stories, but each has an underlying message about something Jesus wanted to teach.

> **Glossary**
>
> **Parable**
> A simple story used to illustrate a moral or spiritual lesson, as told by Jesus in the Gospels.

Unlike fables, parables do not include animals, plants, inanimate objects and forces of nature as characters that can speak and have other human powers.

In a way, parables are even more straightforward. The people involved are typical of the time and place Jesus was living in. In this way, the parables related to the everyday life of the people he was trying to teach.

Jesus used parables to teach about the kingdom of God. In parables Jesus teaches:

- What God is like
- What God's kingdom is like
- How God wants people to live.

Here are some examples of parables with discussion exercises:

1. The 'Lost coin' and 'Prodigal son' describe what God is like. They are told to show that God forgives and loves.

2. The 'Good Samaritan' describes how people need to behave to bring about God's kingdom. It shows that they should help people in need and should not be judgmental of others.

3. The 'Mustard seed' describes God's kingdom as something small that can become something great. He is saying that the smallest idea that is worthwhile can become great and make a huge difference to the world.

4. The 'Sower' describes how people hear and react to the message of God's kingdom. Some people ignore the message, others see it as too much trouble, for others things get in the way, while others listen, do the best they can and reap the rewards of their efforts. When in life does effort need to match intention in order to succeed?

5. The 'Talents' describes how people need to behave to be part of God's kingdom. They should make the most of what they have been given and not waste it. In rugby there is a well-known expression: 'Use it or lose it.' It is about making the most of something you have. How often do people not appreciate or make the most of what they have?

Do you recognise this story?

Is it difficult to forgive people?

How should people treat others?

What small ideas have grown big and made a big difference to people's lives?

The Parable of the Lost Sheep

Now all the tax-collectors and sinners were coming near to listen to him. And the Pharisees and the scribes were grumbling and saying, 'This fellow welcomes sinners and eats with them.'

So he told them this parable: 'Which one of you, having a hundred sheep and losing one of them, does not leave the ninety-nine in the wilderness and go after the one that is lost until he finds it? When he has found it, he lays it on his shoulders and rejoices. And when he comes home, he calls together his friends and neighbours, saying to them, "Rejoice with me, for I have found my sheep that was lost." Just so, I tell you, there will be more joy in heaven over one sinner who repents than over ninety-nine righteous people who need no repentance.'

(Luke 15:1–7)

1. Why did the Pharisees criticise Jesus?
2. In the parable, what has happened to one of the sheep?
3. What does the shepherd do?
4. Who do you think the shepherd represents?
5. Who do you think the sheep represent?
6. What is the message behind this parable?
7. Why do you think Jesus chose to tell this parable at that moment?

The Parable of the Wise and the Foolish Builders, also called The House on the Rock

I will show you what someone is like who comes to me, hears my words, and acts on them. That one is like a man building a house, who dug deeply and laid the foundation on rock; when a flood arose, the river burst against that house but could not shake it, because it had been well built. But the one who hears and does not act is like a man who built a house on the ground without a foundation. When the river burst against it, immediately it fell, and great was the ruin of that house.

(Luke 6:47–49)

 Discuss the meaning of this parable.

The Parable of the Good Samaritan

- **Background to telling the parable**

> *Just then a lawyer stood up to test Jesus. 'Teacher,' he said, 'what must I do to inherit eternal life?' He said to him, 'What is written in the law? What do you read there?' He answered, 'You shall love the Lord your God with all your heart, and with all your soul, and with all your strength, and with all your mind; and your neighbour as yourself.' And he said to him, 'You have given the right answer; do this, and you will live.'*

What did the lawyer want to know? How did Jesus answer him?

- **The parable**

> *But wanting to justify himself, he asked Jesus, 'And who is my neighbour?' Jesus replied, 'A man was going down from Jerusalem to Jericho, and fell into the hands of robbers, who stripped him, beat him, and went away, leaving him half dead. Now by chance a priest was going down that road; and when he saw him, he passed by on the other side. So likewise a Levite, when he came to the place and saw him, passed by on the other side. But a Samaritan while travelling came near him; and when he saw him, he was moved with pity. He went to him and bandaged his wounds, having poured oil and wine on them. Then he put him on his own animal, brought him to an inn, and took care of him. The next day he took out two denarii, gave them to the innkeeper, and said, "Take care of him; and when I come back, I will repay you whatever more you spend." Which of these three, do you think, was a neighbour to the man who fell into the hands of the robbers?' He said, 'The one who showed him mercy.' Jesus said to him, 'Go and do likewise.'*
>
> (Luke 10:25–37)

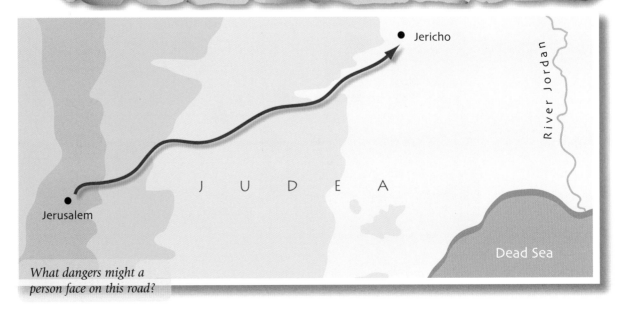

What dangers might a person face on this road?

● **The message of the parable**

The story of the Good Samaritan is told to tell the lawyer who his neighbour is. In this story Jesus describes how people should treat each other. They should be like the Samaritan. The other important message in this story is about how people judge each other. Samaritans were disliked by most Jews at the time because they were not considered 'pure' Jews. People had a very bad opinion of them and treated them as outsiders. The story has a Samaritan as the good character, so it challenges the prejudices people had about them. This story demonstrates that the kingdom of God is open to everyone, but it is not open to prejudice. Within the kingdom people should behave like the Good Samaritan and treat others as their neighbour.

Classwork

1. Who are people prejudiced about in today's society?
2. Rewrite the story in modern times, replacing the people with modern versions.
3. Act out the story as a play.

Over to You

Research the story of the Prodigal Son and find out what happens. This story is about forgiveness, repentance and love. Write a page on how this story is Jesus' way of teaching about the kingdom of God.

Miracles – Jesus the healer

The day was drawing to a close, and the twelve came to him and said, 'Send the crowd away, so that they may go into the surrounding villages and countryside, to lodge and get provisions; for we are here in a deserted place.' But he said to them, 'You give them something to eat.' They said, 'We have no more than five loaves and two fish – unless we are to go and buy food for all these people.' For there were about five thousand men. And he said to his disciples, 'Make them sit down in groups of about fifty each.' They did so and made them all sit down. And taking the five loaves and the two fish, he looked up to heaven, and blessed and broke them, and gave them to the disciples to set before the crowd. And all ate and were filled. What was left over was gathered up, twelve baskets of broken pieces.

(Luke 9:12–17)

A leper came to him begging him, and kneeling he said to him, 'If you choose, you can make me clean.' Moved with pity, Jesus stretched out his hand and touched him, and said to him, 'I do choose. Be made clean!' Immediately the leprosy left him, and he was made clean. After sternly warning him he sent him away at once, saying to him, 'See that you say nothing to anyone; but go, show yourself to the priest, and offer for your cleansing what Moses commanded, as a testimony to them.' But he went out and began to proclaim it freely, and to spread the word, so that Jesus could no longer go into a town openly, but stayed out in the country; and people came to him from every quarter.

(Mark 1:40–45)

Miracle
An amazing event brought about by God's intervention.

Apart from the Gospels, evidence suggests that Jesus did have a reputation for performing miracles. The Jewish historian Josephus wrote, 'About this time arose Jesus, a wise man ... he was a doer of wonderful deeds, and a teacher of those who gladly receive the truth.'

Choose one of the miracle stories above. Draw and write it out as a comic strip.

Types of miracle

Throughout his time as a teacher, Jesus is said to have performed miracles. These are usually categorised as follows:

- Healing – leprosy, paralysis, blindness.
- Nature – feeding of the five thousand, calming the storm.
- Exorcism – casting out demons.
- Restoration to life – bringing people back to life from death.

A few points need to be made about the miracles. At that time, this kind of healing was a much more common practice than it is in today's society. People did not understand many illnesses as we would today, so the idea of possession by an evil spirit was not as strange to them as it is to us. They sometimes viewed illness as a sign of punishment from God. By healing the people, Jesus was not only bringing comfort but was teaching certain values and ideas.

Jesus' miracles as part of his teaching

The miracles show God's love and power. Healing people with physical and mental illnesses was a way for Jesus to show God's love for them. They show that God's kingdom is for everyone and they teach about caring for all people. In those times, nobody would normally go near lepers and demon-possessed people, let alone try to heal them. They also show that God's power is greater than demons or whatever was responsible for the illness.

The miracles also teach about sharing (for example, the feeding of the five thousand). They can also teach about faith or a person putting their trust in God (for example, the calming of the storm). Finally, when Jesus restores people to life this demonstrates that God has power over life and death. All the miracles are signs that God's kingdom is present or that God's will is being done.

Table fellowship

What does it mean to share a meal?

It can mean a sense of:

- Acceptance
- Inclusion
- Community.

Why do families often eat together?

> **Glossary**
>
> **Table fellowship**
> To share food or a meal with others. It is a very common cultural idea that food brings people together.

Who did Jesus eat with?

- The outcast
- The poor
- Pharisees
- Disciples
- Anyone
- Everyone.

Sharing a meal or food brings people together. Jesus shares food in significant ways. For example, when he eats with the tax collector, Zacchaeus, he is eating with an outsider. Jesus will share a meal with anyone and by doing so shows that the kingdom of God is for all.

At the last supper, he eats with his followers and begins the tradition of the Christian community sharing a meal together. At the meal, the bread and wine hint at the sacrifice Jesus is to make. For a long time Christians shared an actual meal together. This developed and is remembered in the sharing of the bread and wine in church services today.

In words and actions, Jesus taught and showed:

- That no one is an outcast (the lost sheep, healing of lepers, eating with a tax collector).
- Sharing with others (miracle of the loaves and fish, disciples).
- Care for others (the good Samaritan).
- God is powerful (calms wind and waves).
- God has the power over life and death (raising Lazarus).
- God forgives and God cares (prodigal son, healing of paralysed man).

The Church of the Beautitudes. Why might people still visit this site today?

The Beatitudes

One of Jesus' most famous teachings is known as the Beatitudes, meaning the 'blessed' sayings, as each one begins with the word 'blessed'. This is a section from the Sermon on the Mount, which took place near the Sea of Galilee. In this sermon, Jesus challenges the ideas people have about who is blessed. Those who have power, wealth and status are not the blessed: in other words, what people saw as important was not important. The blessed are those who show mercy and compassion, are humble and want peace in the world. The sermon sets out ideals that focus on love and humility.

Located on a small hill overlooking the Sea of Galilee and built on the traditional site of Jesus' delivery of the Sermon on the Mount, pilgrims are known to have visited the Church of the Beatitudes since at least the fourth century.

Discipleship

The followers of Jesus were known as disciples. The word means 'student' or 'learner'. The disciples sometimes referred to Jesus as Rabbi, a Hebrew title which means 'master' or 'teacher'. Religious teachers do sometimes have a group of followers who are inspired by their teachings. Most of Jesus' disciples came from the same region as he did. They heard his teachings and were inspired by what he had to say. The Gospels mention many followers of Jesus. These include men and women, who were mostly ordinary people and were all Jewish.

Discipleship
Being a follower of a religious teacher.

In the Gospels, twelve disciples are singled out for special mention. In the Old Testament, the number twelve is significant. There were twelve tribes of Israel, named after the sons of Israel or Jacob. These twelve tribes were seen as making up the people of God. The gospel writers are using twelve to indicate that the disciples were people of God and leaders of a new relationship or covenant between the people and God.

According to Matthew, Mark and Luke, the first four disciples were fishermen. These were James, John, Andrew and Simon Peter. Another disciple was the tax collector Levi. The others were Simon, Philip, Bartholomew, Thomas, James, Thaddeus and Judas. The disciples were taught by Jesus and in time became the early leaders of Christianity and continued his mission.

What type of people would work and live here?

The disciples in the stories

Simon the fisherman is given the name 'Peter', meaning 'rock', by Jesus: 'I tell you, you are Peter, and on this rock I will build my church.' (Matthew 16:18)

He is often depicted as the leader of the disciples, yet he is very far from perfect. He misunderstands much that Jesus teaches, he has little faith at times and, at the end, when Jesus is arrested, he pretends he never even knew him.

Miracle, faith and the disciples

In one of the miracle stories, it was a stormy night and the disciples were battling against the waves as they crossed the Sea of Galilee. As dawn was breaking, they saw Jesus coming out to them, walking on the water. They were terrified, thinking it was a ghost, but Peter asked Jesus to call him out onto the lake with him. Peter took a few steps towards Jesus on the water but fear and doubt then made him sink. Peter is remembered in this episode for his lack of faith but, as some point out, although he failed he was the only one to try.

> 'Then after a little while the bystanders again said to Peter, "Certainly you are one of them, for you are a Galilean." But he began to curse, and he swore an oath, "I do not know this man you are talking about."'
>
> (Mark 14:70–71)

Did you know? Peter died in Rome during the reign of Emperor Nero, probably in 64 CE. He died as a Christian martyr. According to tradition, Peter was crucified upside down because he declared himself unworthy to die in the same manner as Jesus. Excavations under St Peter's Basilica in Rome may have unearthed his tomb.

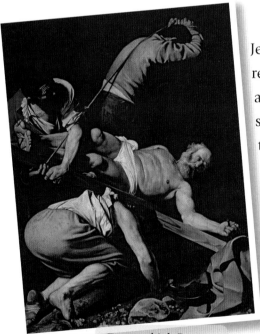

Do you think Peter was a person of faith?

Another disciple, Judas, is famous for betraying Jesus by handing him over to the authorities in return for money. Other disciples are seen to argue with each other and most of them are shown at times as weak, afraid and confused. Yet they become really important after Jesus' death and without them Christianity would not exist today. Their experiences following Jesus' death changed them into strong believers with courage to match their convictions. Their courage was demonstrated by the fact that many of them became martyrs for their beliefs – they were killed for being Christians and professing that faith.

Discipleship and the kingdom of God

The story of the call of the tax collector Levi

After this he went out and saw a tax-collector named Levi, sitting at the tax booth; and he said to him, 'Follow me.' And he got up, left everything, and followed him. Then Levi gave a great banquet for him in his house; and there was a large crowd of tax collectors and others sitting at the table with them. The Pharisees and their scribes were complaining to his disciples, saying, 'Why do you eat and drink with tax-collectors and sinners? Jesus answered, 'Those who are well have no need of a physician, but those who are sick; I have come to call not the righteous but sinners to repentance.'

(Luke 5:27–32)

This is an interesting story for a number of reasons:

1. Jesus is calling on a tax collector. The people hated tax collectors, so he is including an outcast, someone many other people don't want to associate with. This shows the 'inclusive' aspect to the kingdom of God and Jesus' mission.

2. He is criticised by the Pharisees, the group within Judaism who emphasised the need to practise the Jewish law or Torah. He is often in conflict with them, not because he doesn't agree with the law but because he disagrees with the way they interpret it.

3. The mention of a banquet shows how Jesus uses meals to teach. Sharing food was a sign of acceptance. Tax collectors are not to be treated as outcasts but are welcome, like anyone who shows repentance, into God's kingdom. This shows God's forgiveness to all who are sorry.

4. Sharing a meal also indicates a sense of community and the requirement for all disciples to share what they have with others.

Jesus' vocation and mission

Jesus' mission is seen in what he did and said during the three years of his public ministry. For Christians, his death is also part of that mission (it will be dealt with in the next chapter). His work was to bring an understanding of the kingdom of God to people. That was done through teaching, healing and leading others. He asked his followers to take

Mission
An important assignment or aim. In religion, it is a calling to spread the faith or to do something and it is strongly felt.

Glossary

Vocation
The sense of having a calling to do something in terms of career or occupation.

on his work and to continue it after his death. In the Gospels, the mission of the twelve disciples is made clear and it really is a continuation of the work that Jesus was carrying out. It also shows that the lifestyle of Jesus and his followers was not one of comfort or ease, but that there was a commitment to serve others.

Luke, Chapter 9, outlines the mission of the twelve disciples: to cure, to proclaim the kingdom of God and to bring the good news. They are told to take nothing for the journey but to rely on the hospitality of strangers. They are not to attach importance to worldly goods.

Discipleship – past and present

Being a disciple was a choice and something that was not easy. For Christians today, the choice of following Jesus and being a disciple involves working for the kingdom of God now. They make the same decision to believe and to make Jesus' teaching relevant in a new age. Christians today are continuing the mission of the earliest followers of Jesus and making a commitment to serve.

Summary

Jesus' teaching and preaching took place mostly among the ordinary people of Galilee. Here he collected followers, taught people about the kingdom of God, carried out healings, shared meals, clashed with some authority figures and preached a revolutionary message about what matters to God. Through his actions and words he challenged people, shared his ideas and questioned the way things were. For Christians today, that message hasn't changed and the mission is now theirs.

Jesus told the people that the 'kingdom of God' is an idea that is small like a mustard seed but something that could grow huge. It is a world where:

- All are welcome.
- People think of others – 'Love your neighbour as yourself'.
- Everyone is a neighbour (the good Samaritan).
- Everyone matters.

Discuss How should Christians show they understand the message of Jesus as he showed it through his actions and words?

Key Terms

kingdom of God, parable, miracle, table fellowship, discipleship, mission, vocation

Chapter Questions

1. Where was Jesus born?
2. Where did he grow up?
3. Who baptised him?
4. What temptations did he face in the desert?
5. What does *disciple* mean? Name three of the disciples.
6. What was the main theme of Jesus' teachings?
7. What is a parable?
8. What type of miracles is Jesus said to have performed?
9. Where did the Sermon on the Mount take place?
10. What does table fellowship mean?

Exam Practice

Ordinary Level 2004: Short question
An historical source of evidence for the life of Jesus is: Jacob/Job/Josephus/Joshua.

Ordinary Level 2004: Short question
Jesus was baptised in the river: Ganges/Jordan/Nile/Tiber.

Higher Level 2010: Short question
Jesus was born in the province of: Galilee/Judea/Samaria.

Ordinary Level 2010: Short question
The person Jesus appointed to lead his followers was: Jairus/Peter/Zacchaeus.

Higher Level 2005: Short question
Discipleship means _____.

Higher Level 2006: Short question

One parable from the Gospels that Jesus told is: Daniel in the Lion's Den/the Burning Bush/the Good Samaritan/the Raising of Jairus' Daughter.

Higher Level 2007: Short question

An example of a meal Jesus shared with another person is: the Calming of the Storm/ the Good Samaritan/the Meeting with Zacchaeus.

Ordinary Level 2007: Short question

One group of Jewish religious leaders at the time of Jesus were the: Centurions/ Governors/Pharisees.

Higher Level 2008: Short question

A miracle that Jesus performed during his life was: The Healing of the Lepers/The Parting of the Red Sea/The Return of the Prodigal Son.

Higher Level 2005: Short question

One example of Martyrdom from the founding story of Christianity is _____.

Higher or Ordinary Level 2010: Picture question

Name **one** person whom Jesus called to be his disciple. The name of the sea where Jesus called his disciples was

_____.

State **two** things that Jesus asked his disciples to do.

Higher or Ordinary Level 2006: Picture question

Pick **one** thing from the drawing that shows how people reacted to the miracles of Jesus.

Name **one** other miracle that Jesus performed.

State **two** characteristics of the kingdom of God that can be seen in one of Jesus' miracles.

Higher Level 2005: Section 5, question 2

'In the parables Jesus tells people what the kingdom of God is like; in the miracles he shows people the kingdom of God among them' Mark Link

Outline what is revealed about the kingdom of God in **one** parable and **one** miracle you have studied.

Higher Level 2009: Section 4, question 2

Name **one** parable Jesus told his early followers.

Outline **two** points that Jesus taught his followers about the kingdom of God in a parable you have studied.

Mini-Project

Research three miracles that Jesus is said to have performed and make a presentation on them. Find out where each took place and who was involved in each.

The Death and Resurrection of Jesus

9

Key Concepts

conflict with authority, Passover or Pesach, Eucharist, memorial, sacrifice, martyrdom, resurrection, transformation, presence

The part of Jesus' life that he spent as a public figure – teaching and healing people – did not last very long. Most scholars agree it was approximately three years. He spent most of that time in the northern province of Galilee. Here he did come into conflict with authority figures such as the Pharisees. However, it was in Judea and especially in Jerusalem that the conflict he was attracting was most dangerous. His message, though inclusive, was not what everyone wanted to hear. At times, it made some people very uncomfortable, especially the rich and powerful. His final journey to Jerusalem brings him to the last week of his life. Although it is only one week, a great deal is written about it. For Christians, this is the most significant week of Jesus' life and has some of the most important teachings about God.

To recap – politics

Israel was a country in the Roman Empire. It was divided into three provinces: Galilee, Samaria and Judea. The Romans had allowed the local ruler, Herod the Great, to rule on their behalf until his death in 4 CE. Following this, they allowed his three sons to take over the provinces. One son, Herod Antipas, ruled Galilee, which is the region Jesus came from. Another son, Archelaus, was replaced as ruler of Judea (where the capital Jerusalem was) by a directly appointed governor. Pontius Pilate was governor during the time of Jesus.

... and religion

Judaism, the main religion of the area, was centred on the Temple in Jerusalem. There were numerous synagogues throughout the provinces. The Pharisees were a religious group that focused on the need to follow the Jewish law and were quite critical of some of the practices in the Temple. The Sadducees were the group most associated with the Temple and its rituals. They accepted Roman rule and the Romans in turn helped maintain a status quo which gave them a privileged position.

1. Who did Jesus come into conflict with during his time in Galilee?
2. Why was Jerusalem more dangerous for him?
3. Who had taken power as governor of Judea?
4. What did the Pharisees consider most important?
5. Why did the Sadducees accept Roman rule?

Conflict with authority
When an individual or a group clashes with the people who hold power, make decisions and enforce obedience. The authority figures in Jesus' time were the Romans and the leaders of the Jewish religion.

Jesus' last week

Jesus' last week takes up a large part of the Gospels. This is a really important part of the story of Jesus for Christians.

Entry into Jerusalem

Jesus entered Jerusalem at the beginning of the week leading up to Passover, one of the major Jewish religious festivals. He arrived on the day that has become known to Christians as Palm Sunday. He is said to have arrived on a donkey. Why? This story fulfils the Old Testament prophecy found in the book of Zechariah, Chapter 9: 'Lo, your King comes to you; triumphant and victorious is he, humble and riding on a donkey, on a colt, the foal of a donkey.'

This is very significant too, since a young donkey is in complete contrast with a war horse. A king would arrive mounted on horseback and a horse would be the sort of animal the expected messiah might ride. For Christians, Jesus is the Messiah, but a very different messiah from the one of Jewish expectations at that time.

Now imagine an important visitor was coming to your school or county or even to Ireland. What might people line the streets with? Flags are very often waved at people as a greeting. The other thing that usually greets modern VIPs is a red carpet. The next detail of Jesus' arrival into Jerusalem is an ancient version of rolling out the red carpet and waving flags. The palm branches waved at Jesus as he arrived into Jerusalem and people throwing down their coats on the road appear like the greeting reserved for a VIP and a reminder of the expected welcome of a king. The people called out words found in the Book of Psalms in the Old Testament: 'Blessed is the one who comes in the name of the Lord. We bless you from the house of the Lord.'

They then added the words: 'Blessed is the coming kingdom of our ancestor David.' This is the sort of gathering a king might expect and also has echoes of the prophecies of a messiah sent to restore a kingdom of Israel.

Are there any other occasions when people wave flags?

Over to You

1. Outline all the significant points in the story of Jesus' arrival to Jerusalem.
2. Think of a leader in history or fiction who would fit the Jewish expectation of a messiah.
3. Draw a picture of Jesus' arrival in Jerusalem on Palm Sunday.

So, it seems to be going well for Jesus. Yet less than a week later, he is nailed to a cross and executed in one of the most painful ways possible. Why?

What happens next?

The Monday after Palm Sunday is hugely important in the story of Jesus' death. On this day, he visited the Temple in Jerusalem, the heart of the Jewish religion and centre stage of the regional politics of the time. Now Jesus didn't stay quiet and talk in hushed tones about his disapproval of what was happening in the Temple. Instead he carried out a very dramatic protest, which brought him straight to the attention of the religious authorities and the Romans. Both groups would have seen his actions as dangerous and regarded him as a troublemaker.

What had upset Jesus?

The system in the Temple was that people bought animals to sacrifice to God. Jewish pilgrims would travel from all over the country and further afield to come and carry out this sacrifice. People would bring with them the Roman coins that they used every day, but these could not be used to purchase the sacrificial animal. Why? The coins bore the head of the emperor – a Roman god. Jewish people, while forced to use such coins in daily life, did not wish to use something they saw as a false idol to buy something for such an important religious ritual. So the first thing they had to do in the Temple was to go to the money changers' tables and buy temple coins. With this temple money, they went to the stalls of the animal sellers to purchase the animal for sacrifice. At both stages the people were being exploited. The money changers and animal sellers could see a captive market who had little chance of arguing about the price, so they used the system to make more money. Jesus, as a Galilean carpenter with followers who were in the main poor people, was outraged. Good Jewish pilgrims going to the house of God to do the right thing but being exploited for it was too much to ignore.

Outside which buildings in Ireland do people protest?

> Then they came to Jerusalem. And he entered the temple and began to drive out those who were selling and those who were buying in the temple, and he overturned the tables of the money-changers and the seats of those who sold doves; and he would not allow anyone to carry anything through the temple. He was teaching and saying, 'Is it not written, "My house shall be called a house of prayer for all the nations"? But you have made it a den of robbers.'
>
> (Mark 11:15–17)

What was the job of the money changers?

Discuss

Do you think Jesus was right in acting the way he did? Are there situations when it is right to be angry and to protest?

Reaction

To say that the leaders in the Temple were upset would be an understatement. They were annoyed and afraid. They had come to fear any trouble because, with the Romans always looming in the background, the leaders of Judaism were very conscious that the consequences of any disturbances might fall back on them and the people they led. Judaism was in a difficult position, tolerated by the Romans in as far as they allowed them to have their own temple and worship their one God. But Jews were far from free and always under the threat of persecution. From the Roman point of view, they would have been aware of what occurred in the Temple and while the religious points Jesus was making would not have bothered them, the elements of tension and protest in what he did would have concerned them a great deal. Troublemakers, as we have noted, were not tolerated by the Romans and especially not during this festival week when large crowds gathered in the city.

What message were the Romans sending to people?

The significance of Passover

All the events that took place during Jesus' last week were happening during the week of the Jewish festival of Passover. The Passover festival commemorates and celebrates the Exodus, when the people of Israel were led by Moses out of slavery in Egypt. It is a very big event in Jewish history and a story that means a great deal to the Jewish people to this day. Moses is a hugely important figure, responsible for giving the people the law or Torah, making them the 'people of the covenant'. The tension of the week was caused by so many people flooding into Jerusalem for the Passover festival. This tension was increased by the fact that the people – while celebrating a moment when they achieved freedom – were anything but free. There were some who wanted to fight for freedom and the week was an occasion when such people might decide to act.

Further conflict with the authorities

> *So they asked him, 'Teacher, we know that you are right in what you say and teach, and you show deference to no one, but teach the way of God in accordance with truth. Is it lawful for us to pay taxes to the emperor, or not?' But he perceived their craftiness and said to them, 'Show me a denarius. Whose head and whose title does it bear?' They said, 'The emperor's.' He said to them, 'Then give to the emperor the things that are the emperor's, and to God the things that are God's.' And they were not able in the presence of the people to trap him by what he said; and being amazed by his answer, they became silent.*
>
> (Luke 20:21–26)

In the above passage, there is evidence of more conflict with the authorities. This discussion about taxes may have been an attempt by some to catch Jesus out or to find out how dangerous his views on a controversial subject were.

Judas' betrayal of Jesus

On Tuesday or Wednesday, Judas, one of Jesus' followers, went to the leaders of the Temple and offered to hand Jesus over to them. The reason that he did so may never be understood, but either way it was an act of betrayal and ultimately led to the execution of Jesus on the cross. Perhaps Judas had become disillusioned by Jesus, maybe he thought that if he gave Jesus over to the authorities he might force him into action, or maybe he simply wanted the money. He received thirty pieces of silver for his trouble. According to Matthew's gospel, Judas, realising that Jesus was condemned, went back to the leaders in the Temple. He told them he had made a mistake and Jesus was innocent, but they weren't interested. So Judas threw away the money and hanged himself.

Judas has become the archetype of the betrayer in Western culture, with a role in virtually all literature telling the Passion story. From Dante to Elgar, Caravaggio to Lady

Do you know the origin of the phrase 'the kiss of death'?

Gaga, the story of Judas and his betrayal has become the theme of many works of art, whether paintings, plays, classical music or pop songs. The name of 'Judas' has also been used for many a football star who has changed teams. To call someone Judas signifies that they have carried out a serious act of betrayal.

> **Over to You**
>
> Write a diary entry for Judas on the day he betrayed Jesus.

The Passion

The Passion is the story of Jesus Christ's arrest, trial and suffering. It ends with his execution by crucifixion. The word 'passion' comes from the Latin word for suffering. The crucifixion of Jesus is recorded in the Gospels and in the writings of the Jewish historian Josephus and the Roman historian Tacitus. The Passion begins with one of the most famous meals in history – the Last Supper.

The Last Supper – Passover and Eucharist memorial

Jesus and the disciples shared a last meal together in a room loaned by a friend in Jerusalem. It took place either during Passover or on the eve of Passover and was probably a *Seder* meal, eaten at night, as was the custom. At the meal, Jesus followed the normal Jewish custom of thanking God. He then proceeded to break the bread and gave it to the disciples, saying: 'This is my body which is given for you. Do this in remembrance of me.' After the meal, Jesus blessed some wine and gave it to the disciples, saying: 'This cup that is poured out for you is the new covenant in my blood.' (Luke 22:19, 20)

It is especially significant that this event took place during Passover. Passover in Judaism is a sign of the covenant with God. It commemorates a major event in Jewish history when Moses eventually succeeded in getting the Pharaoh

Glossary

Passover or Pesach
A Jewish festival that commemorates the story of the Exodus, in which the ancient Israelites were freed from slavery in Egypt.

What did Jesus teach about table fellowship?

to allow the people to leave Egypt. They were being treated as slaves and it was only after a series of ten plagues that the Pharaoh allowed the people to go free. The final plague was the death of the firstborn and the Jewish people sacrificed a lamb and painted the blood on their doorposts. It was the sign for the Angel of Death to 'pass over' their homes. It was a sign of the covenant and after the night of the Passover the people left Egypt. Here in the Last Supper, Jesus hints at his sacrifice and says that his blood is the new covenant, shed for the forgiveness of sins. In the words of John's gospel, Jesus for Christians is 'the lamb of God who takes away the sin of the world'.

The Last Supper is the foundation of the Christian sacrament of the Eucharist, which is also known by names such as Holy Communion, Mass and the Lord's Supper. Although different Christian denominations have many ways of celebrating the Eucharist and understand it in different ways, they all developed from the Last Supper.

Eucharist *Glossary*

Means 'thanksgiving'; Christian service, ceremony or sacrament commemorating the Last Supper, in which bread and wine are consecrated (made sacred) and consumed.

Memorial *Glossary*

An action or object intended to commemorate someone or something.

Over to You

1. What does 'the Passion' refer to?
2. Who recorded the crucifixion?
3. Where did the Last Supper take place?
4. What did Jesus do with the bread and wine?
5. What Jewish festival were they celebrating?
6. Why is that significant?
7. What Christian ritual commemorates the Last Supper?

The arrest

After the meal, Jesus headed off to the Garden of Gethsemane to pray. Here he told the disciples to keep watch, but they fell asleep, leaving him having to face things alone. He asked God if he could escape his fate: 'Father, if you are willing, take this cup from me; yet not my will, but yours be done.'

Despite this prayer, he willingly submitted to God's will and continued to prepare himself. It is recorded that his distress was such that 'his sweat was like drops of blood'.

Why do you think Jesus was arrested here and not in the Temple?

115

Here in the garden, Jesus was arrested under cover of darkness by a group of temple guards. Judas, one of his disciples, had a pre-arranged signal with the guards to point him out – the famous kiss of death. The disciples were really afraid now and more or less ran off to hide. Although Peter followed to see what would happen next, he too was afraid and when asked if he was a follower of Jesus he denied even knowing him.

Peter's denial

While Peter was below in the courtyard, one of the servant-girls of the high priest came by. When she saw Peter warming himself, she stared at him and said, 'You also were with Jesus, the man from Nazareth.' But he denied it, saying, 'I do not know or understand what you are talking about.' And he went out into the forecourt. Then the cock crowed. And the servant-girl, on seeing him, began again to say to the bystanders, 'This man is one of them.' But again he denied it. Then after a little while the bystanders again said to Peter, 'Certainly you are one of them; for you are a Galilean.' But he began to curse, and he swore an oath, 'I do not know this man you are talking about.' At that moment the cock crowed for the second time. Then Peter remembered that Jesus had said to him, 'Before the cock crows twice, you will deny me three times.' And he broke down and wept.

(Mark 14:66–72)

 Discuss   Why do you think Peter denied ever knowing Jesus?

Trial and interrogation

Jesus was questioned by a group of Jewish religious leaders. The Gospels give slightly different accounts of the trial and interrogation of Jesus, and of who was present. It has been suggested that the interrogation by the religious authorities was illegal because it took place at night and not enough members of the council were present. Caiaphas, the Chief Priest of the Temple, wanted to remove Jesus before he caused a rebellion that would enrage the Roman authorities.

During questioning Jesus said enough for the Romans to see him as a rebel and the Jews to regard him as a blasphemer.

Why were the religious authorities annoyed with Jesus?

- Jesus had *challenged their authority* – earlier in the week Jesus had gone to the Temple and protested against the money changers. In this way he had attacked what the Temple stood for.

- He was *reinterpreting Jewish law* and they believed he had broken the laws concerning the Sabbath.

- They believed that Jesus had claimed to be the Messiah, a claim that the authorities thought was blasphemous. This claim also suggested he was preparing some sort of rebellion, probably against the Romans. Such *a revolt would endanger the relationship between Roman and Jewish authorities.*

- He had predicted the *destruction of the Temple*.

The political authorities – the Romans

Following the interrogation by the Jewish religious authorities, Jesus was handed over to the Roman governor Pontius Pilate and he was charged with treason. Most accounts suggest that Pilate was not convinced that Jesus was guilty of a capital crime.

He also handed Jesus over to Herod Antipas, the ruler of Galilee, where Jesus was from. Herod had no interest in any of the crimes Jesus was accused of and simply made fun of him.

Pilate decided to use the custom of releasing a prisoner during Passover. He gave the people a choice. At the Antonia fortress where Jesus was being held, he offered the crowd either Jesus or a criminal called Barabbas. The leaders persuaded the crowd to ask for Barabbas and so Jesus was condemned to death. Pilate sentenced Jesus to be whipped first and then executed by crucifixion. Although the Gospels show Pilate as a weak man who ignored justice rather than stand up to the crowd, other sources say that he was tough and authoritarian, and unlikely to have been pushed around by anyone.

Discuss Pilate's role in Jesus' execution.

Did you know? Pilate was eventually ordered back to Rome and tried for the cruel way in which he treated the people under his government.

The crucifixion

What message were the Romans sending to the people?

Alone and deserted by his friends, Jesus was whipped and then, to mock the claim that he was 'King of the Jews', given a crown of thorns and dressed in a purple robe. At this stage, having lost a lot of blood, he was forced to carry the crossbeam to the place of crucifixion. It is noted that he was helped along the way by a man called Simon of Cyrene.

The crucifixion took place at a location called Calvary or Golgotha, meaning 'place of the skull'. Jesus was nailed to the cross by his wrists and a sign was placed above his head that said: 'King of the Jews'. Two criminals were crucified alongside him. After some hours, the soldiers checked that Jesus was dead by stabbing him in the side. Blood and water gushed out. At the very end, the Roman centurion declared, 'Truly this man was God's Son!'

What did Jesus say on the cross? The Seven Last Words:

1. 'Father, forgive them; they do not know what they are doing.' (Luke 23:34)
2. 'I tell you this; today you shall be with me in Paradise.' (Luke 23:43) Jesus said this to one of the criminals who was crucified with him.
3. 'Mother, there is your son. Son, there is your mother.' (John 19:26)
4. 'My God, my God, why have you forsaken me?' (Mark 15:34)
5. 'I thirst.' (John 19:28)
6. 'It is finished.' (John 19:30)
7. 'Father, into your hands I commit my spirit.' (Luke 23:46)

Did you know? The Seven Last Words formed the basis of a famous piece of music by the Austrian composer Franz Joseph Haydn. Commissioned in 1786, it was first performed on Good Friday, 1787 in Cadiz, Spain.

At the moment of Jesus' death on the cross, the curtain hanging in the centre of the Jewish Temple is said to have 'torn in two, from top to bottom'. This dramatic event is recorded as a symbol of the death of Jesus having removed the barrier between God and people.

Where was Haydn from?

What does Golgotha mean?

Over to You

Write a newspaper report on the trial and execution of Jesus.

Christian understanding of Jesus' death

The curtain or veil was a barrier between man and God. It was placed in the centre of the Temple to prevent anyone from carelessly entering God's presence. Even the high priest who entered the Holy of Holies on the Day of Atonement had to make preparations. He had to wash himself, put on special clothing, bring burning incense to let the smoke cover his eyes from a direct view of God and bring blood with him to make atonement for sins. 'But only the high priest entered the inner room, and that only once a year, and never without blood, which he offered for himself and for the sins the people had committed in ignorance.' (Hebrews 9:7)

For Christians, Jesus' sacrificial death on the cross changed this belief. *Christians believe that his death meant that God's presence was now accessible to all.* When Jesus cried out on the cross, 'It is finished!' he was proclaiming that God's plan was now complete. The ultimate offering had been sacrificed.

No one person or group can really be

Where was the curtain placed?

Glossary

Sacrifice
In ancient times, an act of slaughtering an animal or surrendering a possession as an offering to a God. It also means to give up something valued for the sake of something else that is regarded as more important or worthy. When sacrifice is used in Christianity, it may refer to Jesus' offering of himself in the crucifixion.

> **Martyrdom** (Glossary)
> The death or suffering of a martyr (someone who is killed for their beliefs).

blamed for Jesus' death. The Romans were the ones who carried it out, of course, but in many ways his death was a result of complicated circumstances. In Christianity, the emphasis is on the idea that his death was a part of his mission to bring people close to God, to repair their broken relationship with God, and so he sacrificed himself for others. As the high priest brought blood to offer a sacrifice for the people's sins, Jesus offered his own blood for everyone's sins. In Christian understanding, Jesus' death on the cross is a symbol of victory over death and sin, opening a new opportunity for life, forgiveness and love.

Jesus' body was taken down and buried

Following his death on the cross, Jesus' body had to be taken down. The normal preparations for burial could not be carried out because it was Friday and the beginning of the Sabbath, the Jewish holy day. The friends and followers of Jesus did not have time to prepare his body properly, but they asked for it none the less, and a wealthy member of the Jewish council, Joseph of Arimathea, offered a tomb in which it could be placed. The body was left in the tomb and guarded until the Sunday morning.

Resurrection

When a group of women followers went to anoint Jesus on the Sunday morning, they found the tomb empty and were told: 'He has been raised, he is not here.'

Just when the disciples thought it was all over! Understandably Jesus' friends were upset and most of them were prepared to do what needed to be done and then head home. But the events of the first Easter Sunday changed everything. When the women found the tomb empty and heard the news of the resurrection, they told the others. While some disciples were quicker than others to believe the news, they were all shocked and eventually transformed by it.

Who first discovered the empty tomb? What did it come to symbolise?

> **Resurrection** (Glossary)
> Restoring a dead person to life in a transformed way, beyond the power of death. In Christianity, it refers to the belief that Jesus rose from the dead.

This is the point when the disciples went through a complete transformation from being disappointed, confused and afraid to becoming leaders, martyrs and the people who would begin a new religion. In this way, for the early Christians, the resurrection was a transformative event. For modern Christians, it is celebrated and remembered as such, but even more than that, Christians believe it has the power to transform people's lives today.

Transformation
To undergo a marked change.

The empty tomb is the symbol for the belief that Jesus rose from the dead. The resurrection is fundamental for Christians because:

- It forms the basis for the belief that there is life after death.
- It means that Jesus is the Messiah.
- It is evidence of the power of good over evil.

The Sunday that Christians believe the women found the empty tomb became known as *Easter Sunday*. It is one of the most important days in the Christian calendar as it celebrates the resurrection of Jesus.

In Christian understanding, when Jesus was resurrected he was not the same as he had been before; he was present in a new way. While the risen Jesus' appearances continued for forty days, when he left the disciples for the last time on Ascension Thursday, they were told he would be with them always: 'Go therefore and make disciples of all nations, baptising them in the name of the Father and of the Son and of the Holy Spirit, and teaching them to obey everything that I have commanded you. And remember, I am with you always, to the end of the age.'

Presence
The state or fact of existing, occurring or being present. It can also refer to a person or thing that exists or is present in a place but is not seen.

Christians believe that Jesus was God incarnate or 'in the flesh'. In this way, God knows what it is like to be human and humans are no longer separated from God. The presence of God was fully realised in the life of Jesus, but in the resurrection that presence is promised continually till the end of time.

Over to You

1. What happened to Jesus' body after he died on the cross?
2. When did the followers go to the tomb to anoint his body?
3. What did they discover?
4. What does resurrection mean?
5. How did the disciples change after Easter Sunday?
6. When was the last time the disciples saw Jesus?
7. What was their role after his death?

Key Terms

conflict with authority, Passover or Pesach, Eucharist, memorial, sacrifice, martyrdom, resurrection, transformation, presence

Revision

Go through all the key terms for the chapter, explaining each and describing its relevance to the last week of Jesus' life.

Exam Practice

Higher Level 2011: Short question
The Roman governor in Palestine at the time of Jesus was: Peter/Philip/Pilate.

Higher Level 2010: Short question
The crucifixion of Jesus is most associated with which **one** of the following places: Gaza/Gilgal/Golgotha.

Higher Level 2006: Short question
According to the Gospels, **one** person Jesus appeared to after his death and resurrection was _____.

Ordinary Level 2004: Short question
The Last Supper was a meal associated with which of the following religious celebrations?
Bar Mitzvah/Hanukkah/Passover/Sukkot

Ordinary Level 2010: Section 4, question 2
The person most associated with the arrest of Jesus in the Garden of Gethsemane was: Barabbas/Herod/Judas.
Outline **two** ways in which the first disciples were affected by the arrest of Jesus in the Garden of Gethsemane.
Imagine you were an eyewitness to the last events of Jesus' life.
Describe what happened.

Test Yourself
eTest.ie

Mini-Project

Research three famous works of art based on the Passion. Find out how the artist interprets the story.

Faith in Christ

10

Key Concepts

martyr, Pentecost, missionary, people of God.

Higher level only: **Son of Man, Son of God, Messiah/Christ, New Creation**

The story of Christianity does not end with Jesus' death. Now the largest religion in the world, Christianity has begun in a small country in the eastern Mediterranean with the life and death of a Jewish teacher named Jesus. How did it spread? What happened following the crucifixion?

The beginning of Christianity

It is really only after Jesus' death that you can talk about Christianity as a religion. The word Christianity itself derives from a title for Jesus: the Christ. It refers to the belief that Jesus was the Messiah, the anointed or chosen one. It was only after his death that his followers understood that and began to see what type of messiah he was. So they became known as Christians or followers of Christ.

Did you know?

The fish was one of the earliest Christian symbols. The first Christians did not use the cross, which was a reminder of Jesus' painful execution as a criminal. The fish had connections with the disciples, many of whom were fishermen, and with miracles Jesus was said to have performed. The letters of the Greek word for fish (*ichthys*) translate as the first letters of the words 'Jesus Christ, God's Son, Saviour'.

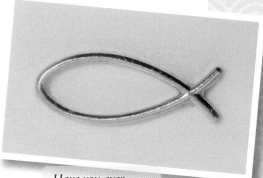

Have you ever seen this symbol? Where?

123

Can you name three letters that Paul wrote?

As we have noted, the disciples became the early leaders of a new religion, which was still very much connected with Judaism; so much so that for many decades after Jesus' life there were people who are best described as 'Jewish Christians'. Their experiences after Jesus' death varied but most involved considerable hardship, danger and frequently martyrdom. Peter was executed by crucifixion. James, the brother of Jesus, who became leader of the new Christian movement in Jerusalem, was beaten to death. Paul, the famous writer and leader, who went through a dramatic conversion to Christianity on the road to Damascus, was also executed, as indeed were many more up to the fourth century. The ideas or teachings of Jesus, however, could not be killed and despite three centuries of persecution, the movement continued to grow and develop.

We saw how the disciples changed after the resurrection. They believed and understood much more of what Jesus had told them in his lifetime. One account of this sort of transformation and new understanding is told in the story of the 'Road to Emmaus' in Luke 24:13–35.

Glossary

Martyr
A person who dies for their beliefs.

In this story, two disciples were walking on the road seven miles from Jerusalem to Emmaus and while on the journey were joined by a stranger. They explained to him why they were so sad: all about Jesus, his execution and the empty tomb. The stranger was Jesus but they were unaware of this. He explained to them about the idea of a messiah who would suffer for the sake of others, through teaching them what it says in the scriptures. They reached Emmaus and asked Jesus to join them. He broke bread with them: 'When he was at the table with them, he took bread, gave thanks, broke it and began to give it to them. Then their eyes were opened.' Just as they realised who he was, he was gone. They said to each other: 'Were not our hearts burning within us while he was talking to us on the road, while he was opening up the scriptures to us?'

It is significant that the disciples recognised Jesus when he broke bread. Many Christians today, when they have the bread and wine during the sacrament of the Eucharist, believe that they too can experience the risen Jesus. Christians believe that it is in the ongoing life of the community, sharing and gathering together, that the possibility of recognising Jesus becomes real.

Classwork

Read the full story in Luke, Chapter 24 and act it out as a drama or draw a picture of the story.

Pentecost

Forty days after Easter, on Ascension Thursday, Jesus said farewell and was taken up into heaven. Now the disciples had to start their mission for real. They had been told that Jesus would be with them, but the sign they really needed, enabling them to carry out their mission, took place ten days later. This event is known as Pentecost.

Pentecost, or *Shavuoth*, is a Jewish festival, which takes place fifty days after the Passover, seven weeks plus one day. It is a harvest festival, which also commemorates Moses receiving the law on Mount Sinai. The apostles were celebrating this festival when the Holy Spirit descended on them.

When would you be likely to see this in a church?

The story took place in Jerusalem, where Jesus' disciples, family and friends were marking the festival. As they prayed together in a room, a sound like rushing wind filled the house and tongues of fire (a symbol of the Holy Spirit) descended on them.

So Pentecost is also a Christian festival, which celebrates the gift of the Holy Spirit. For many, it is the moment of the beginning of the Christian Church, the moment from which Christians started a mission to the world. It takes place fifty days after Easter and is also sometimes called Whit Sunday.

Pentecost
A Christian festival celebrating the gift of the Holy Spirit.

Glossary

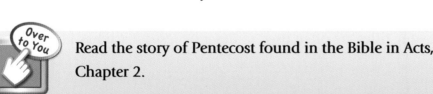

Over to You — Read the story of Pentecost found in the Bible in Acts, Chapter 2.

Missionary
A person sent on a religious mission, especially one sent to promote Christianity.

Glossary

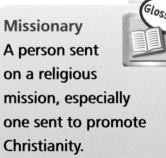

What effect did Pentecost have on the early followers of Jesus? They became missionaries, or people who try to encourage others to share their faith. Their mission spread everywhere and Christian communities emerged throughout the Roman world, in Egypt, Turkey, Greece, Syria, Italy etc.

The early development of Christianity

Some groups of early Christians were not always clear about what they needed to do or believe and some of the early Christian writings give such people advice, e.g. Paul's letters to Christians in places like Corinth (Corinthians), Philippi (Philippians) and Thessalonica (Thessalonians). Paul was a very important leader of the early Christian movement. He travelled a good deal and established many communities of Christians in the Roman world. Like the other leaders, his mission was to bring about a new community, believing in Jesus as the Messiah and living their lives as the people of God. In one of his letters to the community at Corinth, Paul warns the people about division and fighting: they are to be one people, who share their unity in Christ.

> **Glossary**
>
> **People of God**
> Refers to the idea of Christians as a community united by faith in Christ.

Christianity was developing at a very difficult time for Judaism. The Romans persecuted the Jewish people severely after revolts in 70 CE, when the Temple in Jerusalem was destroyed, and again in 135 CE, when they were dispersed from their homeland. The Jewish people had to redefine their identity outside the Promised Land. The Judaism that became dominant was most like the teachings of the Pharisees in its emphasis on the law or Torah. New writings emerged, such as the *Mishnah* and the *Talmud*. Christians also suffered but unfortunately the two groups, although so closely connected, were suspicious of each other. The close relationship became increasingly problematic, especially in their understanding of God's plan for the people. Who was right? Was Jesus the Messiah? Had God changed the covenant? All these sorts of questions led to a painful parting of the ways, which has had repercussions to the present day.

Titles for Jesus

For Christians, the following titles are often used to describe Jesus. Each has its own meaning and origins.

Son of Man

In Mark's gospel, the disciples are confused when Jesus speaks of a figure called the 'Son of Man'. In the Gospels, it is the most frequent term used for Jesus. The term 'Son of Man' is found in the Old Testament book of Daniel, where it refers to a character who receives authority, honour and royal power from God. Jesus, however, lived out this role through suffering and warned his followers about the fate of the Son of Man: 'Then he began to teach them that the Son of Man must undergo great suffering, and be rejected by the elders, chief priests, and the scribes, and be killed, and after three days rise again.' (Mark 8:31). For Christians, Jesus as Son of Man went through a final battle with evil during the crucifixion, which his resurrection shows he triumphed over.

Son of God

In Mark's gospel, Jesus is also shown as the 'Son of God' and the title is placed at very important moments in Mark's story: at Jesus' baptism (Mark 1:11), at his transfiguration (Mark 9:7) and at his crucifixion (Mark 15:39). It is also used in all the other gospels and in the book of Acts. The term refers to the special relationship between Jesus and God. It is an important part of his identity and work, since the Gospels are not only telling the story of his life but encouraging faith in Jesus as God's son. Son of God was also a title commonly used by Roman emperors and by calling Jesus this, early Christian writers may be stating their belief in Jesus' power, rather than the emperor's.

Messiah/Christ

The title 'Messiah' in Hebrew translates into 'Christ' in Greek. The early Christians were named as followers of the Christ or Messiah. In Hebrew, this means 'anointed one'. Anointing someone indicated that the person was chosen by God. The idea of a messiah to deliver the Jewish nation developed during periods of oppression in Old Testament times. Jesus was born at a time when this idea was widespread in Judaism, as the people looked to God to free them from the Romans. They saw the Messiah as someone who would be a warrior king to set them free. For Christians, Jesus is regarded as the Messiah of Hebrew prophecies and the saviour of the world.

New Creation

For Christians, after the ascension Jesus' victory over evil is complete and he is understood to be the Christ who will restore order out of chaos and renew the harmony of the universe. The old way of the world with suffering and oppression has been ended by Jesus' victory over death. When Christians refer to 'New Creation' they are expressing a belief that through Jesus the entire world, all of God's creation, is redeemed. With Jesus' victory over evil, people have the ability to live at peace with nature and in community with each other.

Key Terms

martyr, Pentecost, missionary, people of God.

Higher level only: Son of Man, Son of God, Messiah/Christ, New Creation

Chapter Questions

1. Why is it appropriate to describe many early followers of Jesus as Jewish Christians?
2. Where did Paul undergo a dramatic conversion?
3. What was his role in the early church?
4. What is a martyr? Name two Christian martyrs.
5. What happened on Ascension Thursday?
6. What is important about Pentecost for Christians?
7. Why did the relationship between Jews and Christians become difficult early on?
8. What titles are used to describe Jesus? Explain two.

Exam Practice

Higher Level 2003: Short question

Christians call the coming of the Holy Spirit upon the disciples after the death of Jesus: Ascension/Pentecost/Resurrection.

Higher Level 2004: Short question

Son of God is a title the first Christian communities used when referring to: James/Jesus/John/Joseph.

Higher Level 2005: Short question

One example of martyrdom from the founding story of Christianity is

_____.

Higher Level 2011: Section 5, question 2

Examine how the experience of one of the below played a part in the development of the first Christian communities: Memorial/Mission.

Higher Level 2007: Section 4, question 2

Describe **one** incident from the life of Jesus that led to his death.

Outline **two** reasons why the incident you have described above led to the death of Jesus.

Outline how Jesus' death affected the people who were following him.

Higher Level 2006: Section 5, question 2

Outline what **one** of the titles below shows about the early Christians' understanding of Jesus: Son of God/Son of Man.

Mini-Project

Research Peter, James or Paul as an early Christian leader and tell their story.

Useful Websites for Section B: Foundations of Religion – Christianity

For this section of the course, the aims are to explore the context into which Jesus was born, to identify the Gospels as the main source of knowledge about Jesus, and to examine the meaning of the life, death and resurrection of Jesus for his followers, then and now.

To find out more about many of the origins of Christianity and how the New Testament came to be written, the following are useful websites:

www.scoilnet.ie – this is an excellent portal to numerous websites and resources. Click on Junior Cert Cycle, Section B, Foundations of Religion.

www.bbc.co.uk/religion/religions/christianity

www.reonline.org.uk

www.rejesus.co.uk

www.christianityinview.com

There are many useful and worthwhile books to read for further information. The following are very good for work with students. They include lots of pictures, diagrams and maps:

The Lion Illustrated Encyclopaedia of the Bible by John Drane

The Lion Handbook of the Bible by John Drane

The New Lion Bible Encyclopaedia by Mike Beaumont

Suggested DVDs include:

The Miracle Maker, a stop motion animated film about the life of Jesus Christ told from the perspective of a young girl, Tamar, the daughter of Jairus. Directed by Derek Hayes and Stanislav Sokolov, it features the voices of Ralph Fiennes and Julie Christie.

Jesus of Nazareth, a 1977 television mini-series directed by Franco Zeffirelli, dramatises the birth, life, ministry, crucifixion and resurrection of Jesus, largely based on the New Testament.

The Lion, the Witch and the Wardrobe, based on the novel of the same name by C. S. Lewis, is an allegory of Christ's crucifixion. It is an interesting way to explore the theme of Christ's suffering and death, and his sacrifice for sin and faith.

Section

Foundations of Religion – Major World Religions

This section of the syllabus aims:

- To explore in detail a major world religion (Buddhism, Hinduism, Islam or Judaism).
- To examine the impact of this religion on its followers today and on other individuals and communities.

Judaism: Context and Evidence

11

Key Concepts

location, cultural context, founder, revelation, dream/vision, inspiration, prophet, evidence, oral tradition, sacred text

Location *Glossary*

Where something takes place. The region in which the religion started is the location for its beginning.

Cultural context *Glossary*

What an area was like when something took place: the religion, way of life, form of government, customs, practices, influences, beliefs etc.

Judaism

This is the oldest of the monotheistic or 'one God' religions. The Jewish religion goes back to approximately 1850 BCE, to a time when most people worshipped a variety of Gods. For those people, these Gods made the sun shine and the rain fall, and worship of them was important for survival. As the founder of Judaism was from Ur in Mesopotamia, roughly where modern-day Iraq is, he lived among such people. His name was Abraham and he is recognised as the first person to believe in one God.

History of Judaism

The story of the beginning of Judaism is about the Patriarchs or founding fathers: Abraham, Isaac and Jacob. Their stories are told in the Bible in the book of Genesis, the first book of the Jewish law or Torah.

Stage one: into the Promised Land

Abram, from Mesopotamia, was a nomad who had moved from Ur to Haran. Archaeology of the region suggests that the people there built temples, known as *ziggurats*, to worship a moon God. They may have sacrificed people to their Gods. Abram encountered God and made a covenant or agreement with God. The encounter with God was a revelation. The agreement was to worship one God; God would bless him, and give him land and descendants as numerous as the 'stars in the sky'. God told Abram that from then on he was to be called Abraham.

 Discuss Why do you think God gave Abram a new name?

 Did you know? The Jewish practice of circumcision dates from the time of Abraham and is a sign of the covenant or agreement with God.

Believing in God, Abraham (as he was now called) took his family to the Promised Land. The Promised Land was the land of Canaan, roughly where Israel now is. In one of the most famous stories about Abraham, he was asked by God to sacrifice his only son, Isaac. Showing great willingness to obey God, Abraham and Isaac climbed the mountain to carry out this sacrifice, but God stopped Abraham from going through with it. The story is frequently used to emphasise the importance of obedience to God. For ancient Judaism, it was also a way of saying that God does not want human sacrifice, a practice that was common in other religions at the time.

How would Isaac and Abraham have felt?

135

Stage two: out of the Promised Land

Abraham's son Isaac and grandson Jacob continued the covenant with God. Jacob, who received the name 'Israel' from God, had twelve sons. The sons became known as the 'twelve tribes of Israel'. One of his sons, Joseph, went to Egypt and the people followed when there was a famine. The descendants of Abraham, while still continuing the covenant with God, were no longer living in the Promised Land.

Did you know?

The name Israel means 'God strives' and was given to Jacob after he struggled with a stranger one night, only to discover he had been struggling with God. See if you can learn the names of his twelve sons, the twelve tribes of Israel: Judah, Asher, Zebulun, Reuben, Issachar, Naphtali, Gad, Levi, Simeon, Dan, Joseph and Benjamin!

Glossary

Dream/vision

An image that passes through the mind like foresight or imaginative insight; a view of what is to be or could be.

JACOB'S VISION. A. STRÄHUBER. Genesis, ch. xxviii, ver. 12.

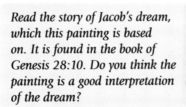

Read the story of Jacob's dream, which this painting is based on. It is found in the book of Genesis 28:10. Do you think the painting is a good interpretation of the dream?

Over to You

1. Who are the Patriarchs?
2. Where was Abraham from?
3. Name Abraham's grandson.
4. Who are the twelve tribes of Israel?
5. How do the people end up in Egypt?

After the period of the Patriarchs, the people found themselves strangers in a foreign land. The next stage in their history is about the struggle to get back to their homeland and is dominated by a colossus of the Old Testament: Moses. His story is told in the book of Exodus, the second book of the Jewish law.

Stage three: the Exodus

After many generations in Egypt, the people had become slaves to the Pharaohs, the rulers of Egypt. They cried out to God to help them. The Egyptians were polytheists (they had many Gods); the Pharaoh was also considered to be a God. The work of slaves would very often include building the magnificent pyramids and temples, that can still be seen in Egypt. This period, when Moses brought the people out of slavery in Egypt, is known as the Exodus, meaning 'departure'. The date was approximately 1250 BCE.

An inspirational early leader: who was Moses?

According to the book of Exodus, the beginning of Moses' life was fraught with danger. As a Hebrew (the name the Jews were known by at this time), he was destined to be killed on the orders of the Pharaoh, who had decided that the 'Hebrews were becoming too numerous', so he ordered the murder of Hebrew boys. His survival, due to his mother's decision to place him in a water-tight basket on the River Nile, showed his destiny was important. He was taken from the water by an Egyptian princess who hired a Hebrew woman to nurse him, who was, in fact, his own mother.

One of the biggest films of 1956 was *The Ten Commandments*, starring Charlton Heston as Moses. It was an epic movie, directed by Cecil B. DeMille. In 1998 Steven Spielberg produced the story again as an animated film, *The Prince of Egypt*. The voice of Moses is American actor Val Kilmer, while the Pharaoh is voiced by British actor Ralph Fiennes.

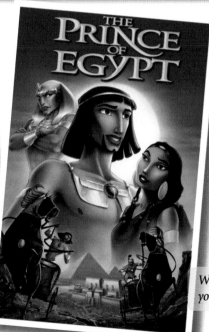

Which film poster do you prefer? Why?

Later, having grown up as an Egyptian noble, Moses rescued a Hebrew slave who was being beaten by an Egyptian taskmaster. Moses accidentally killed the Egyptian. He fled and ended up in Midian, an area outside Egypt, where he married Zipporah, the daughter of a Midianite priest called Jethro. He lived and worked here, until one day while herding sheep, he encountered God in a dramatic way.

Moses saw a bush on fire, but it was not burning. The flames represented the presence of God. The voice that came from the flames told Moses to take off his shoes, for he was 'walking on sacred ground'. Moses dutifully did so. In this revelation, Moses was told by God to go back to Egypt to help free the people. Moses was fearful of this mission or task that he had to do, but was told he would be helped by his brother, Aaron. Moses asked who he should say had sent him and the response was: 'I am the God of your father, the God of Abraham, the God of Isaac, and the God of Jacob' (Exodus 3:6).

Inspiration
The process of being stimulated to do or feel something, the quality of being inspired. In many religions, inspiration is seen as coming from God.

This was the one God, the God of the Patriarchs. Moses' importance is further demonstrated by the fact that he was told the name of God. In Judaism, this name is never spoken and where it appears in the sacred texts it is replaced with *Adonai* or 'the Lord'. This encounter with God inspired and motivated Moses and he went to the Pharaoh to ask for the freedom of the people.

The book of Exodus tells how the Pharaoh would not agree with Moses to let the people leave Egypt and it was only after a series of ten plagues that he gave in. Moses and the people left in a hurry. While they were fleeing Egypt, the Pharaoh changed his mind and sent his troops after them. The sea dramatically opened up, allowing the people to go free. The Egyptians caught up with them but it was too late; when they reached the sea, they became submerged in the water.

On Mount Sinai, Moses received the Torah (law) from God, including the Ten Commandments. The law was to become one of the most central parts of Judaism. It is the foundation for many Jewish traditions and practices. Moses himself led the people towards the Promised Land, but they spent a generation (a time of preparation) in the wilderness before they were ready to re-enter it. Moses died without having reached it.

> **Did you know?** Numbers are very significant in the Bible and some numbers have special meaning. There were twelve tribes of Israel. Who had twelve followers? The people spent forty years in the wilderness. During the flood, it rained for forty days and nights. Can you think of any other numbers that recur like this?

The significance of the Exodus

In Judaism, the Exodus is one of the most important moments in its history. It is remembered annually in the festival of Passover, during which special foods are eaten and the story of the Exodus is told. It shows the special covenantal relationship Jews have with God. God had not abandoned them, but had brought them out of slavery in Egypt and back to the Promised Land.

Why do people send cards during festivals?

The Torah is a very early form of regulation of human behaviour. Judaism is significant for being one of the first religions to emphasise the fact that religion is more than worship of God or carrying out certain rituals. It is about how people treat other people. It teaches that love of God is shown through love of others.

After Moses, the religion developed its own identity, customs and practices. The turbulent history in and out of the land, however, continues.

Over to You

1. Why did the people cry out to God from Egypt?
2. What does Exodus mean?
3. Where did Moses receive the Torah?
4. Who was the first king of Israel?
5. Why do you think the prophets told the people they did not need a king?
6. What is Solomon famous for?
7. Who is the most successful king? Do you know anything named after him?

Over to You

Research more information about Moses and write an account of his life and importance to Judaism.

Stage four: the kingdom of Israel

Back in the Promised Land, the people looked to God to give them a king. At first, the prophets warned the people that they did not need a king. The role of the prophets is to remind people to be faithful to the covenant and, therefore, God.

Glossary

Prophet
A person regarded as an inspired teacher or a messenger of the will of God. There are many figures regarded as prophets in Judaism, including Moses and Abraham.

139

Eventually God agreed to their request and Saul was chosen as their first king. David succeeded Saul as the second king. He is described as a very successful king and his reign is seen as one of the most glorious periods in the history of Israel. David's son, King Solomon, famous for his wisdom, built the Temple. Along with the land and the Torah (law), the Temple became another focus of identity for ancient Judaism.

Stage five: the divided kingdom

At the end of the reign of Solomon, the kingdom divided into two parts:

1. Israel in the north.
2. Judah in the south.

Both were weakened by the division and by constant rivalry, and were taken over by other states. The northern kingdom was taken over and destroyed by the Assyrians at the end of the eighth century BCE. In 586 BCE, the southern kingdom of Judah was taken over by the Babylonians and the Temple in Jerusalem was destroyed.

Many people from Judah (the Jews) were taken as captives to Babylon. There, without a homeland or temple, they came to believe that their law or Torah was the most important part of their identity.

Stage six: return to Israel

After the Babylonian exile, the new Persian rulers allowed the people to go back to their homeland and rebuild the Temple. This is known as the Second Temple Period. During this time, the land was constantly being taken over by big empires. The Romans took over in 63 BCE. The people began to hope for a messiah. They had religious leaders called rabbis (teachers) and they met together in synagogues to worship God.

Why do you think this wall is so important to Jews today?

Stage seven: revolt and dispersal

The Jews rebelled against the Romans twice. In 70 CE the Romans destroyed the second Jewish Temple. The only part left standing to this day is the Western (Wailing) Wall. In 135 CE, after the second Jewish revolt, the people were expelled from the land by the Romans and dispersed all over Europe and the Middle East – the community that spread throughout the world is referred to as the diaspora.

Outside their homeland and without a temple, they still had their identity based on the law, the Torah, and so their understanding of themselves as the people of the covenant has continued to the present day.

The final stage shaped Judaism for many years to come. The modern state of Israel was not founded until 1948 and while many Jewish people live there, many more live in the United States of America, Europe, Australia and South Africa.

 Discuss

How important is the covenant in Judaism?

Find out how many people live in Jerusalem today. Check out the news to see what events are happening there.

 Over to You

1. Who took over the northern kingdom of Israel?
2. What event took place in 586 BCE?
3. What did the people do when they returned to the Promised Land?
4. What happened in 70 CE?
5. What part of the Temple is still visible today?
6. What is the diaspora?
7. What did the Jews come to understand was the most important part of their identity?

Now that we have looked at the long history of Judaism, we must ask: where is this history recorded?

The Tanakh

The evidence or information about the story of Judaism is found in the Jewish sacred writings known as the *Tanakh*. The Tanakh is divided into three parts: the Torah or law, which is the first five books, the *Nevi'im* or prophets, and finally the *Ketuvi'im* or writings, which include the proverbs and psalms. The Jewish writings are a mix of history, poetry, wisdom literature, songs, psalms and stories.

 **Glossary**

Evidence
The available body of facts or information.

 Did you know?

The first part of the Christian Bible, the Old Testament, is the same as the Jewish Tanakh. The word 'testament' in fact means 'covenant' and refers to the covenant made first by Abraham.

The Torah

Jews consider the Torah, or law, to be the most important part of the Tanakh and they treat this section with such importance that a copy is found in every synagogue. This copy of the Torah is written by hand on scrolls and kept in a special location known as the 'Ark'. It is taken out during services and read. A special stick called a *yad* is used to follow the text to avoid marking the scrolls. The writing is in Hebrew, the language of

What is your most precious possession? How do you look after it?

ancient Judaism still used today. It is read from right to left. The Torah gives guidance on various aspects of life, including family, work, personal hygiene and diet. A unit of law is called a *mitzvah*, which is a commandment or good deed. There are 613 *mitzvot* (commandments) in the Torah.

The Tanakh was written over a period of about 700 years. Much of it was at first told by word of mouth. This is known as the oral stage of its history.

Glossary

Oral tradition
When the stories of a religion were passed on by word of mouth rather than written down.

Other religious texts: Mishnah and Talmud

The writings of Judaism also include the *Mishnah*, a compilation of oral teachings written down in the third century CE. It formed the basis of the *Talmud*. The Talmud, meaning 'teaching', is a written interpretation of the Tanakh. There are two Talmuds – the Babylonian and the Palestinian or 'Jerusalem' Talmud. These writings are a huge collection of Rabbinic teaching from between the fourth and seventh centuries.

What are the two Talmuds known as?

Sacred text

Glossary

The important religious writings of a particular religion; the source of information or authority for people in that religion. As well as containing the teachings of the religion, most sacred texts contain stories of the founder or the beginnings of the religion and include key moments in the history of the religion. They are also important for use in worship and during religious celebrations or festivals.

1. What is the Tanakh?
2. What are its three parts?
3. What is contained in the Torah?
4. What is a yad?
5. Where is the Ark and what does it contain?
6. What does Talmud mean?

Key Terms

location, cultural context, founder, revelation, dream/vision, inspiration, prophet, evidence, oral tradition, sacred text

Chapter Questions

1. Who is responsible for starting the belief in one God?
2. Where did Judaism begin?
3. What is the covenant?
4. Who led the people out of slavery in Egypt?
5. What was the role of the prophets?
6. What did the people learn during the Babylonian exile?
7. Name the Jewish sacred text.

Exam Practice

Higher Level 2005: Short question

In major world religions a prophet is someone who _____.

Higher Level 2006: Short question

A key person in the founding story of Judaism is: Abraham/Gandhi/Gautama/Jesus.

Exam Practice

Higher Level 2007: Section 4, question 3

Tick **one** of the world religions that you have studied: Buddhism/Hinduism/Islam/Judaism

Name **one** key person/group of people associated with the founding story of the world religion you have ticked above_____.

Explain why the person/group of people you have named is important in the founding story of the world religion you have ticked above.

Outline **one** way in which the story of the earliest followers influences members today.

Explain how the world religion you have ticked is linked to another major world religion.

Ordinary Level 2009: Section 4, question 3

Tick **one** of the world religions that you have studied: Buddhism/Hinduism/Islam/Judaism

In religious tradition the term 'revelation' means _____.

Describe **one** example of revelation from the story of the founder/earliest followers of the world religion you have ticked above.

Higher Level 2009: Section 5, question 3

Discuss the importance of a sacred text in one of the major world religions that you have studied: Buddhism/Hinduism/Islam/Judaism

Mini-Project

Draw a timeline of the history of Judaism and write in the key events and names of important people. Or: draw a map of ancient Israel and write a page on the history of Judaism in relation to the movement of the people in and out of the land.

www.jewishvirtuallibrary.org

Judaism: Sacred Time and Place

12

Key Concepts

ceremony, rite, rite of passage, ritual, prayer, meditation, practice, sign, symbol, sacred time, creed/ethic, festivals, calendar, pilgrimage, places of worship

Nearly all religions celebrate important moments in a person's life. They also make some stages in a person's spiritual life significant with rituals or ceremonies. These are known as rites of passage. In other words, they are ceremonial acts to mark the transition from one stage in life to another, e.g. marriages and naming ceremonies.

> **Glossary**
>
> **Ceremony**
> A set of actions performed in a particular setting that mark a particular occasion.

Jewish rites of passage

In Judaism, the following ceremonies take place to mark times of significance in a person's life.

At birth

For boys the 'covenant of circumcision' or *Brit Milah* takes place at eight days old. This is when the foreskin of the penis is removed. Usually a Hebrew name is given to the child. For girls the ceremony of *Zeved Habet*, meaning 'gift of a daughter' takes place, when they too are given a Hebrew name. It is common for family and friends to come to the home of the child for a celebration at this time.

> **Glossary**
>
> **Rite**
> A ceremonial act.

At maturity

One of the most significant rites of passage takes place at this stage. This is known as *bar mitzvah* or *bat mitzvah*. It occurs when a Jewish boy is 13 years old or for a girl when she is 12 years old. It signifies that they have become an adult in their faith.

- Bar mitzvah means a 'son of the commandment/law'.
- Bat mitzvah means a 'daughter of the commandment/law'.

Whether or not a ceremony occurs, once a child has reached this age, they have become bar or bat mitzvah. For most Jewish people, however, an important ritual takes place. They have to learn Hebrew and read from the Torah scroll in the synagogue. Afterwards they usually have a big party to celebrate.

What rite of passage do some Christian children celebrate at a similar age?

At marriage

What do you think is the symbolism of the canopy?

In the past, marriages were very often arranged and this still occurs in some Jewish communities. For many Jews, however, this is not the case any more. The wedding traditionally takes place under a canopy or temporary shelter set up where the ceremony is taking place, rings are exchanged and vows made. Then, the tradition has become to break a glass. This is done to remind people of the destruction of the Temple. It can also demonstrate how fragile life and relationships are and that they should be taken care of.

At death

In Judaism (and in Islam) a person's funeral will usually take place within twenty-four hours of death. An important ritual is the closest relative saying the *Kiddush* or the prayer for the dead. Relatives make a small tear in their clothes which shows the gap in their lives brought about by the loved one's death. It indicates recognition of the value of life over material things.

Following the death, a week of mourning takes place. This is known as *shiva* (seven). People will sit on low chairs and cover mirrors and pictures in their home, close friends and relatives visit bringing food and, of course, company. Less intensive mourning goes on for thirty days and children are supposed to mourn parents for twelve months. An annual remembrance day follows when children or the closest relative recites the Kiddush in the synagogue.

Over to You

1. What is Brit Milah?
2. Explain the ritual that Jewish boys and girls go through when they become adults in their faith.
3. Describe either the rituals involved in a Jewish wedding or at death.

Rite of passage *Glossary*

A ceremony or an event marking an important stage in a person's life, usually occurring at birth, the transition from childhood to adulthood, marriage and death.

Other rituals in Judaism
Prayer

Prayer is about communicating with God. In all religions where worship of a God of Gods take place, prayer is usually of importance. In Judaism, a person's relationship with God is very significant and this can be enhanced, developed and improved through prayer. People may pray for different reasons: to show their belief, to feel part of a community, to seek help from God or to worship and thank God.

It is the tradition in Judaism to pray three times a day: morning, afternoon and evening. The Jewish prayer book (called a *Siddur*) has special services set down for this.

The skullcap, tallit and tefillin

Orthodox Jewish men cover their heads by wearing a skullcap, known in Hebrew as a *kippah* or in Yiddish as a *yarmulke*. Liberal or Reform Jews see the covering of the head as optional. It is nearly always worn during prayer. The skullcap is about showing respect to God and recognising God's greatness. At morning prayers, men wear a *tallit* or prayer shawl, which has tassels at the four corners. This is because of a command in the Torah. They may also wear the *tefillin* or black leather boxes containing

Ritual *Glossary*

A religious or solemn ceremony consisting of a series of actions performed according to a prescribed order.

Prayer *Glossary*

Prayer is conversation between human beings and God. It is from the heart and can be carried out in a number of ways.

Meditation *Glossary*

Meditation is to concentrate deeply on something. In some religious traditions, it is used to help people focus on what is important.

Practice
Glossary
Something people do regularly because of their religious beliefs.

Sign
Glossary
A sign is an image, gesture or object that represents something; it has one fixed meaning.

texts of the Torah strapped onto the forehead and left upper arm, opposite the heart. This is not worn during Sabbath or festivals but the tallit would be.

How do you think people might react to someone dressed like this?

Over to You

1. Why do Jewish people pray?
2. How often do they pray?
3. What is the Siddur?
4. Describe three symbols of prayer in Judaism and say why they are used.

Symbol
Glossary
Symbol is similar to sign, but it has many meanings and depends on who is looking at it, where it is and what experience of it the person has previously had.

Sacred time
Glossary
Time set aside for special religious understanding.

Shabbat

The Sabbath day (*Shabbat* in Hebrew) is from sundown on Friday to sundown on Saturday and is an important day of rest for Jewish people. Observing it is part of the covenant with God. The day involves prayer, food, reading the sacred writings and relaxing with family and friends. It is a special day of joy and celebration, and a time to thank God. There is a fuller account of the Jewish Sabbath in Section E, The Celebration of Faith.

Mezuzah

This is a small box placed on the doorpost of a Jewish person's home. It contains a small scroll with the words of the *Shema*: 'Hear, O Israel, the Lord our God is one.' It is there because of the instruction in the Torah to keep the laws on your doorpost. The tradition is to touch the *mezuzah* on the way in and out of your house to demonstrate that God is always at the centre of your life.

And you shall love the Lord your God with all your heart, with all your soul, and with all your strength. And these words, which I command you today, shall be upon your heart. And you shall teach them to your children, and speak of them, when you sit in your house, when you walk by the way, and when you lie down and when you rise. And you shall bind them as a sign on your hands, and they shall be ornaments between your eyes. And you shall write them on the doorposts of your house and upon your gates.

(Deuteronomy 6:5-9)

Over to You

What rituals have developed because of this passage?

Creed

A creed is a statement of faith or belief. The Shema is a form of creed said by many Jews.

Ethic is the moral principle on which a religion is based. The ethic for Judaism is to follow the law as handed down by Moses and found in the Torah.

Do members of any other religions that you know have symbols of their religion in their homes?

Other special objects found in Jewish homes

- A *menorah* or special candlestick, used for the Sabbath. It has seven branches, representing the days of the week.
- A special *Hanukkah* candle or eight-branched menorah, used for the festival of lights in December.
- The *Seder* dish, used during the Passover festival.
- Goblets used for the Sabbath and during special festivals.

Would you know that this symbol indicates that the food is kosher?

Food laws

Possibly one of the most noticeable features of being Jewish is the food laws. Within Judaism, there is much variation on how strictly the food laws are interpreted and followed. The food laws are known as *kashrut*. Food that may be eaten is known as *kosher*, i.e. clean and fit for consumption.

The kosher home is a cornerstone of Jewish life. The selection and preparation of food according to the dietary laws have served to protect the well-being of Jewish people since earliest times. The dietary laws are rooted in the Torah and cover every aspect of food preparation, from when it is selected to when it is served at the table.

- For meat to be kosher, animals must have cloven hooves and chew the cud. Pork is, therefore, not allowed. Beef, lamb and veal are fine.
- Kosher birds include domestic fowl like chicken and turkey but not birds of prey.
- Fish has to have fins and scales, so shellfish is forbidden.

Animals must be prepared so that when slaughtered all the blood runs out. A kosher species must be slaughtered by a *schochet*, a ritual slaughterer. Since Jewish law prohibits causing any pain to animals, the slaughtering has to be carried out in such a way that unconsciousness is instantaneous and death occurs almost instantaneously.

Meat and dairy cannot be mixed, stored together, put in the same dish or prepared with the same utensils. In some Jewish households, there are two sinks: one for washing dishes that have been used for dairy foods and one for dishes used for meat.

- Foods that are meat or meat products are called *fleischig*.
- Foods that are milk or milk products are called *milchig*.
- Foods that are neither milk nor meat are called *pareve*; these include fish, eggs, fruit and vegetables. They can be mixed with milk or meat products.

Did you know?

Some traditional Jewish foods include:

Bagel – A bread roll made of yeast dough.

Blintzes – Very thin, rolled pancakes filled with fruit, cheese or meat.

Challah – Sabbath twists of white bread.

Knishes – Stuffed dumplings.

Latkes – Pancakes.

Strudel – Paper-thin pastry rolled and filled with sweet fillings.

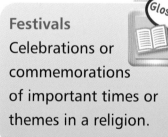

Over to You

Research some traditional Jewish recipes and if possible try to make some.

Festivals

There are many Jewish festivals throughout the year. Like Christians, Jews have their own calendar, which sets out the various significant days in the course of a year.

The main ones are:

Rosh Hashanah	New Year	Autumn
Yom Kippur	Day of Atonement	Autumn
Sukkoth	Festival of Tabernacles or Booths	Autumn
Simchat Torah	Rejoicing in the Torah	Autumn
Hanukkah	Festival of Lights	Winter
Purim	Festival of Lots	Spring
Pesach or Passover	Commemoration of the Exodus from Egypt	Spring
Shavuoth	Festival of the Torah	Summer

Glossary

Festivals
Celebrations or commemorations of important times or themes in a religion.

Glossary

Calendar
The sequence through the year of significant religious events, celebrations and commemorations.

Rosh Hashanah and Yom Kippur

While for Christians the year begins in Advent, for Jewish people, it begins in September at *Rosh Hashanah* or New Year. The tradition for Rosh Hashanah is to dip an apple (sometimes bread) in honey and wish others a 'sweet new year'. A ram's horn or *shofar* is then blown to call people to the ways of God. The New Year is followed immediately with ten days of reflection before a very important day, *Yom Kippur* or the Day of Atonement. To atone is to make up for wrongdoing and seek forgiveness. This day is a very serious and solemn one in the religious calendar. It is a day of spiritual renewal when Jews pray and fast, and look to make a fresh start for the year ahead.

Why do people make New Year resolutions?

Two of the big festivals of Judaism are Hanukkah and Pesach (Passover). Both are commemorating important events in Jewish history. Both offer a time to celebrate, to bring family and friends together, and to hope for good times ahead.

Hanukkah – Festival of Lights

This is a festival that remembers a time when the Jewish Temple was restored to its proper use for the worship of God. Hanukkah means 'dedication'.

What does it celebrate?

The event took place in 165 BCE, after the Temple had been taken over by the King of Syria, Antiochus IV Epiphanes, who tried to force all the people to worship the Greek Gods. Of course the Jews refused to do so. A priest named Judas Maccabaeus and his four brothers led the people to victory against the Syrians. They were anxious to rededicate the Temple to God and to remove any traces of idolatrous worship. They lit the great menorah (seven-branched candlestick) and placed it on the altar, but there was only enough oil for one day. It was going to take eight days to get more. However, by a miracle, the oil burned for the full eight days.

How is it celebrated?

This festival lasts eight days. The central custom of the festival is the Hanukkah lights. A special eight-branched menorah is used. A ninth branch holds the candle use to light the other eight. On the first night, one candle is lit and on each succeeding night an additional candle is lit. As with so many festivals, people celebrate by exchanging presents, wearing new clothes, visiting family and friends, and having a big meal. Hanukkah is a cheerful festival and an occasion for spending time with family.

This candlestick is a symbol. What do you associate candles with?

Passover and the Feast of Unleavened Bread

Passover or Pesach, along with the Feast of Unleavened Bread, is an eight-day spring festival. Many Jewish people will try to be at home to celebrate this festival with family. This festival celebrates the deliverance from slavery in Egypt.

What do the pictures mean?

In preparing for Passover, Jewish homes are thoroughly spring cleaned, with particular emphasis on removing any traces of leaven (*hametz*), raising agents used in baking. People may get new clothes for Passover, special dishes are taken out and lots of food is bought.

The highlight of the festival is the first evening with the ritual of the *Seder* (meaning 'order of service') meal. At the table, Jewish people tell the story of *Haggadah* and reflect on how it must have felt to be a slave in Egypt. Nowadays during Passover, modern issues of freedom, oppression and slavery are often discussed.

The Seder is for everyone to be involved in. Everyone participates and the youngest child will sing in Hebrew: 'Why is this night different from all other nights?' There is chanting, singing, discussion, storytelling, games and riddles.

Four glasses of wine represent the four stages in redemption from the Exodus to the coming messiah. Another glass is sometimes poured and left untouched for the prophet Elijah.

The Seder meal includes many symbolic foods. It is placed on a beautifully decorated Seder plate.

Passover foods and their meaning

Matzot – Three wafers of unleavened bread, to symbolise the bread eaten by the Israelites when they left Egypt in a hurry.

Maror – Bitter herbs, to represent the bitterness of slavery.

Charoset – A sweet paste made from almonds, apples and wine, to represent the mortar used in building in Egypt and to symbolise suffering, while its sweet taste symbolises the sweetness of freedom.

Parsley – Dipped in salt water, to represent the tears of the slaves.

A roasted lamb bone – To represent the lamb sacrificed by the Hebrews as a sign for the angel of death to 'pass over' them.

Roasted egg – A symbol of the ancient festival offering.

What do the different foods represent?

Other Jewish festivals

Sukkoth: Feast of the Tabernacles, a joyful harvest festival to thank God for looking after the people in the desert. Jewish people build temporary shelters as a reminder. Traditionally people lived in these for the week, but today, for most people, they are more symbolic. This ends with the service *Simchat Torah* or 'rejoicing in the law'.

Purim: Festival of Lots, which lasts one day and recalls the story of Esther's victory over Haman of Persia. He had cast lots to decide when to kill the people.

Shavuoth: Also called Pentecost, it takes place fifty days after Passover. Remembering the giving of the law, the Ten Commandments are read out in synagogues. It is also a harvest festival, marking the harvest of first fruits and plenty.

Over to You

1. Compare a Jewish festival to one from a different world religion. What do they have in common? What is different about them?

   Or

2. Design a poster showing four different Jewish festivals.

Pilgrimage

The most important site in the world for Jewish people is the Western Wall or Wailing Wall in Jerusalem. This is the only surviving part of the once great Jewish Temple, which was destroyed by the Romans in 70 CE. At one time a central part of Judaism, the Temple is still an important symbol. It represents the covenant or agreement between the people and God. How? It was built to worship God on the holy land that the Jewish people were promised according to the Tanakh or sacred writings. For some Jews, just visiting Israel is in itself a pilgrimage. It is, after all, the Promised Land, a central part of the story of Judaism. Unlike some other religions, there is no obligation to take part in a pilgrimage.

Where is this wall found?

Synagogue

Like most religions, Jews have a place to worship God as a community and, as with other religious communities, the place of worship is an expression of what the community believes. A Jewish place of worship is called a synagogue, which means 'meeting place'. They became centres of Jewish life after the destruction of the Temple in 70 CE. They are built to face Jerusalem. Worship in synagogues includes readings, prayers, hymns, psalms and sermons.

If we look in detail at the synagogue, we can see many parts that reveal what Jewish people believe about God, themselves and how to practise their religion.

> **Pilgrimage** — Glossary
> A journey to a place of significance for a particular religion, carried out to show one's devotion.

> **Places of worship** — Glossary
> Buildings designed for the members of a religion to go to for worship.

Star of David

Easily the most recognised symbol of Judaism, the Star of David is frequently used to decorate synagogues. It is named after King David, the most successful king in Jewish history, who united the people in a glorious kingdom. His was a time of plenty, good foreign relations and strength. The Star has six points with interlocking lines, which show diversity and unity. Sadly, one of the most remembered uses of the Star of David is when the Nazis forced Jews to wear a yellow star in order to identify and persecute them.

What Jewish symbol is most visible?

Ner tamid

This is the perpetual light, always shining. It represents the ongoing covenant between the people of God. When Judaism had a temple, there was always a lit menorah or candlestick and the *ner tamid* is a reminder of that.

Aron Hakodesh – the Ark and the Torah scrolls

One of the most important features of any synagogue is the Ark, inside which are the Torah scrolls, known as the *Sefer Torah*. The Torah is fundamental in Judaism, as fulfilling it is the way people keep faith with God and the covenant. The Ark is a box-like cupboard placed in a wall facing the city of Jerusalem. During services, the scrolls are taken out and unwrapped, as a beautiful cloth normally protects them. They are then rolled out and read from at the *bimah* or raised platform. A *yad* or pointer is used by the person reading from the scrolls. This copy of the Torah is handwritten and must contain no errors. The person who writes it must start over again should they make a mistake. This shows the importance of the Torah for Judaism. It is a symbol of the everlasting agreement or covenant between God and the Jewish people.

Ten Commandments

It is very common to have a copy of the Ten Commandments on the wall of a synagogue. Written in Hebrew, they would be placed near the Ark and ner tamid.

Seating

Traditionally in orthodox synagogues, there are separate sections for men and women. They may have seating for women upstairs in a balcony or gallery, or in some synagogues in a room adjoining the prayer hall. In reformed or progressive synagogues, men and women sit together. Seats are often in a circle or arc, facing the bimah or platform.

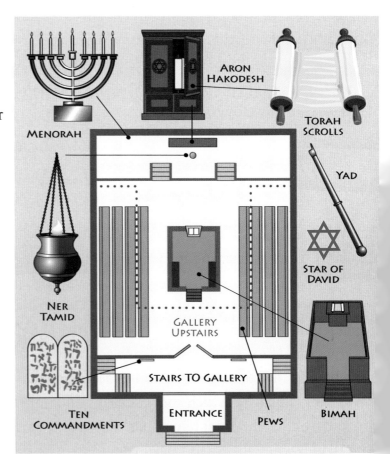

Are any of the features similar to those found in any other place of worship?

The rabbi, cantor and minyan

A rabbi (meaning 'my master') is the leader of a synagogue community. The rabbi's role is to lead services, give sermons and look after the building. In the community, a rabbi is leader, teacher and advisor. He takes care of the well-being of the community and conducts weddings, funerals, bar and bat mitzvahs, and naming ceremonies. He will also represent the community at other religious and non-religious events. In some Jewish communities, women are allowed to be rabbis, while in traditional orthodox communities only men can have this role.

The *cantor* is the person who leads hymn singing, chanting of prayers and psalms. The *minyan* is the minimum number of people necessary for communal prayer to take place in a synagogue. Traditionally this had to be ten men.

Over to You

Draw a diagram of a synagogue and label it fully.

Key Terms

ceremony, rite, rite of passage, ritual, prayer, meditation, practice, sign, symbol, sacred time, creed/ethic, festivals, calendar, pilgrimage, places of worship

Chapter Questions

A. True or false?
1. Jewish people believe in more than one God.
2. Bar mitzvah is a Jewish rite of passage.
3. Hanukkah is the Jewish New Year.
4. Rome is an important pilgrimage site for members of the Jewish community.
5. A menorah is a candlestick and an important symbol in Judaism.

B. Define the following words: Rosh Hashanah, tefillin, kosher, ner tamid, mezuzah.

C. Choose one Jewish festival and compare it with any festival of one other major world religion.

Exam Practice

Higher Level 2005: Short question

Unleavened bread is used in celebrating the Passover meal: true or false.

Higher Level 2007: Short question

The title 'Rabbi' is most associated with a leader in which of the following world religions? Buddhism/Hinduism/Judaism

Ordinary Level 2008: Short question

The Western Wall or Wailing Wall is a place of religious importance associated with Judaism: true or false.

Higher Level 2011: Section 5, question 3

You are visiting a friend whose family are celebrating a religious festival. Outline what happens during the celebration of a religious festival associated with **one** of the following major world religions and explain the reasons why the festival is celebrated today.

Buddhism/Hinduism/Islam/Judaism

Higher Level 2010: Section 5, question 3

Imagine that you have been asked to write an article about the religious practice of members in **one** of the following major world religions. Outline the points that you would make in your article referring to the religious practice of early followers and members today.

Buddhism/Hinduism/Islam/Judaism

Higher Level 2007: Section 5, question 3

Describe a time of the year that is important for members in **one** of the following world religions. In your answer you should explain why that time of year is important for followers today. Buddhism/Hinduism/Islam/Judaism

Higher Level 2007: Section 5, question 5

'Ritual can help people to express their faith.'

Discuss the importance of ritual for members of one of the following major world religions: Buddhism/Christianity/Hinduism/Islam/Judaism

Ordinary Level 2005: Section 4, question 5

World religions have different places of worship. Tick **one** of the following places of worship and name the world religion associated with it: Church/Mosque/Shrine/Synagogue/Temple

World Religion_____.

Name **one** religious symbol that can be seen in the place of worship you have ticked above.

Explain the meaning of this religious symbol.

Mini-Project

Make a poster of the symbols of Judaism. Include at least five symbols and write an explanation of each.

www.bbc.co.uk/religion/religions/judaism

Judaism: Commitment and Community

13

commitment, persecution, development, expansion, follower/disciple, schism, community structure, tradition, leadership, education, dialogue

Every person, while part of a community, is an individual with personal views on their religion and how best to practise it.

Commitment

Commitment
Dedication to something or someone.

Commitment refers to dedication to something. Jewish people show commitment to their religion by following the Torah or law. Of course, not all Jewish people have exactly the same interpretation of the law or understanding of how it should be followed. Love of God and of other people is central to Judaism, and to be committed to Judaism is really about trying to demonstrate this belief in everyday life.

Persecution

Jews have suffered persecution many times in history. During the time of Moses, the Egyptians treated them as slaves. The Babylonians sent them to exile in Babylon.

Persecution
Suffering inflicted deliberately on a person or a group of people. The persecutors are often those who make up the majority of a population, some of whom may be in positions of power and influence. People have been persecuted because they have a different religious, political or ethnic identity.

The Greeks desecrated the Temple. The Romans too destroyed the Temple and sent the Jews out of Israel. Right up to the present day, Jews have lived in many different countries, mostly in Europe and America. For centuries, Jews often faced some degree of persecution in many European countries. In some they suffered severe persecution, while in others they suffered lesser degrees of discrimination. The worst period of the persecution of the Jews was in Germany during the 1930s and 1940s.

Development

Judaism is a very ancient religion and it has developed enormously over the many, many centuries since its foundation. From the time of Abraham to Moses, the religion developed in numbers as a new nation was begun. Under Moses, the religion further developed many of the traditions and practices that are still associated with it today. During the period of the kings, the Temple was built and worship there developed. In the Roman period, Judaism survived despite persecution and when the Jews were forced out of their homeland by the Romans in 135 CE, it dispersed throughout first Europe and then the rest of the world. As it spread, the teachings written down in the *Mishnah* and *Talmud* helped develop Judaism as a world religion.

In some parts of Europe large Jewish communities developed with different traditions. The *Ashkenazi Jews* of the River Rhine and the *Sephardic Jews* of Spain had many famous leaders, and developed their own customs and traditions throughout the centuries.

It is not usual to use the word sect or even denominations when talking about the different movements within Judaism; they are more commonly referred to as different schools of thought. The enlightenment within Judaism traces back to the figure of Moses Mendelssohn (1729–86). He encouraged Jews to be more involved in European culture and translated the Torah into German. He advocated Jewish civil rights and helped Jews to interpret their religion in the light of new knowledge.

In the nineteenth and twentieth centuries, many Russian Jews suffered severe persecution under first the Tsars and later the communists. Many left Russia to go west. During this period many Jews arrived in Ireland. The area of Dublin near the South Circular Road and Portobello became known as 'little Jerusalem', because of the large Jewish community living there.

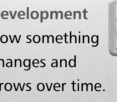

Development
How something changes and grows over time.

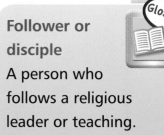

Expansion
The growth and spread of something in size or influence.

Follower or disciple
A person who follows a religious leader or teaching.

A famous fictional story, *Fiddler on the Roof*, about a Jewish dairyman living in late nineteenth-century Russia, was based on a collection of short stories written by Solomon Rabinowitch, a Ukrainian writer who used the pen name Sholom Aleichem. He wrote in Yiddish and was widely hailed as the 'Jewish Mark Twain'. The story deals with the oppression of Jewish people in Russia at that time and has themes of faith, values, family and love at its heart. It was made into an Oscar-winning movie in 1971, with the director, Norman Jewison, going to great lengths to recreate the feel and look of a traditional nineteenth-century Jewish village in Eastern Europe.

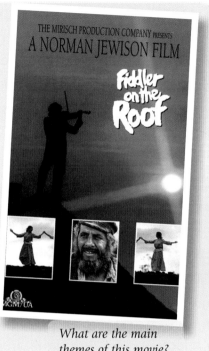

What are the main themes of this movie?

Did you know? During the late nineteenth century, Zionism, a movement to establish a permanent and national homeland for Jewish people, emerged. Zionists organised their first congress in 1897 in Basle, Switzerland. The main organiser was Theodor Herzl.

This beautiful pre-war synagogue was completely destroyed. What else were the Nazis aiming to destroy?

Later, the Nazi period brought catastrophe to the Jewish population of Europe, known as the *Shoah* or *Holocaust*, after which only one third of the European Jewish population remained. Many pre-war communities and their synagogues, traditions and way of life were completely destroyed.

Discuss what would be a suitable caption for this photograph.

The Holocaust Education Trust of Ireland

The trust was formed in 2005 to promote awareness and education about the Holocaust. It is a non-profit charity that designs, facilitates and supports education programmes. The aim of the trust is to combat anti-Semitism and all forms of racism and intolerance in Ireland. The Holocaust Education Trust helps the government organise the annual Holocaust Memorial Day commemoration, which takes place in the Mansion House, Dublin at the end of January every year.

Community

After the war, it was very difficult for surviving Jews to return home and many chose to go to either America or Israel to start a new life. These two countries now have the largest Jewish communities. Modern Judaism is a mixture of different groups, including the orthodox, conservative, hasidic, secular and reformed.

The terms generally used for the different schools of thought in Judaism are:

- Reform – A more liberal group
- Conservative – Preserves traditional practices but takes the view that the law may be reinterpreted in light of modern understanding
- Orthodox – A more traditional group
- Hasidic – An ultra-orthodox group, symbolised by a total separation of Judaism from the modern world

There are also humanistic Jews, secular Jews, Jewish groups who support the state of Israel, those who don't, and many in between.

In Ireland, the Jewish community is quite small. The current population is around 1,900. The community is normally located near a synagogue, as the tradition is to walk to the synagogue on Saturday morning or Friday evening. In Dublin, there are two main synagogues and a Jewish school, all within a small area.

The modern state of Israel was founded under international law in 1948. Why do you think it was founded at that time?

Schism — *Glossary*
A split or division within a group or community.

Community structure — *Glossary*
How a community organises itself and the different roles within it.

Tradition — *Glossary*
Teachings and practices handed down through history, which help to inform members today.

Leadership Glossary
The role of leading and taking responsibility for an organisation or group of people.

Education Glossary
Facilitating learning and the development of a person's intelligences and skills.

In Ireland, the position of Chief Rabbi is currently vacant. The leader of the Orthodox Jewish community is Rabbi Lent. He looks after the community and the synagogue of the Dublin Hebrew Congregation. There is also a Progressive Jewish synagogue in Dublin, which has visiting rabbis.

Rabbis lead their congregation in worship and they look after weddings, bar and bat mitzvahs, and funerals. They take care of the administration of their community and community relations. Some rabbis teach and others may write for religious publications. They are responsible to a board of trustees of the congregation. To be ordained a rabbi, a person must complete study at a Jewish seminary, usually for four to six years.

Stratford College. Why is it important for religious communities to have their own school?

Involvement in the wider community

Jewish people are, of course, involved in many different areas of life in Ireland. Like any other group of people, some are musical, others sporty, academic, artistic, political, business people and craftspeople. Jewish people are involved in a number of inter-religious groups, including the Irish Council of Christians and Jews, the Three Faiths Forum and the Dublin Inter-Religious Council. In public life, members of the Jewish community include Alan Shatter, who became Minister for Justice, Equality and Defence in 2011, and Ben Briscoe, a former lord mayor of Dublin.

Dialogue Glossary
A two-way process of communication. In religion, it usually refers to the discussion between two individuals or groups that aims to improve the understanding and relationship between them.

בית המדרש הגדול

IRISH JEWISH MUSEUM
OPENED BY
THE PRESIDENT OF ISRAEL
CHAIM HERZOG
JUNE 1985 ~ TAMMUZ 5745

The Irish Jewish museum is an interesting collection on Jewish life in Ireland over hundreds of years. Try to organise a visit for your class or yourself.

Key Terms

commitment, persecution, development, expansion, follower/disciple, schism, community structure, tradition, leadership, education, dialogue

Chapter Questions

1. What does commitment mean?
2. Give an example of when the Jewish people experienced persecution.
3. Who was Moses Mendelssohn? What did he do?
4. What does Zionism refer to?
5. What was the Shoah?
6. Name three types of Judaism.
7. How does one become a rabbi?

Exam Practice

Higher Level 2005: Short question
Discipleship means _____.

Higher Level 2009: Short question
A tradition is a newly established practice: true or false.

Higher Level 2008: Short question
In religious traditions 'schism' means _____.

Higher Level 2003: Section 5, question 3
You have been asked to write an article about a leader in **one** of the following world religions: Buddhism/Hinduism/Islam/Judaism
In your article you should outline the role of the leader in relation to **two** of the following points:

- Community Structure
- Follower/discipleship
- Tradition

Higher Level 2008: Section 5, question 3
In the history of world religions there are key moments that shape their development.
Profile the way in which **one** of the following world religions has been shaped by
experiencing a time of *either* persecution *or* expansion.
Buddhism/Hinduism/Judaism/Islam

Mini-Project

Research and write about the history of the Jewish community in Ireland.
www.jewishireland.org

Hinduism

14

Key Concepts

The key concepts in this chapter are the same as those for Chapters 11, 12 and 13.

Hinduism is the oldest of the major world religions. It is connected with the subcontinent of India and it is from the River Indus that the word Hinduism originates. It is, in fact, such an ancient religion that no one knows for certain who started it, so the founders are referred to as *rishis* or wise men.

Copy the map of India and write out the origins of the name Hinduism.

Beliefs

Unlike other world religions, Hindus have no set creed or statement of belief. They do share many beliefs and ideas about life, death and God.

They have many Gods and one divine source of all life known as *Brahman*. For Hindus, all life comes from Brahman and all life is trying to get back to this universal soul. Hinduism has a very cyclical view of the world and life. The world and people go through cycles of creation, preservation and re-creation. For people, this takes form in the process known as reincarnation.

The ultimate goal for a Hindu is not to be reincarnated but rather to break this cycle. This happens when a person lives the perfect life. When this happens, a person has reached *moksha* or reunion with Brahman. The soul or *atman* in every person is part of Brahman and thus wishes to achieve this union.

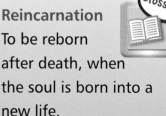

Glossary

Brahman
The universal soul. All life is part of Brahman.

Glossary

Reincarnation
To be reborn after death, when the soul is born into a new life.

Not usually worshipped directly, Brahman is considered to be unknowable. What is the ultimate goal for Hindus?

Dharma
Glossary
Sacred duty in Hinduism.

Karma
Glossary
The law of cause and effect in Hinduism: from good comes good, from evil comes evil.

Hindus also believe in *dharma* or sacred duty. This means that people have an obligation or duty to do the right thing for whatever stage in life they are in. They believe that people go through stages in life from childhood to adolescence, marriage and old age. A person's dharma, therefore, depends on which stage they are at. For example, a young person has the duty to do well at their studies and respect their parents. They also have rights, for example, to be cared for, loved and provided for. A parent's dharma is to look after their family, while in old age, when children have grown up and left home, a person's dharma is to look after their own spiritual life and prepare for death and reincarnation.

Karma is something that Hindus also believe in. This is the law of cause and effect. It means that from good comes good, while from bad comes bad. In other words, if a person does something good, good will come of it and vice versa. This will also affect a person's next life, so there are serious consequences from how you live your life. Hindus therefore aim to live in a way that will cause each of their lives to be better than the life before.

Aum is the main symbol of Hinduism. This is the sound heard in deepest meditation and is said to be the name most suited to God.

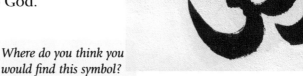

Where do you think you would find this symbol?

Over to You

1. Who is the founder of Hinduism?
2. What makes Hinduism different from many other faiths?
3. For Hindus, who is Brahman?
4. Explain reincarnation.
5. What does karma refer to?

Gods

Hinduism has many, many Gods. Apart from Brahman, the main ones are named Brahma, Vishnu and Shiva. These three are known as the *Trimurti*. They are also referred to as the creator, preserver and destroyer.

Brahma – the creator

This God is represented with four faces and four arms. He also holds some symbolic objects. The faces are symbolic of the four Vedas or writings of Hinduism. Brahma's four arms point in all directions, symbolising the belief that he is everywhere. He holds a water jar, as all life came from the ocean; beads representing time cycles; a book to represent his intellect, necessary for creation; and finally, he bestows his fourth hand in grace to the people.

Why does he have four faces?

The consort (wife) of Brahma is Saraswati, the goddess of knowledge. Her symbols include a string of beads, a musical instrument and a swan or goose, which symbolises her beauty and grace and her ability to use knowledge for the good of humankind. She is worshipped by anyone interested in knowledge, especially teachers, students and scientists.

The swan is said to be able to distinguish pure milk from milk mixed with water. This indicates the power to make distinctions between things. What can the Goddess herself distinguish?

Over to You

1. How is Brahma depicted?
2. Why does he carry a water jar?
3. Why does he need a great intellect?
4. Who is the consort of Brahma? Describe her.
5. What kind of people do you think would worship this God?

Vishnu – the preserver

Vishnu has descended in different forms to earth. Vishnu arrived to preserve the earth when it was in danger. As a being who has descended to earth, Vishnu is known as an *avatar*. The forms that Vishnu has taken have been both animal and human. The most famous forms are probably Rama (hero of the *Ramayana*), Lord Krishna (hero of the *Mahabharata*) and the Buddha. In the past, Vishnu has descended nine times and it is said he will descend one more time, when the earth is in danger. The next will be the last time and he is given the name Kalki, a man on a white horse.

For whenever the law of righteousness (dharma)
Withers away, and lawlessness (adharma) raises its head,
Then do I generate myself on earth
For the protection of the good,
For the destruction of evildoers
For the setting up of righteousness
I come into being, age after age.

(Bhagavad Gita, 4:7)

To whom is the passage referring?

The 10 incarnations of Vishnu are:

1. Matsya
2. Kurma
3. Varaha
4. Narasimha
5. Vamana
6. Parasurama
7. Rama
8. Krishna
9. Buddha
10. Kalki

The consort or wife of Vishnu is Lakshmi, the goddess of fortune. Her name comes from the Hindu word *lakshme*, which means 'goal'. She represents the goal in life, which

What are their names?

includes spiritual as well as worldly prosperity. Lakshmi is especially worshipped during the festival of Diwali for prosperity. It is said she came from the ocean and she holds a lotus flower, the symbol of purity. Lakshmi has one hand in the giving position and people often place coins in her hand, to make the connection with fortune.

1. What is an avatar?
2. How many times is Vishnu said to appear on earth?
3. What is the purpose of his visits?
4. Who is Lakshmi?
5. What does her name mean?
6. When is she worshipped? Why?

Shiva – the destroyer

An intimidating-looking God, Shiva holds his weapon, the trident, and is usually depicted with a snake. His body can sometimes be shown covered in ashes, representing the transcendental aspect of the universe. He has three eyes: symbols of the moon, sun and fire. The bull, Nandi, is his vehicle, and a symbol of strength and constancy. Shiva can often be shown crushing the demon, the symbol of ignorance. Shiva has three consorts or wives: Parvati, Durga and Kali. Parvati and Shiva are parents of one of the most popular Hindu Gods, the elephant-headed God Ganesh.

Ganesh is the God of success and the remover of obstacles. He is worshipped by anyone undertaking a new venture or going on a journey. There is a festival for Ganesh, called *Ganesh Chaturthi*, during which people put clay statues in their homes and carry out a *puja* (act of worship) to the God. There is much celebrating at home and in the community. Food, presents and new clothes may be bought. The God is a friendly, helpful and lucky spirit in the home.

Who are the parents of Ganesh?

171

Temples or mandirs

Hindu worship can take place at home or in a temple. An act of worship is called a puja. Unlike some other religions, Hindus do not have to go to a temple, but many

do so anyway. In temples, daily worship, festivals and family celebrations take place. They vary in design and can be anything from a small shelter to the huge ornate temples found in the big cities of India, for example Chennai, formerly known as Madras.

To separate daily life from the sacred space of a temple, there is an outside wall. Temples have a gateway through which people enter. Before entering, people remove their shoes and wash their hands. A bell is placed at the entrance and people ring it to announce their presence. Inside the outer wall, there may be a small shrine or shrines to different Gods or Goddesses, with statues of them. The main image or shrine is found at the back, in a dark chamber with light coming from oil lamps placed around it. Worshippers may walk around the image to show reverence to the God. Most temples have a tower, which creates a link between heaven and earth.

People can visit a temple alone or with family. They will usually offer the God or Goddess milk and sweets. One of the main rituals is the *arti* service or worship of the sacred flame. Devotional singing usually takes place. The priest will mark the worshipper's forehead with red powder to show they have carried out an act of worship. Sweets are returned to the worshipper, who will eat some and give the rest to family and/or the poor. People might visit a temple on the way to work, give offerings and then go on with their daily life.

> There is a full account of the arti service in Chapter 22, Rituals.

Writings

The writings of Hinduism are divided into *Shruti*, considered to be revealed by the Gods, and *Smriti*, which are remembered or passed down as an important source or tradition. The main texts are called the Vedas. These are stories of the Gods and contain key teachings for Hindus to follow. The others are the *Ramayana, Mahabharata,* the *Upanishads* and the *Puranas*.

Rites of passage

Birth: Some rituals take place even before birth, e.g. the lighting of the sacred flame to ensure a healthy child. After birth, a pen is dipped in honey and the word 'Aum' written on the baby's tongue, as a symbol of the hope that they will speak the truth. The first haircut removes any badness from a previous life. The naming of the child takes place at twelve days old, when the baby is washed and dressed and then placed in a cot with oil lamps lit around it. The name is announced by a priest and all repeat it. There is hymn singing and prayers, and afterwards a celebration. The first outing of the child is also special and usually includes the first visit to a temple.

Child/adolescent: The sacred thread ceremony means the child has reached the stage in life when the scriptures can be studied. The sacred flame is again lit and placed around the person as a sign of their willingness to learn. There is reading from the texts and a celebration afterwards (see Chapter 21 for a full account of this ritual).

Marriage: Hindu weddings can last for days. The significant moments include the seven steps around the sacred flame. Each step represents something: love, life, happiness, children, wealth, God and strength. The couple sit beside the fire, the bride's sari is attached to the groom's scarf and they feed each other cake or sweets. Prayers and readings are said. The couple are showered with petals or rice as a wish for happiness and peace.

Death: Hindus are generally cremated. The fire is necessary to release the soul for reincarnation. The flame is lit by the nearest relative. A priest will say prayers and the ashes are usually scattered on a local river. The River Ganges is a popular place to scatter ashes.

What is the common feature of the four different rites of passage?
Compare the rites of passage for Hindus with rituals in any other religion.

Symbols

Shri yantra: A symbol used for meditation, it prevents the mind wandering.

Swastika: A symbol of success, fortune and welcome. Often painted near an entrance. (Note: the swastika is an ancient Hindu symbol. The Nazis used it as a symbol of Aryan identity and nationalist pride. Hinduism does not have any connection to Nazism.)

Peacock: Represents the beauty of creation.

Coconut: Hard on the outside, sweet milk on the inside. It represents how the soul or pure spirit inside a person is what matters and not their exterior.

Lotus flower: Beautiful even in muddy water, it reflects the soul untouched by the badness of the world that surrounds it.

Bindi: The third eye, it protects from evil. The custom was for married women to wear a bindi.

Sacred cow: The cow is a giving animal and its gentle nature reflects the Hindu ideal called *Ahimsa*. Milk, yogurt, cheese, butter and oil (used for lighting the sacred flame in religious services) all come from cows. Hindus don't eat beef.

Over to You

Draw three of the Hindu symbols and explain their meaning.

Pilgrimages

One of the most significant places for Hinduism is the River Ganges – this river is considered to be a God itself and a source of life in India. People visit the stepped banks of the river in the cities of Benares and Varanasi. At different steps, particular rituals are carried out, including prayer, bathing and offerings. The water of the Ganges is believed to be able to wash away bad karma.

The *Kumbh Mela* is an incredible Hindu ritual involving pilgrimage to the confluence of the Ganges and Yamuna rivers. It takes place every twelve years and is the largest religious ritual in the world with up to ten million people taking part. Hindu mythology says that the rivers churned the ocean to produce the nectar of immortality.

Another important place for Hindus to go on pilgrimage is Badrinath in the mountains of the Himalayas, which is considered to be the home of the Gods.

Why might people imagine this as the home of the Gods?

Festivals
Holi

This festival takes place in the spring, which is a turning point in the year and represents the ideas of new life and nature being replenished. This can easily be interpreted to represent ideas of the triumph of good over evil or life over death.

To celebrate this festival, people light bonfires and acts of worship take place, especially worship of the sacred flame. One of the activities most associated with this festival is the play of colours, when people throw coloured powders and coloured water on each other. Tricks played are associated with Lord Krishna, the Hindu God who, it is said, played tricks on people as a boy.

Diwali or Deepavali

This festival takes place in the autumn and is known as the festival of lights. *Deepavali* means 'row of lights' and this festival celebrates the victory of goodness over evil and light over darkness. The festival commemorates the story of how Lord Rama returned to his kingdom, having defeated the forces of evil after he rescued his kidnapped wife Sita.

Before this festival, people clean their homes, and to celebrate they wear new clothes, give presents, light candles, have a big meal, and visit family and friends. During *Diwali*, people pray to Lakshmi, the Goddess of wealth, prosperity, light and wisdom, and place coins in the hands of her statue. It marks the beginning of the New Year and people send each other wishes for a prosperous new year. People also worship Ganesh, the remover of obstacles and Lord of Beginnings.

How do the images on the cards relate to the festivals?

175

Caste

Society in Hinduism is divided into different social groupings called *castes*. Each caste has its own privileges and limitations, which are transferred from one generation to the next. They are as follows:

- *Brahmins* are priests.
- *Kshatriyas* are rulers, warriors or landowners.
- *Vaishyas* are merchants.
- *Sudras* are unskilled workers, farm workers or craftspeople.

Outside of the caste system are the *Harijans* or 'children of God', once known as the 'outcasts' or 'untouchables'. Although caste discrimination is now illegal in India, bias is still a problem.

Hinduism in Ireland

The Hindu community in Ireland, established in the 1980s, is biggest in Dublin, Cork, Galway and Limerick. As Hinduism originated in India, the main Hindu community in Ireland is of Indian ethnic origin. Other members are from Malaysia, Sri Lanka, Nepal, the Philippines and South Africa. There are, of course, ethnic Irish Hindu followers too.

Key Terms

The key terms in this chapter are the same as those for Chapters 11, 12 and 13.

Chapter Questions

1. Is Hinduism a monotheistic or polytheistic religion? Explain your answer.
2. Name the three main Hindu Gods.
3. Name one Hindu Goddess.
4. Explain the following words – moksha, arti and atman.
5. What do Hindus believe happens when a person dies?
6. Vishnu is said to have ten avatars. What is an avatar?
7. What is the name of a Hindu temple?
8. Name one of the Hindu sacred texts.
9. What animal do Hindus consider sacred? Why?
10. Where did Hinduism originate?

Exam Practice

Higher and Ordinary Level 2006: Picture question
Pick **one** thing from the photograph that shows this
ceremony is celebrating religious faith.
Name **one** other ceremony that celebrates a stage in the
growth in religious faith.
Taking part in a religious ceremony is one way of expressing
religious faith. Name **two** other ways of expressing religious faith.

Ordinary Level 2007: Section 4, question 3
Choose **one** of the following world religions you have studied:
Buddhism/Hinduism/Islam/Judaism
Name **one** place of pilgrimage that is most associated with the world religion you have
chosen.
Describe what can be seen in the place of pilgrimage you have named above.
Give **two** reasons why people go on pilgrimage to the place you have named above.
Describe what can be seen in a mandir.

Test Yourself
eTest.ie

Mini-Project

Research the Hindu sacred writings. Outline two stories from them and draw a picture
of the main characters.

Islam

15

Key Concepts

The key concepts in this chapter are the same as those for Chapters 11, 12 and 13.

What is the function of a sacred text?

Islam is another of the world's major religions and is said to be the fastest growing in today's world. The followers of Islam are called Muslims. There are millions of Muslims around the world with a range of opinions on what it means to be a Muslim. They look to the sacred text, the Qur'an, for guidance, and to the example of their founder, Mohammad, on how best to be a good Muslim.

How Islam began

Islam started in the seventh century when a man named Mohammad first encountered God. Mohammad was born in 570 CE and by the time he was six, he was an orphan. His uncle raised him and Mohammad grew up to become an important businessman. His reputation for honesty and integrity earned him the name al-Amin, the 'trustworthy one'. He married a woman named Khadijah and they had children – four daughters and two sons. This all took place in the city of Mecca.

At that time, most people in Mecca worshipped many Gods. In the city, there was a building called the Ka'ba with statues to the many Gods. The Ka'ba is said to have been built hundreds of years before Mohammad by Ibrahim and his son Ismail. So, by the time of Mohammad, the Ka'ba, which Ibrahim and Ismail had built to honour God, was being used by people to worship many Gods.

From Ireland, in which direction is Mecca? Did any other religions start near here?

What benefit did the Ka'ba have for the people in Mecca at that time? Since people flocked to Mecca to go to the Ka'ba to worship there, it was good for business in the city. To Mohammad, the people were being exploited and he was unhappy with this.

When did all this change?

Although life seemed good for Mohammad and he was happily married with a good business, he was not at peace. He would spend time alone, praying and fasting in the hills outside the city. In 610 CE, while in the hills, Mohammad had his first experience of God. This is known as a revelation. Speaking through the angel Jibril, God told Mohammad that he was to be a prophet of God. The angel spoke to Mohammad and gave him the first words of the Qur'an.

Mohammad told Khadijah about his experience and she became the first convert to Islam. The word Islam means 'peace'. This peace is brought about through submission to Allah. Allah is the name for God in Islam. Therefore Islam is based on the idea that to follow God is to do God's will – a Muslim is one who submits. Muslims find out God's will by looking to the sacred writing, the Qur'an, and to the life of the prophet – the example of the prophet is known as the *Sunnah*.

Mohammad's message of one God did not go down well in Mecca. He and his followers were persecuted and had to flee the city. They left in an event known as the *Hijrah* or 'departure', and went to the city of Yathrib, later known as Medina or the city of the Prophet. Mohammad had been invited there to help run its administration. The date of the Hijrah, 622 CE, is the first year of the Islamic calendar. His emphasis was on justice and equality, and he attracted many followers. He criticised the exploitation of the weak, especially the poor, widows and orphans. In Medina, the development of Islam really began. Here the rituals most associated with Islam took shape, e.g. prayer, fasting and almsgiving. One of the main teachings of Mohammad was the importance of *Umma* or community and it is still an important emphasis in Islam today.

On his way to Medina, Mohammad was followed by Meccans who wanted to assassinate him, so he hid in a cave for three days. Legend says a spider spun a web over the entrance to the cave, leading his pursuers to think no one could have gone in there.

Return to Mecca, 630 CE

Mohammad was now a political leader and he decided to go back to Mecca with a group of followers. His main concern was that the Ka'ba should be rededicated to God and, thus, restored to its original purpose. He successfully took over Mecca and restored the Ka'ba. It is said that when the Ka'ba was being restored, there was a dispute over who should place the black stone into the wall. Mohammad ordered that the stone be placed on a large sheet and a member from each tribe should take a corner of the sheet. In that way, they all got to move the stone. He himself then placed it in the wall. It is still there today.

Copy the map on the previous page and write a short account of the significance of Mecca and Medina for Muslims.

Mohammad's death, 632 CE

Shortly after giving his final speech at the Mount of Mercy, Mohammad died. He was succeeded by Abu Bakr (632–634) and the next three *Caliphs* (deputies of the prophet) were Umar, Uthman and Ali. However, a dispute arose and Islam split when Ali's son Hussain was killed by Muslim rivals at the Battle of Karbala. The two main branches of Islam that exist today, called the *Sunni* and the *Shi'a*, emerged from this split.

Sunni takes its name from the *Sunnah*, the example of the Prophet. The name Shi'a is from 'followers of the party of Ali' and comes from those who believed Ali,

Mohammad's son-in-law, had the qualities and authority of their founder. They believed these qualities made him suitable to become their religious leader or imam. The majority of Muslims are Sunni, making up approximately 90 per cent of the Islamic world.

Write about the importance of Mohammad for Muslims.

The Ka'ba – the house of God

A Muslim's daily prayer is directed towards the city of Mecca and the Ka'ba. The Ka'ba, built by Ibrahim and Ismail, is a symbol of submission to Allah and respect for Allah. During the annual pilgrimage to Mecca, Muslim pilgrims circle the Ka'ba seven times and try to touch the black stone, which absorbs their sins. As an earthly focus for prayer for hundreds of years, the Ka'ba unites the community.

What does this building represent?

The Qur'an

Why are decorated copies of religious texts made?

The most fundamental things in Islam are belief in one God, Allah, and recognition of his prophet, Mohammad. The prophet Mohammad is said to be the last of the prophets or the 'seal of the prophets'. For Muslims, what Mohammad taught is that which God wants, God's final message to the people. He gave the people the Qur'an as the word of God and Muslims believe it is the direct word of God. Therefore the text of the Qur'an is very special. Even the physical object is respected, e.g., a Muslim would not leave it on the floor. The Qur'an's themes include Allah, nature, human beings, prophethood, revelation, society and much more.

After Mohammad's death, the Qur'an was written down, at first on pottery, dried-out palm leaves and anything else that came to hand. The writing of the Qur'an is in itself a religious act. It is written in Arabic from right to left, with the hand drawing in towards the heart. Nowadays the Qur'an has been translated into many different languages and can be accessed in book shops, libraries and even on computer. Some people choose to learn the 114 chapters of the Qur'an by heart. The name for someone who has done this is *Hafiz*. Those who learn the Qur'an by heart will have the words of Allah present in their mind at all times. Being Hafiz is believed to bring blessings on the person and their family. In fact, some Muslims believe that this brings paradise to seven generations.

1. Why is the Ka'ba so important for Islam?
2. Where did Mohammad give his farewell speech?
3. Name the two main branches of Islam.
4. What does Sunnah mean?
5. How is the Qur'an written?
6. What is a person called who learns the Qur'an by heart?

The Five Pillars of Islam

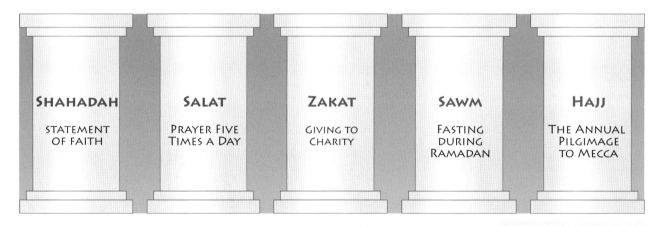

SHAHADAH	SALAT	ZAKAT	SAWM	HAJJ
STATEMENT OF FAITH	PRAYER FIVE TIMES A DAY	GIVING TO CHARITY	FASTING DURING RAMADAN	THE ANNUAL PILGIMAGE TO MECCA

The Five Pillars of Islam.

The Shahadah

This is the statement of belief that Muslims recite. It simply sums up what is central to their faith: 'There is no God but Allah and Mohammad is the Prophet of Allah.'

The *Shahadah*, along with four other rituals, make up the Five Pillars of Islam. These are obligations for Muslims. The other four rituals are to pray five times a day, to fast during Ramadan, to give money to charity and to go on the pilgrimage to Mecca.

Salat – prayer five times a day

Prayer five times a day is one of the most significant rituals in Islam. It is carried out at five set times and involves specific words and actions. Children join in prayer from an early age and are expected to know the proper form of Salat and *Wudu*, ritual washing before prayer, by adolescence.

> There is a full account of Salat in Chapter 22, The Experience of Worship.

Which direction is this person facing?

Significant action: Zakat – almsgiving or charity

Islam teaches that everyone should be grateful for the blessings they have received from Allah. They must recognise that everything comes from God; no one owns anything and people must share with each other. The Qur'an lists categories of people who should receive welfare, including orphans, widows, students and those in debt. The annual amount should be 2.5 per cent of a person's wealth, but more can be given. No one should know how much another person gives or should know who receives Zakat. It is a person's own moral duty to give Zakat. However, in many Muslim countries the government collects Zakat as a form of tax.

Should religions encourage people to give charity to others?

Significant ritual: fasting during Ramadan

Another of the Five Pillars is fasting during the holy month of Ramadan, when Muslims should also concentrate on prayer. This is a special time of the year for Muslims. It indicates a willingness to obey Allah and to devote time to Islam. The intention of the fast is to thank God and discipline the soul to wait for God. During Ramadan, people abstain from food and drink during the daylight hours for the entire month. The sick, children and the very old do not have to take part in this ritual. It brings the community together and it increases attendance at the mosque.

Significant action: the Hajj – pilgrimage to Mecca

For all Muslims, Mecca is of huge importance. They pray towards it every day, five times a day. The fifth and last pillar of Islam is the duty for all Muslims to try, at least once in their life, to visit the holy site of the Ka'ba during the annual pilgrimage known as the Hajj. It takes place during the twelfth month of the year, called *Dhu al Hijjah*. A person should only go on the Hajj with sufficient money and in good health.

Rituals of the Hajj

- Men wear an unsewn white garment and women wear a simple dress and head covering with no jewellery. This indicates being in a state of *Ihrman* or entering into the spirit and rites of the Hajj. It symbolises the equality of all before God.

- *Tawaf* is when pilgrims walk around the Ka'ba seven times in an anticlockwise direction. They salute the black stone as they pass by.

- *Sa'y* means running between the hills of Safa and Marwa, where Hagar searched for water for Ismail. This is done seven times. Pilgrims drink the water from the spring of Zamzam and put some in bottles to bring home.

- Journey to the Plain of Arafat and the Mount of Mercy, where Mohammad gave his farewell speech. Here Muslims pray for hours for the mercy and forgiveness of God.

What is the purpose of prayer?

- Stoning the pillars in Mina, recalling the temptation faced by Ibrahim and Ismail. Here pilgrims throw pebbles at three pillars in a symbolic act which indicates a rejection of temptation in their lives from now on.

- *Eid-ul-Adha* – the Hajj ends with the 'festival of sacrifice'. Prayers are said.

- Now pilgrims return to Mecca to repeat Tawaf.

When a person has completed the Hajj, a man has the title *al-Hajj* and a woman has the title *al-Hajjah*. Should a person be unable to go on Hajj because of ill health, they may pay the expenses for someone else to make the pilgrimage on their behalf. If a person dies while making the Hajj, it is considered a great blessing and they will have the honour of being buried there.

Did you know? The black cloth that covers the Ka'ba, known as the *Kiswa*, is embroidered with verses from the Qur'an. During Hajj, it is raised to reveal the stone walls and it is renewed at the time of Hajj. The old one is cut up and pieces are taken home by pilgrims as a memento.

Over to You Write an essay on the commitment needed for a person to follow the Five Pillars of Islam

Significant place: the mosque

Mosque means 'place of prostration' and refers to the fact that during prayer Muslims prostrate themselves or lie with their forehead on the ground. Mosques have many features that reflect Muslims' beliefs. They include the following:

- The minaret is a tower from where the call to prayer is made. The *Muezzin* is the person who makes the call.

- *Mihrab* is the alcove in the *Qiblah* wall, both of which show the direction to Mecca. All Muslims direct their prayers in this direction.

- *Minbar* – like a pulpit from where the imam gives the sermon and leads prayers.

- Mosques have no seats because everyone sits on the floor to pray facing Mecca. There may be some seats along the sides for the very old or infirm. Praying together on the floor emphasises the equality of all before Allah.

- As they have no images of Allah, Mohammad or any person, mosques are decorated with calligraphy and geometric patterns.

- The main symbol of Islam, the star and crescent moon, is often seen on the top of a mosque.

What features indicate that this is an Islamic place of prayer?

The mosque is important for the Muslim community as it is the place where worship, prayer, festivals, marriages and funerals take place. They may also function as schools and community centres. The mosque is led by an imam, the spiritual leader of the community. His role is to lead prayers, give sermons and conduct marriages and funerals. In mosques, women and men pray in separate areas. Before entering a mosque to pray, Muslims must remove their shoes, indicating that they are entering a sacred space, and they must also carry out ritual washing called wudu.

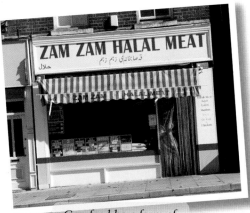

Can food be a form of religious expression?

Food

Muslims have to be careful with regard to what they eat. There are types of food that are forbidden (*Haram*), including pork, blood and animals that are carrion or have died of natural causes or illness or have been slaughtered incorrectly. Fish are generally permitted (*Halal*), as are vegetables. When an animal is slaughtered for meat, it should be done as painlessly as possible, without the animal witnessing the suffering of any other animal. No more should be killed than is necessary. Hunting and shooting for sport is forbidden in Islam. Alcohol is completely forbidden in Islam.

If someone's life was in danger and a food that was clearly Haram could preserve their life, then they may eat it.

1. What does the word 'mosque' mean?
2. Describe three features you would find in a mosque.
3. Who is the leader of a mosque?
4. Where do people sit in a mosque?
5. What functions do mosques have?
6. Explain Haram in relation to food for Muslims.
7. How do Muslims view hunting?

Rites of passage

There are two rites of passage in Islam.

Birth

The first ritual that takes place straight after birth is the call to prayer (*Adhan*) whispered in the baby's ear by the father. Prayers are said and gifts given. Next is the naming ceremony at seven days old. Names associated with Mohammad and his family, and names of prophets or derived from the names of God in the Qur'an are popular. At this time, the first haircut is weighed in either gold or silver and given to the less fortunate. There may be the sacrifice of an animal and the meat can be shared with family and friends. Boys are circumcised in Islam.

Death

When it is clear that a person is dying, they are placed in such a way as to face Mecca. People may recite the Shahadah to them, to remind the dying person of these words. In Islam, it is believed that angels record all your deeds during your life and when you die you are held to account for these. When the person dies, the body is prepared for burial as quickly as possible and is treated with the utmost respect and dignity. The body is placed in a simple shroud for burial. Some men are placed in the garment they wore on the pilgrimage to Mecca.

The funeral takes place in the home or mosque, though the body would not be placed in the prayer hall of a mosque. Prayers are led by the imam or the most senior male relative. The prayers said at the funeral invoke God's mercy for the dead person. The body is placed in the grave so that the head faces in the direction of Mecca. Prayers at the grave remind the deceased of the oneness of Allah and the prophet Mohammad. After the funeral, people may share meals and recite the Qur'an together. A period of forty days of mourning is the tradition for many Muslims. Widows may mourn for a period of four months and ten days. Over the grave, a marker may say the name of the deceased and verses from the Qur'an.

Festivals

Eid–ul–Fitr takes place at the end of the holy month of Ramadan to thank God for a successful fast. It means the 'festival of fast-breaking'. In many countries this is a national holiday. Muslims go to the mosque, pray, wear new clothes, give extra money to charity, give presents and cards, visit family and friends and have a celebratory meal.

Eid–ul–Adha, the 'festival of sacrifice', takes place at the end of the Hajj. The festival was started by Mohammad. The first part is prayers at the mosque. A sheep is sacrificed as a symbol of devotion to Allah. This festival commemorates Ibrahim's willingness to sacrifice Ismail to Allah. When God saw the faith of Ibrahim and Ismail, he provided a sheep to sacrifice instead. The food is shared with family, friends and the poor. Again much celebration takes place, with a family meal, cards and visits to family and friends.

Why do people send cards for religious celebrations?

The Irish Islamic community has been growing steadily since the 1950s, with mosques, cultural centres, schools and shops now established in Ireland. The community is involved in some interfaith groups such as the Three Faiths Forum and Dublin Inter-Religious Council.

There is more information about the Muslim community in Ireland in Chapter 3, Communities of Faith.

Key Terms

The key terms in this chapter are the same as those for Chapters 11, 12 and 13.

Chapter Questions

1. Who founded Islam?
2. Where did Islam originate?
3. What is the Muslim name for God?
4. Who built the Ka'ba?
5. When did Islam split?
6. What is the name of the Islamic sacred text?
7. Where do Muslims pray?
8. What are the Five Pillars of Islam?
9. Describe one rite of passage in Islam.
10. What does Eid-ul-Adha commemorate?

Exam Practice

Ordinary Level 2010: Section 4, question 3

Tick **one** of the following world religions that you have studied: Buddhism/Hinduism/Islam/Judaism

Name the part of the world most associated with the founding story of the religion you have ticked.

Describe **one** example of the way people lived in this part of the world when the religion was founded.

Name *either* one person *or* one group associated with the founding story of the world religion you have ticked above.

Outline how *either* one person *or* one group played an important part in the founding of the world religion you have ticked above.

Higher Level 2011: Section 5, question 3

You are visiting a friend whose family are celebrating a religious festival. Outline what happens during the celebration of a religious festival associated with **one** of the following major world religions and explain the reasons why the festival is celebrated today: Buddhism/Hinduism/Islam/Judaism.

Test Yourself
eTest.ie

Mini-Project

Research and present in pictures a study of the city of Mecca and its importance for Islam.

Useful Websites for Section C: Foundations of Religion– Major World Religions

For this section of the course, the aims are to explore in detail a major world religion and to examine the impact of this religion on its followers today and on other individuals and communities.

To find out more about Judaism, Hinduism or Islam the following website is highly recommended:

www.bbc.co.uk/religion/religions

For religious communities in Ireland today the following websites are useful:

www.hindu.ie
www.jewishireland.org
www.islamireland.ie
www.islaminireland.ie

For more on Judaism, the following may be useful:

www.jewfaq.org (Judaism 101)
www.jewishvirtuallibrary.org

Information on the Holocaust can be found at:

www.ushmm.org

The Chester Beatty Library in Dublin has a wonderful display called the *Sacred Traditions Exhibition*. Two of the collections that it houses, the Islamic Collection and the East Asian Collection, are relevant when studying this part of the course.

Section

d

The Question
of Faith

This section of the syllabus aims:

- To explore the situation of religious faith today.
- To identify the beginning of faith in the asking of questions and the search for answers.
- To recognise expressions of human questioning in modern culture.
- To identify the characteristics of religious faith.
- To examine challenges to religious faith today.
- To offer opportunities for the exploration of and reflection on personal faith positions.

The Situation of Faith Today

religious belief, religious practice

Understanding belief and practice

Belief means to hold certain things to be true or of ultimate importance in a person's life. Practice means to carry out actions. Someone might say, 'My family is the most important thing in my life.' This belief shows itself in practice by the person spending as much time as possible with them.

Religious belief
Belief in God, a way of life and what is important in life.

Religious practice
Actions carried out as a result of religious belief.

Classwork

In pairs, suggest some things that people believe. How do people practise these beliefs? Share your ideas with the class.

Having a belief is important, but it is only visible by acting a certain way, and saying and doing things that show a person has a particular belief. For example, most Irish people believe in having elections to choose a president. The belief is that this is the best way of making the decision about who should be head of state. The action is going to vote in the election. In this way, belief underlies practice.

If people indicate that they are a Christian, Jew, Muslim, Hindu or Buddhist, it means they hold certain beliefs to be true. They share basic beliefs about the world and God with others in their religion. When they go to a church, synagogue, mosque or temple, they are carrying out that belief. They are involved in religious practice. To practise one's religion, a person may carry out rituals or ceremonies, wear special clothing, eat special food, go to a special place for worship or gather with others from their faith.

1. Religious belief is put into action in a variety of ways. Write out three ways a person practises religion.
2. Carry out a survey of religious belief and practice among your friends and classmates.

Religious practices at life's important times demonstrate what people believe. There are many special times in life – the most significant ones are birth, marriage and death. Nearly all religions hold special ceremonies for such times. This religious practice is an indication that the important times are made more so because of their connection with religious belief.

What practice is this? What belief is behind the action of the people carrying it out?

Practices in life that show what people believe

Religious practices at birth:

- In Judaism, the covenant of circumcision is carried out when a boy is eight days old and the naming ceremony for a girl celebrates the gift of a daughter.
- In Islam, the call to prayer is the first thing a baby should hear after birth.
- In Christianity, baptism is the first ritual for most people, welcoming the baby into God's family or as a member of their particular Christian community.

Religious practices for marriage:

- In Hinduism, the couple step around the sacred flame, the central symbol of the divine source of all life, Brahman.
- In Judaism, marriage beneath a canopy indicates the belief that God will provide.
- In Christianity, a celebration of the Eucharist alongside the wedding ceremony shows the belief that the love of the couple is a sign of God's love for the world.

What religion do these people belong to?

What do the bread and wine symbolise? Why would this take place at a wedding?

Religious practices at death:

- In Hinduism, the funeral pyre is lit near the skull to release the soul for reincarnation.
- In Islam, the body is buried in such a way that it faces the holy city of Mecca. This symbolises the belief that God has asked Muslims to pray towards the sacred mosque.
- In Buddhism, family and friends bring the body to a temple and celebrate the belief that the person is released from suffering.

What do Hindus believe happens after death?

Change in religious practice in Ireland

Religious practice does not stay the same. How people practised their religion in the past and how people do so now may be different. The fact that people practise differently does not necessarily mean they don't believe in the same things. It just means that they show their belief in another way.

Over to You

Do a survey about how parents/guardians/grandparents practised their religion when they were children. If they were not members of any religious tradition, ask them about how other people did so.

Place your findings in a chart with the following details:

Did they go to a place of worship – once a year, month, week or day?

Did they have to go to a place of worship during festivals?

Did they go to a school where only one type of religion was taught?

Did they have many friends who were members of religions differing from their own – none, some, many?

Did they feel they had to believe in one God or many Gods?

Compare the results with the beliefs and practices of your own age group.

In Ireland today, religion is very different from what it was in the past. First, there are far more people who are not members of the largest religious tradition, the Roman Catholic Church. Ireland is a much more multi-cultural and multi-denominational country. Second, the position of power that the Roman Catholic Church once had no longer exists and people feel much freer to express a belief that is not in agreement with it. Third, fewer people practise their religion in the traditional way. While many still believe in a God, they do not feel they have to express that belief in the way the Church may expect them to or in the way their parents or grandparents did.

People have also become increasingly influenced by other world views and ideas, such as materialism, atheism, agnosticism, humanism and secularism. Such ideas have influence on people's beliefs and, therefore, will also influence people's religious practices. Other things that will influence a person's religious belief are family, friends, school and the media.

Did you know? In Britain, an advertisement campaign was put up on buses with the slogan, 'If you're not religious, for God's sake say so.' It was launched for the census of 2011, though it was later changed since it was viewed as causing offence.

Materialism – When material things are more important than spiritual ones.

Atheism – The belief that God doesn't exist.

Agnosticism – The belief that God may exist but more proof is necessary.

Humanism – Human beings are the most important thing – actions can be measured by how they benefit human life. Some humanists are atheists while others are, in fact, religious humanists, such as Christian humanists.

Pluralism – To recognise that truth or truths may be found in more than one religious or non-religious perspective. A pluralist recognises that there is a place for more than one outlook in society.

Secularism – Religion should be kept separate from other aspects of everyday live.

How most people practised religion in Ireland in the mid-twentieth century:

- Going to church at least every week.
- Praying in the home at set times and in formal ways.
- Fasting during holy days.
- Going on a pilgrimage to seek forgiveness.
- Not eating meat on a Friday.
- Helping in the community.
- Getting married in a church.

How many people practise religion today:

- Going to church at important or special moments in life.
- Praying at bedtime or when the need arises, using your own words.
- Having a special meal during religious holidays.
- Taking part in a youth group within their religious community.
- Taking time off to be with family one day a week.
- Volunteering to do work for a charity.
- Thinking about how what you buy affects the lives of others.
- Choosing to love others and showing it.

*Contrast the way the people in the two
pictures are expressing what they believe.*

Key Terms

religious belief, religious practice

Chapter Questions

1. In your own words, describe the difference between religious belief and religious practice.
2. List two beliefs of a member of any religious community. How might a person show these two beliefs?
3. Has religion in Ireland changed in the past century? Explain your answer.
4. What ideas influence people's belief?
5. Do you have to be an atheist in order to be a humanist?
6. Explain secularism.

Exam Practice

Higher Level 2007: Short question
Agnosticism holds the view that _____.

Ordinary Level 2009: Short question
People express religious beliefs by the way that they live. State **one** other way in which people can express their religious beliefs.

Ordinary Level 2008: Short question
A humanist can be described as someone who gives religious answers to questions about the meaning of life: true or false.

Higher Level 2010: Short question
Secularism holds the view that the laws of a country should be based on religion: true or false.

Ordinary Level 2007: Picture question

Pick **one** thing from this photograph that shows that these people are practising their religion.

State *another* way in which people can practise their religion.

Describe **one** thing that can influence the way in which people practise their religion.

2009 Higher Level: Document question, section 3

Jo: What was it like growing up in Ireland in the 1950s?

Mr Murphy: Things were very different then, compared to how they are today, in many ways.

Jo: What about religious practice, has that changed much since the 1950s?

Mr Murphy: The way people practise their religion has changed a lot. When I was young most people attended religious services every week. In my family we went to Mass every Sunday. The whole family would get up early and put on our best clothes. We would go without any breakfast because we had to fast before receiving Holy Communion. My mother and sisters always wore scarves on their heads when they went to religious services.

Jo: Did you enjoy going to religious services with your family every week?

Mr Murphy: Yes I did. I enjoyed spending time with my family and it also gave me a chance to meet my friends and everyone in my parish. However participating in religious services then was different to how it is today.

Jo: In what way was it different?

Mr Murphy: For a start, Mass was said in Latin which I did not understand so, as you can imagine, I found it very hard to be involved. The priest had his back to the people and they were not as involved in the prayers during Mass. Whereas today when I go to Mass the priest is facing me, he is speaking a language that I can understand and I can be more actively involved.

Jo: Do you still go to religious services every week?

Mr Murphy: Yes I do. I believe it is very important to be active in my parish and I still enjoy meeting my family and friends at religious services. Unfortunately I see less people at religious services each week and this makes me very sad.

From your reading of the above interview, outline **two** examples of changes in religious practice that have taken place in Ireland since the 1950s.

Explain **one** reason why religious practice is important for people of religious faith.

Higher Level 2005: Section 4, question 4

'When I was young everyone I knew believed in God and churches all over Ireland were crowded every Sunday ...' (Pat, born 1940)

Is there a difference between religious practice in Ireland today and religious practice when Pat was young?

Explain why you think there is or is not a difference in religious practice in Ireland today.

Apart from going to church, outline **one** other way in which young people today express religious belief.

The findings of surveys show that many young people today believe in God. Give **two** reasons why many young people today believe in God.

Agnosticism and humanism can be described as non-religious ways of looking at the world. Briefly explain the way *either* agnosticism *or* humanism has of looking at the world.

Higher Level 2011: Section 4, question 4

Describe what is meant by the terms:
i. Atheism   ii. Agnosticism.

Explain how the religious belief of a person could be challenged by *either* atheism *or* agnosticism.

Mini-Project

Design an article for a youth magazine dealing with the religious belief and practice of young people today. For ideas you could check out *Face Up* magazine.

The Beginnings of Faith

17

Key Concepts

question/questioner, search, meaning/meaninglessness, reflection, awe and wonder, humanism

If you had one question you could put to God, what would it be? What is the one thing you would really like to know?

A world of questions

People are always asking questions. Many can be answered without too much difficulty. Others require more time and effort, but ultimately do have an answer. Some questions have more than one answer and others are yet to be answered. Sometimes the answer to a question changes when new information becomes available.

Some questions may not have an answer that can be found easily, or maybe human understanding is too limited to find out the answer. These sorts of questions can arise time and again over the course of a person's life.

Glossary

Question
Something that requires an answer.
Questioner
A person who seeks an answer to a question.

People may find from time to time that they are satisfied with not knowing and at other times people become troubled by unanswered questions. It may not be possible to find the answers in the realm of history or science. Philosophy has at times addressed such questions and religions often try to give people direction in their search for answers to them.

Classwork

1. List some easy-to-answer questions.
2. Now list some difficult questions.
3. Finally, list some questions that you may never be able to answer.

Searching for meaning

The search for meaning has been around for as long as human beings have existed: from Newgrange and Stonehenge in the ancient world, to modern expressions of the search for meaning in popular music or film, or the efforts to find meaning in philosophy and science. It is a human characteristic to want to make sense of the world and find a purpose for our existence in it.

Search
An attempt to find something.

Suggest what these ancient monuments were used for.

The following are some questions that people ask at different stages of their life:

- What is life about?
- Where was I before I was born?
- Why are we here?
- What happens when we die?
- Why do bad things happen to good people?
- Is there a point to existence?
- Where does the point come from?
- Where does meaning come from?

Meaning
A reason or purpose to something.
Meaninglessness
There is no reason or point to something.

Over many centuries, people have reflected on such questions in different ways. They have found expression in music, art and poetry. These and other questions are all part of humankind's search for meaning.

Expressions of the search for meaning

Expressions of the search for meaning can be found through the centuries, in the form of images and writing.

Art

What stories do these paintings show?
What question do people want answered that is being addressed in these paintings?
Where did that answer come from?

What is the theme of the painting?
What is the story behind this painting?
What does this painting teach us about?

The statue of the Buddha contains some important Buddhist teaching. What does it teach?
What ultimate goal or purpose is found in what Buddhism teaches?

Questions are part of the search for meaning, which is characteristic of being a human being. People want to know about life, the world and the universe. Not only what is in it or how it works, but also why? What it is about? Is there an ultimate purpose? Is there an overall story that people are part of? Will those who do wrong be held to account and those who do good get their reward in the end?

Poetry

Read the following poem, 'Youth Calls to Age', by Dylan Thomas, and discuss how it reflects the search for meaning.

You too have seen the sun a bird of fire
Stepping on clouds across the golden sky,
Have known man's envy and his weak desire,
Have loved and lost.
You, who are old, have loved and lost as I
All that is beautiful but born to die,
Have traced your patterns in the hastening frost.
And you have walked upon the hills at night,
And bared your head beneath the living sky,
When it was noon have walked into the light,
Knowing such joy as I.
Though there are years between us, they are naught;
Youth calls to age across the tired years:
'What have you found,' he cries, 'what have you sought?'
'What you have found,' age answers through his tears,
'What you have sought.'

1. What questions does 'Youth Calls to Age' address?
2. Where might people find answers to such questions?
3. Do you know any other poems that deal with questions about life and death?

Literature

The book *Sophie's World*, by Jostein Gaarder, is about philosophy and the questions we ask about life. The story is about a fourteen-year-old girl who is introduced to philosophy and finds out that she is in the centre of a mystery. To solve the mystery, she uses her knowledge of philosophy and discovers a strange truth. The book introduces readers to the thoughts of Socrates, Descartes, Hegel and many other great philosophers. It raises profound questions about the meaning of life and the origin of the universe.

Is there anything in life you see as a mystery?

Modern music

The Irish band U2 wrote the song I Still Haven't Found what I'm Looking For'. Read the lyrics and listen to the song, then answer the following questions.

1. What is the song's theme?
2. What images does it contain?
3. What is the overall mood of the song?
4. As the question is never answered, does it leave a feeling of disappointment or openness to finding out the answer?

Listen to or read the lyrics of the Coldplay song 'Speed of Sound'.

1. Do these lyrics suggest any religious understanding of the world?
2. What questions are being addressed?
3. Are any answers given?

The song 'You've Got the Love' has been recorded by Florence and the Machine. Play the song and listen to the words.

1. What does the singer feel keeps her going when she is in despair?
2. What is the only thing that is real for her?
3. Does this song answer any question of meaning?

Finding meaning in life

As we have seen, humankind's search for meaning finds expression in art, literature, poetry and music. But where can meaning come from? The following are some of the areas in life that people find give them a sense of meaning and purpose.

Family: Love is one of our most basic needs. It is important for our development and self-fulfilment. The love of family and the role one has within a family give a person a sense of place, belonging and identity.

Friends: Like family, friends give people a sense of identity, acceptance and belonging.

Work: For some people, their work and the fulfilment that they get from it give them a sense of purpose. The need for belonging and identity is fulfilled in this area of life. To help others as a doctor or nurse, to find cures for illness through science, to discover new ways of doing things with technology, to express human emotions through art, to govern people well, to build a home for someone, to administer justice, to teach others, or to provide services, are all roles in human societies which people may find fulfilling. In carrying out roles like these, many people feel they are achieving their potential and find a reason to live and to do the right thing.

Sport and hobbies: Some people find that the meaning in life is found in doing something to the best of their ability. Using a talent for dancing, running, music or some other hobby is what gives a sense of purpose and identity. To have a supportive community and a framework of meaning helps the person to cope with the stresses of life. In this way, sport or some other pastime can provide an antidote to meaninglessness.

Philosophy: 'I think therefore I am.' (Rene Descartes). Philosophy is the study of knowledge, reality and existence. A Greek word, it literally means 'love of wisdom'. Philosophy has long tried to provide the answers to the question of what life is about. Philosophers have asked questions about existence, purpose, life and death, behaviour and everything in between.

Over to You

Research one philosopher and find two questions they tried to answer and what answers they arrived at.

Religion: In religion, there is the belief that God created people for a purpose, for people to have a loving relationship with God and with our fellow human beings. For many people, this is enough to give their lives meaning and purpose.

Religion gives people a view that things do not happen by chance, that there is an ultimate purpose in life and that the world is all part of a bigger story in which all people have their part to play. Religion provides answers to moral questions regarding what is right and wrong, and implies accountability, whereby people will be judged by their actions.

The sociologist Max Weber's study of religion became known as the 'meaning theory'. He emphasised the way religion gives meaning to human life and society in the face of suffering and injustice. Good and bad fortune fit into a broader picture of reality that goes beyond our everyday understanding.

In Judaism, being part of God's people, and of the covenant between people and God, provides a source of life, moral guidance and a purpose to living.

In Hinduism, the ultimate source of all life is Brahman. This universal soul, or God, is in all life and all life is trying to get back to this source. Through reincarnation, people are either moving closer to achieving *moksha* or union with Brahman, or moving further away from it. The purpose, source and question of life and death are in this way answered.

For Buddhists, the ultimate goal is for each person to achieve a personal Nirvana or enlightenment. Through following the eightfold path, as laid down by the Buddha, each Buddhist tries to reach Nirvana. Enlightenment suggests an overall purpose to life and an ability to discover what that is.

> 'What is the purpose of life? I believe that the purpose of life is to be happy.'
> **Dalai Lama, Tibetan political and spiritual leader**

Christians believe that God's care for people is shown by Jesus coming into the world to teach people how to know God and how to love each other. Jesus' death and resurrection repaired the relationship with God and showed the extent of God's love for the world. This all helps Christians to understand the world and their place in it.

> 'We have not come into the world to be numbered; we have been created for a purpose; for great things: to love and be loved.'
> **Mother Teresa of Calcutta**

Muslims understand the world as a gift from Allah. They believe that they can know God; they have the Qu'ran and the example of the prophet Mohammad as a guide to live by. Following the Five Pillars of Islam helps give a structure and meaning to life.

Science: For many people, scientific understanding is the best source for finding meaning to life. Being able to understand how things happen, the way the planet works, through biology, physics or chemistry, fulfils the desire to make sense of the world. In knowing how things work, some people find they are satisfied in the meaning that this understanding in itself brings. For others, however, this is only part of the search. While they want to understand how something happens, they also want to find a reason for why they exist at all.

Brian Cox 'The Wonders of the Universe'

David Attenborough 'Life on Earth'

Thinking about life, the meaning of life, why bad things happen, birth and death, is a reflective process. To reflect means to meditate, consider and think deeply about something.

Sometimes people are struck by a sense of how amazing something is. Spectacular landscapes or natural phenomena, such as the Himalayas, the Grand Canyon, the aurora borealis, the Victoria Falls or the Cliffs of Moher, can make people wonder at the world and what it all means. The amazement felt after the birth of a child is especially thought-provoking. Such experiences can motivate people to reflect on what this all means, on whether there is a reason, a purpose or the possibility that a God is behind this. This can lead people to reflect on big questions about life and the meaning of life.

Reflection
To think deeply about something.
Glossary

Awe and wonder
Amazement and surprise at something.
Glossary

Humanism

Humanism is based on the view that human beings are the most important thing and that actions can be measured by how much they benefit or how good they are for human beings. Some humanists are atheists, while others are religious humanists, such as Christian humanists. As a system of thought, humanism is concerned with human matters, not religious ones, and emphasises human needs and seeks rational ways of solving human problems.

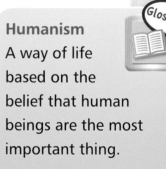

Humanism
A way of life based on the belief that human beings are the most important thing.
Glossary

Key Terms

question/questioner, search, meaning/meaninglessness, reflection, awe and wonder, humanism

Chapter Questions

1. What does the search for meaning refer to?
2. How do people express this search?
3. Where do people look for meaning in life?
4. What does philosophy mean?
5. What is the ultimate goal of Buddhism?
6. What gives meaning to life in Judaism?
7. How does science help with understanding life?
8. Where does humanism seek answers for human problems?

Exam Practice

Higher Level 2010: Section 4, question 4

In searching for answers to questions about the meaning of life, people sometimes turn to: family/friends/music/work.

Choose **two** of the above and explain how each can help people to find answers in the search for the meaning of life.

Higher Level 2006: Section 4, question 4

People today express the search for meaning in many ways. Give **two** examples of how the search for meaning is expressed in today's world and give a brief account of each example.

Higher Level 2004: Section 4, question 4

'And will the new young flowers die?

And will the new young people die?

And why?'

('Poem from a Three Year Old', by Brendan Kenelly.)

Pick **one** of the above questions and explain how it is typical of a child's search for meaning.

Explain how the questions a person may ask in their search for meaning could change as they develop from childhood to adulthood.

People sometimes express questions about the meaning of life in art, music, film and books. Choose **one** and explain how people express questions about the meaning of life in this way.

Mini-Project

Read the book *Sophie's World* and write a review of it.

Or:

research humanism and show how it is a source for meaning.

You can find some information on the website *www.humanism.ie*.

The Growth of Faith

18

Key Concepts

trust, faith, personal faith, childhood faith, mature faith, stages of faith

Glossary

Trust
Firm belief that a person or thing may be relied on.

Glossary

Faith
To have complete trust or confidence in someone or something. A strongly held belief that may be based on a spiritual conviction.

Glossary

Personal faith
Faith that is based on personal convictions and beliefs that a person holds.

When you are a child, you learn trust from the significant people in your life, especially the adults around you. Children brought up in a religious tradition are often encouraged to place trust in God.

Personal faith – what is it and how is it expressed?

Some people feel that faith is best expressed by belonging in a community of faith, while for others that is not important. For some, faith is a very personal thing, which is difficult to express in words. If you judge people on their actions, those actions may well indicate a faith. For instance, if a person shows their faith outwardly in what they wear, what they eat or how they behave, their faith is visible to others.

Some people have a faith that is less visible on the outside but still valid and important to them. It may affect their ideas of right and wrong, their behaviour to others and their views on life, love and relationships.

A person's faith is not a fixed thing. As the great Hindu holy man Mahatma Gandhi once said: 'Faith is not something to grasp, it is a state to grow into.' Faith is developing, changing and reacting constantly to life's experiences. Children's faith develops as they grow. They may reject it later on in life or it may change to a more mature faith. But it will not remain exactly the same.

As children grow up in a faith community, they are taught about their religious traditions. They experience rituals, celebrations and ceremonies that encourage them to think about their faith and what it means. They may question their faith and through personal experiences understand it differently. Some people do not remain in the same religious community they grew up in, but many others do.

Having a mature faith can be a source of strength in a person's life. This type of faith is based on strongly held beliefs which can be questioned. A person with a mature faith is not concerned with what others think. A person with a mature faith can turn to it for comfort in times of difficulty, they trust in what they believe and try to live by this.

> **Childhood faith** *Glossary*
> Beliefs a person holds as a child, which will develop over their life.

> **Mature faith** *Glossary*
> A faith based on experience and a mature understanding of life.

What stage of their faith are these children at?

Over to You

1. What does it mean to trust someone or something?
2. How do people express faith?
3. Does a person's faith change during their life?
4. What affects a person's faith?
5. How do children learn about their religion?
6. What is a mature faith based upon?

Stages of faith

The stages of faith are marked by important rituals in most religious communities. The first stage is marked by a naming ceremony or baptism. Then the child is brought up in that particular faith community and taught about the religion. When old enough, they have the opportunity to take part in a ritual that marks another stage in their faith.

At what age is this ritual carried out?

Stages of faith
How faith develops and changes over time and through one's life.

Glossary

Different religious traditions have different rituals to mark the next stage. Hindus carry out the sacred thread ceremony, which shows a willingness to learn from the sacred writings. Christians may have a confirmation, which indicates a renewal of the vows undertaken at baptism. Jews have a *bar* or *bat mitzvah*, which means the boy or girl is now a son or daughter of the law, and able to understand the need to try to follow the Torah in their life.

Discuss

Is it important to have ceremonies to show the different stages of faith?

A person of faith in Islam – Khadijah

Khadijah is famous as the first convert to Islam and the wife of the Prophet Mohammad. After he first encountered the angel Jibril (Gabriel), Mohammad was afraid and went home. There, Khadijah covered him with a blanket and said to him that Allah (God) would protect him from danger, as he was a man of peace who had offered friendship to all. Khadijah immediately accepted Islam. She was loyal to her husband and a constant source of strength to him. In the early days of Islam when the prophet and his followers suffered persecution, Khadijah showed great patience and courage. She is a famous person of faith from the past and also someone who is a role model for Muslims today.

Over to You

Research a person of faith from another world religion.

Who decides what a child eats?

Understanding traditions from childhood to mature faith
Judaism – food laws or customs

When it comes to food laws, a person of mature faith has and is expected to have a better understanding of why these are adhered to. In Judaism, it is a mother's role to keep a kosher diet for the family. Children do, of course, take part in this important aspect of their beliefs. They do more so because it is the custom and practice of their home and community and less so because they understand the importance of it. As they grow, a deeper understanding of the food laws will develop within them.

Christianity – Lent and Easter

Children often fast during Lent and may understand that it is related to Jesus spending forty days and nights in the desert. They do so because they are encouraged to remember how fortunate they are, to learn to do without a luxury or show some level of devotion to religious tradition. However, a person of mature faith has a greater appreciation of this ritual and the significance of identifying with Jesus' suffering and sacrifice. The preparation for Easter and the commemoration of the most significant week in the Christian calendar, Holy Week, has a greater impact on a person of mature faith.

What do the eggs represent?

Did you know? Fabergé eggs were jewelled eggs made by the House of Fabergé and were popular gifts at Easter. The first one was commissioned by the Russian Tsar Alexander III for his wife Maria Fedorovna in 1885.

At Easter itself, most children enjoy the Easter eggs and getting to eat some long-awaited chocolate. They may know the symbolism of new life that an egg represents. The importance of Easter as a major Christian festival, the idea of resurrection, everlasting life and victory over death are themes that, over time, will mean more to children as they grow up.

What is often emphasised for children during religious festivals?

Judaism – Passover

Children are very much involved in the many rituals around Passover. The youngest member of the household asks the question, 'Why is this night different from all other nights?' They also enjoy the festive foods, presents and games. Nevertheless, it is a person of mature faith who realises the real significance and importance of this major Jewish festival. The symbolic significance of the removal of yeast, the careful preparation of all the food, and the discussion on freedom and oppression are of more importance to a person of mature faith.

Islam – Ramadan

In Islam, the holy month of Ramadan is a month of fasting and prayer. Muslims fast during the hours of daylight and focus on their faith. The obligation to fast, however, is not compulsory for children. This, of course, has to do with it being better for children to eat regularly during the day and the possible ill-effects of fasting. It is also recognised that children are not at the mature stage of faith when they would benefit most from this spiritual exercise.

How would a child learn about the rituals they don't take part in?

Christianity – Advent candles

Often children love to light Advent candles, either at home or in their church. They may know that it is in preparation for Christmas and that there are different colours for the candles: three purple candles, one pink one and a white candle for Christmas Day. While children enjoy the ritual and know about the events that are being commemorated, the time of preparation for encountering Christ may be understood by a person of mature faith in a more relevant way.

When are the candles lit? Find out what the different colours represent.

Childhood faith and Sunday school

In many Protestant churches, children attend a Sunday school or Bible club during the weekly service of worship, while the adults of the congregation listen to the sermon and/or receive Holy Communion. This gives the children an opportunity to take part in activities, which perhaps are more appropriate for their age, such as listening to Bible stories, talking about what they mean, drawing pictures or playing games. The idea of Sunday school is to allow children to learn about their religion in an appropriate way and to develop their faith. It recognises that there is a difference between childhood faith and mature faith.

Over to You

1. Write a diary entry for a young Muslim, Christian or Jew, explaining their religion through a festival and how they understand it.
2. Debate the following statement, with three people against and three for the motion: Children should not be allowed to take part in religious rituals.

Images of God from childhood to mature faith

Childhood faith is shaped by the significant people in a child's life, and by their experience of religion and what they have been taught about God, both within and outside their religious community. The image a child has of God may be what they were told God was like or it may come from images they have seen in books, pictures or television. It may have been an image they received from a story or something they imagined at a young age.

> **Discuss** What images of God did most people have when they were in primary school? Has this image of God changed?

The image of God that a person of mature faith has may be quite different and usually reflects a deeper understanding of God and religion. Many people will no longer see God exactly as they did when they were children. Experience and challenges naturally shape a person's faith. Many people reject the faith they once had, while others develop it to a mature faith. People of mature faith will understand more about God and the relationship they believe God has with them and the world. They will have developed an image that fits better with their understanding of God. Sometimes an image from outside oneself, a picture, description or one evoked by music, can resonate with a person; since it relates to how they view God, it may help a person to form their own image of God. For others, it is just their idea and understanding of God. For example, while some may see God as a man, others may see God as a woman, while others may see God as neither male nor female but pure spirit and a force of good in the world.

Images of God from religious tradition

God is portrayed in many different ways in the various religious traditions. The following is a brief list of some of the well-known ways in which God is described and imagined. Each person's image of God tends to be suited to their understanding of God.

- God the father.
- God the shepherd.
- God the mother.
- God the king.
- God the creator.
- God the judge.
- God the saviour.

> **Discuss** Where do these images of God come from? Describe what each image brings to mind.

'As a mother comforts her child, so I will comfort you; you shall be comforted in Jerusalem.'

(Isaiah 66:13)

Is this an image you are familiar with?

How is God depicted in this work of art?

Could this match your image of God?

In Islam, Allah is never pictured, but there are many descriptions of the characteristics of Allah: the merciful, compassionate, perfect, wonderful, king, holy, guardian, honourable etc. For Hindus, there are so many images of God it is difficult to know where to start. The many Gods are depicted in great detail. There are statues, shrines, images in homes and temples. (The main Hindu Gods are described in Chapter 14.) In Judaism, as in Islam, God is not pictured, but characteristics of God are portrayed through the Tanakh. Many Jewish images are shared with Christians, as they derive from the same texts: father, ruler, liberator, mother and judge.

Modern images of God

More modern images of God are found in music, television, books and movies. There is a song by Faithless that talks about God as a DJ. Johnny Cash sang about his own personal Jesus. Kanye West had a hit song called 'Jesus Walks'. In television and movies too, there are various images of God. *The Simpsons* regularly deals with religion, with either Apu's shrines to Shiva or Ganesh, or the Reverend Lovejoy giving a sermon. They also have shown God as a large male figure walking in the clouds, seen in 'Homer the Heretic'. The film *Bruce Almighty* has the actor Morgan Freeman play God and shows God to have a sense of humour, as well as incredible power and compassion.

Is this a typical image of God?

What is significant about this image?

Over to You

Do any of the images of God in religious traditions, music, film or television resonate with you? Give reasons.

Key Terms

trust, faith, personal faith, childhood faith, mature faith, stages of faith

Chapter Questions

1. How is faith connected with trust?
2. How constant is faith?
3. Compare childhood faith with mature faith.
4. What religious rituals do children take part in?
5. Name three things that may influence a person's image of God.

Exam Practice

Ordinary Level 2006: Short question

To have faith means _____.

Higher Level 2008: Short question

One example of an image of God that can be found in a major world religion is
_____.

Ordinary Level 2009: Short question

To trust is to have confidence in the truth of something: true or false.

Ordinary Level 2010: Short question

In religious traditions the term 'mature faith' means _____
_____.

Ordinary Level 2010: Picture question

Pick **one** thing from this picture that suggests it is
based on an image of God.

State **one** thing this image shows about the child's
understanding of God.

Give **one** other example of an image of God.

Ordinary Level 2007: Section 4, question 4

Describe **two** things that are typical of a child's faith.

Describe **one** thing that is typical of a mature faith.

Higher Level 2010: Section 5, question 4

Adolescent Faith/Mature Faith

Outline the main characteristics of each of the above stages of faith development using the following headings:

i.   Relationship with God/the Divine.

ii. Main influences on faith.

Mini-Project

Research a movie, book, film or song that portrays God and present it to the class. Does the image of God resonate with you? Can you relate to it? Or is it completely different?

The Expression of Faith

19

Key Concepts

prayer, monotheism, polytheism, worship

Much of what this chapter deals with is treated in more detail in other sections of the book. However, what it does explain is that when the question of faith arises, different answers lead to different expressions of what that means. One of the most common expressions of faith in God or Gods is prayer. A person of faith may pray either at home or in the community with others. People may also carry out acts of worship to express their faith. These acts may be directed to one God (monotheism) or many (polytheism).

Prayer – communication with God

A hugely important aspect of many religions, prayer is a way of communicating with God.

Glossary

Prayer
A way of communicating with God, it involves a conversation from the heart between human beings and God.

How does prayer express faith? When people have faith and trust God, they will often turn to God in times of despair, worry or when they have questions relating to the bigger issues of life and death. The way that people communicate with God is through prayer. Prayer is a reflection of a person's faith in God, which may be done in a variety of other ways too,

Why do people pray?

all equally valid. For some, membership of a religious community is very important to them, therefore they prefer to pray with others from that community. It is an expression of their sense of belonging.

People use a variety of types of prayer: thanksgiving, intercession, petition, adoration, penitence and praise. These names for different kinds of prayer are an indication of how prayers are a way of worshipping God, thanking God for something, asking for help for oneself or someone else, asking for forgiveness and acknowledging the respect due to God.

When do people pray? People can pray by themselves at any time and can also join in formal prayers in places of worship at set times.

Why pray? To communicate with God, to show your beliefs are important to you, to seek help from God in times of need, to express appreciation of what you believe God does for you.

> Prayer is dealt with in more detail in Chapter 25.

Monotheism

The religions of Judaism, Christianity and Islam are monotheistic faiths. The members of these three major world religions worship and recognise only one God. They have many different ideas about God and how God has communicated a message to people over thousands of years. Nevertheless, they all believe there is only one God that brings meaning to life. For these religions, God is said to be omniscient (all knowing), omnipotent (all powerful), omnipresent (everywhere), pure spirit, and yet able to communicate with humans and to have a relationship with them.

Monotheism
Belief in one God.

Expressing faith in one God

Hear, O Israel, the Lord our God is One
The Shema
Jewish

I believe in one God, the father almighty.
The Creed
Christian

There is one God, Allah.
The Shahadah
Muslim

Which three religions do these represent? What do they have in common?

221

Polytheism

Hinduism is the third largest religion and the oldest major world religion. It is polytheistic and involves the worship of many Gods and Goddesses. In the ancient world, there were many polytheistic faiths, e.g. the Celts, Greeks and Egyptians. For Hindus, the universal soul or source of life is called Brahman. Since this God is unknowable, they worship the many other Gods that are forms or expressions of the one unchangeable and unknowable God.

Most religions that are about belief in God or Gods see worship as an important practice. Through worship, people are able to show the importance of God in their lives. God is the focus of worship as an indication that no other aspect of life is as important or worthy of the same level of respect. Of course, worship of God may mean different things to different people and may also be expressed in a variety of ways.

Polytheism
Belief in more than one God.

Worship
Showing honour to God, demonstrating the fact that God is worthy of respect.

Worship is dealt with in more detail in Chapter 22.

Key Terms

prayer, monotheism, polytheism, worship

Chapter Questions

1. Why do people pray to show belief in a God or Gods?
2. Name three prayers. What are they for?
3. Define polytheism. Name a polytheistic religion.
4. What is worship?
5. How does worship demonstrate belief in God?
6. Match the religion with the statement:

   Judaism   I believe in one God, the father almighty.

   Islam   Hear O Israel, the Lord our God is one.

   Christianity   There is one God, Allah.

Exam Practice

Higher Level 2009: Short question

One example of a world religion associated with polytheism is _____

_____.

Ordinary Level 2008: Short question

In religious traditions to 'worship' means to _____

_____.

Ordinary Level 2006: Short question

Polytheism is the belief in _____.

Higher Level 2005: Short question

Islam is an example of monotheism. Name another example.

Ordinary Level 2006: Picture question

Pick **one** thing from the photograph that shows
the ceremony is celebrating religious faith.
Name **one** other ceremony that celebrates a stage
in the growth of religious faith.
Taking part in a religious ceremony is one way of
expressing religious faith. Name **one** other way of
expressing religious faith.

Higher Level 2007: Section 5, question 4

'The world is charged with the grandeur of God.' Gerard Manley Hopkins
Describe the key beliefs about God held by believers in **one** of the major world
religions that you have studied. In your answer you should outline how the beliefs
about God influence the way of life of followers of the world religion.

Test Yourself
eTest.ie

Mini-Project

Write a page on one monotheistic faith and how it expresses the belief in one God.
Draw symbols used in this religious tradition that show the belief in one God.

Challenges to Faith

20

This is a higher level only section of the syllabus.

Key Concepts

reflection, world view, atheism, agnosticism, experiencing God, secularism, materialism, religious fundamentalism, creation

Challenges to religious faith

A person's faith or belief is not a fixed thing. Without doubt it is shaped by that person's experiences. As a person's experiences change, faith too is constantly changing. Many people feel their faith goes through ups and downs, and through times of certainty and uncertainty. Some people are more affected than others by what one

Reflection
Glossary
Serious thought or consideration.

World view
Glossary
A set of assumptions a person makes about the world. It is a way of seeing the world and how it works.

might describe as challenges to faith or belief. That may depend on a person's own faith or the strength of other influences. Nevertheless, in society and throughout life, there are always challenges to faith. These do not have to be viewed as a negative thing or something that is dangerous or problematic. Life is full of interesting viewpoints which a person may or may not share, and encountering these can lead a person to question things they once took for granted or to think more deeply about things such as faith and belief. They may reflect on their faith and what it means to them.

Since the word 'challenge' seems like something that must be overcome, it is very easy to see a challenge to faith as something that is trying to undermine or devalue a person's faith or belief. This does not have to be the case. The challenge here is one of reality and the fact that there are many world views which people encounter. Their existence gives all such viewpoints, religious and non-religious, an opportunity to express themselves in relation to each other. They do not always clash and may, in fact, complement each other from time to time. For example, people who have a strong religious belief in God may also have a very scientific understanding of how things happen.

Agnosticism is the view that it is not certain whether or not God exists. More evidence is needed either way. Agnostics are people who basically are not denying the existence of God but not affirming it either. The position that an agnostic takes when it comes to belief in God is that one cannot know or at least needs more proof to believe.

The scientist Charles Darwin, who discovered the evolution of species, once wrote to a friend that he saw himself as an agnostic. He acknowledged a person could believe in both God and evolution, and said of himself: 'I have never been an atheist in the sense of denying the existence of a God. I think that generally (and more and more so as I grow older), but not always, that an agnostic would be the most correct description of my state of mind.'

Atheism
The belief that God does not exist.

Does God exist?
Yes – theism
No – atheism
I don't know – agnosticism.

Agnosticism
The belief that God may exist but more proof is necessary.

Did you know?
Darwin was on a five-year scientific expedition (1831– 1836) when he came up with the ideas he later wrote about in *On the Origin of Species by Means of Natural Selection*. The breakthrough for his ideas came on the Galapagos Islands when he observed the similarities and differences between birds on the various islands in the group.

Experiencing God

Experiencing God
This can be described as awareness of the presence God, which can happen in a variety of ways.

Throughout a person's lifetime, an individual may answer the question of God differently at different times. Each person has experiences that shape ideas about God and life. Some people experience the presence of God through religious ceremonies or rituals. Some encounter God through prayer. Others experience a sense of God's presence at certain times in their life, while others encounter God in the everyday and through people they meet.

It can be difficult to understand another person's experience of God, but there are certainly ways in which the different religions encourage followers to experience God.

Attitudes to faith

Some people believe religion should be a private matter and kept separate from everyday life. Of course, many people who belong to a faith community see it as something important which influences their everyday life.

Secularism
Religion should be kept separate from other aspects of everyday life.

Secularism refers to things not connected to religious or spiritual matters. For a secularist, religious matters should not affect the other aspects of everyday life, such as government, education, lifestyles etc. It is a viewpoint that believes there should be a complete separation between religion and the rest of everyday life.

Materialism
Existence can only be explained through physical matter. Thus material things are more important than spiritual ones and the greatest good is physical well-being and material success.

A materialist sees material things as the most important in life. All that exists is physical and there is no place for a higher reality or God. A materialist doesn't regard the spiritual life as important. Thoughts, ideas and feelings can only be explained with regard to physical matter. Therefore, meaning cannot come from God or spiritual ideas. Materialism is concerned with worldly, not spiritual, matters.

 Discuss Are material things the most important in life?

The book *A Christmas Carol*, by Charles Dickens, tells the story of the transformation of Ebenezer Scrooge from someone who prizes only material wealth to someone who is benevolent, kind and has love in his heart. It is one of the most powerful stories of light, joy and love overcoming a person full of darkness and despair. It is a story of the Christian message of life over death and of what Christmas should be about, that true Christianity is in how people treat each other and especially the less fortunate in society.

Religious fundamentalists generally have a very strict interpretation of what their faith means and often a literal understanding of sacred writings. With most religious fundamentalism, there is little scope for seeing truth or value in religious understanding other than the one the individual professes. This can lead people to close themselves off from engaging with those they see as having an opposing viewpoint or belief.

Marley's Ghost

Why do you think it was through a visit from a ghost that Scrooge was offered a way to change?

> **Glossary**
>
> **Religious fundamentalism**
> A form of a religion that upholds belief in the strict, literal interpretation of scripture and sees this interpretation as the only valid one.

The issue of creation

Many religions describe God as the cause or designer of human existence, and many people see God as the creator of the universe. There are religious accounts of the bringing about of the world. The religious purpose is not, however, the same as a modern scientific account.

> **Glossary**
>
> **Creation**
> A view of how the world and humans came into existence that involves a creator.

Two stories of the creation in the Bible (Genesis)

1   'In the beginning God created the heaven and the earth.' This story comes from about 500 BCE. It divides the story into seven neat sections, each one described as a day. On the first day, light is brought into the world; on the sixth day man and woman are created; and the seventh day is set apart as a day of rest.

2   The other creation story dates even further back, to about 850 BCE. In this story, the time is not clearly defined and the earth is described as a wasteland. The style and detail is very different.

How important is light? What does light sometimes symbolise in religion?

For many people of faith, these stories are symbolic and the descriptions are not necessarily meant to be taken literally. Similar creation stories or myths are told in the other major world religions and also in smaller indigenous religions.

In modern times, people want a scientific account of the beginnings of the world and, indeed, there are many very detailed explanations of this. The creation myths, however, fulfilled a different purpose. They are stories full of symbolism, which aim to dig deeper into basic truths about life. They want to address questions such as: why are we here? Why is the world both good and bad? What is our responsibility in the world?

The two stories mentioned above, though separated by hundreds of years and differing in detail, agree on some very important points: God is behind everything that exists, an orderly world was created and it is intended to be a good place to live. People have a role within the natural world, one which was given to them by God, to preserve and nurture that world. This understanding not only gives people a place in the world but also a responsibility for it.

The beginnings of the earth

A simple scientific account of the beginnings of the earth explains that the earth was formed about 4.6 million years ago, from hot gas and dust that became a ball of hot liquid rock. Over millions of years, the temperature at the centre cooled and gases inside the rock escaped, forming an atmosphere. As the earth cooled, the liquid rock set, clouds formed in the new atmosphere and the oceans filled with water. About three million years ago, the first life forms appeared in these oceans. These were very simple life forms at first, but over time plants grew, animals developed and life moved on to land. The earth is one planet in a solar system that rotates around the sun.

The first humans appeared approximately 2.3 million years ago; these are members of the same genus as humans today. Modern humans, or *Homo sapiens*, are said to have originated around 200,000 years ago in Africa.

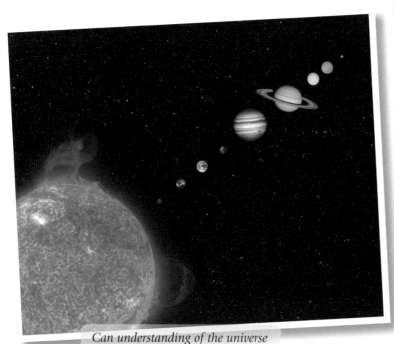

Can understanding of the universe bring people closer to God?

This type of account and many more detailed ones give us incredibly important and useful information about the earth and what it is made up of, how it is developing and the life upon it. These accounts are very worthwhile for a scientific understanding of the world. However, they are not directly concerned with a human search for meaning, a purpose to existence or a moral responsibility. They can inform on such matters but they do not directly aim to address them.

God and the universe

Most religions believe in a strong sense of God's presence in the world. Every detail of the world depends in some way on God for its existence, and in this way God's presence can be experienced in the world.

The following passage from the Psalms sums up this idea: 'Where can I go from your spirit? Or where can I flee from your presence? If I ascend to heaven you are there; if I make my bed with the dead, you are there. If I take to the wings of the morning and settle at the farthest limits of the sea, even there your hand shall lead me' (Psalm 139:7–9).

In many religious traditions, mountains are often the location for experiencing God – why do you think this is so?

At the same time, in most religious understandings of God, God is not only intimately present in the world but is also *transcendent*, above and beyond the world, unlike anything else. God does not depend on anything for existence. The following passage, also from the Psalms, sums up this idea: 'Before the mountains were brought forth, or ever you had formed the earth and the world, from everlasting to everlasting you are God' (Psalm 90.2).

Key Terms

reflection, world view, atheism, agnosticism, experiencing God, secularism, materialism, religious fundamentalism, creation

Chapter Questions

1. Explain reflection.
2. How would an agnostic answer the question, 'Does God exist?'
3. How do members of religious communities experience God?
4. What does it mean when a person is said to have a world view?
5. How would a secularist feel about people publicly expressing religious beliefs?
6. What would a materialist say is the most important thing in life?
7. What key points are made in the story of creation found in the Bible? Are there any lessons to be learned from this story in today's world?

Exam Practice

Higher Level 2004: Short question
A world view can be described as a set of assumptions which a person holds about the basic make up of the world: true or false.

Higher Level 2006: Short question
Atheism means _____.

Higher Level 2007: Short question
Agnosticism holds the view that _____.

Higher Level 2003: Short question
Reflection can be described as a human characteristic that involves a person thinking and becoming aware of their own feelings and actions: true or false.

Higher Level 2007: Section 4, question 4
People sometimes have experiences that make them wonder about the meaning of life. Describe how an experience in life could make a person ask questions about the meaning of life.
Tick **one** of the following and describe what it means: Materialism/Secularism
Explain how the religious faith of a person could be challenged by *either* materialism *or* secularism.

Higher Level 2008: Section 4, question 4

Imagine you are doing a project on the creation of the world. Tick **one** of the following world religions and outline **two** points it teaches about the creation of the world: Buddhism/Christianity/Hinduism/Islam/Judaism

Outline **two** points that science teaches about the creation of the world.

Describe **one** similarity between what a religion says and what science says about the creation of the world.

Higher Level 2011: Section 5, question 4

You are taking part in a school debate about the challenges to religious faith in Ireland today. Outline what you would say about the way in which each of the following could change a person's religious faith: Materialism/Secularism.

Mini-Project

Find out about Charles Darwin and his theory about the evolution of species.

Write a project on his life, discoveries and influence.

You will find some useful ideas on the website www.christs.cam.ac.uk/darwin200.

Useful Websites for Section D: The Question of Faith

For this section of the course, the aims are to explore the situation of religious faith today, to identify the beginning of faith in the asking of questions and the search for answers, to recognise expressions of human questioning in modern culture, to identify the characteristics of religious faith, to examine challenges to religious faith today and to offer opportunities for the exploration of and reflection on personal faith positions.

To find out more about many of the topics from this part of the course, the following may be useful:

Chapter 16

www.croagh-patrick.com
www.ciyd.ie

Chapter 17

www.humanism.ie
www.newgrange.com

Chapter 18 and 19

www.jewishireland.org
www.catholicireland.net
www.ireland.anglican.org
www.islamireland.ie
www.islaminireland.ie

Chapter 20

www.bbc.co.uk/religion/religions/atheism
www.christs.cam.ac.uk/darwin200

Section

The Celebration of Faith

This section of the syllabus aims:

- To show how ritual and worship have always been part of the human response to life and to the mystery of God.
- To identify how communities of faith express their day-to-day concerns in various forms of ritual.
- To explore an experience of worship.

Higher Level Only

- To explore the link between patterns of worship and mystery, which is of ultimate concern to individuals and communities.

The World of Ritual

21

Key Concepts

places of significance, pilgrimage, creed, actions of significance, times of significance, sacredness

Some places are really significant to people. If you visit a foreign country on holidays, you might get a guide book or a list of places of local interest. These might be places of considerable historical interest or places that are geographically spectacular. Very often, the places people visit are associated with an event or person. Places become significant over time because of the things or people they are connected to. This happens in religions too. The places that are significant for the different world

Do you recognise any of these locations?

Places of significance

A place that has special associations and is important to an individual, group or community because of an event that occurred there or its connection with a particular person. In religion, a place is significant because of who or what it is connected to or because it is used for some special purpose.

Glossary

234

religions have become so because of an association with an event or person from that religion. These places very often become places of pilgrimage for members of that particular religion.

Interestingly, many of the big tourist sites in Europe and elsewhere are places of worship, which shows the major impact religion has had on human life.

Places of significance for the major world religions

The following are places associated with each of the major world religions. Members of the religion in question see these places as significant and may go there to show devotion to their religion.

Places of religious significance

Religion	Location	Significance
Hinduism	Benares	City dedicated to the Lord Shiva
Judaism	Wailing Wall	Only remaining part of the Temple
Buddhism	Bodh Gaya	Where the Buddha reached Nirvana
Christianity	Jerusalem	Site of Jesus' crucifixion and resurrection
Islam	Mecca	Location of the Ka'ba

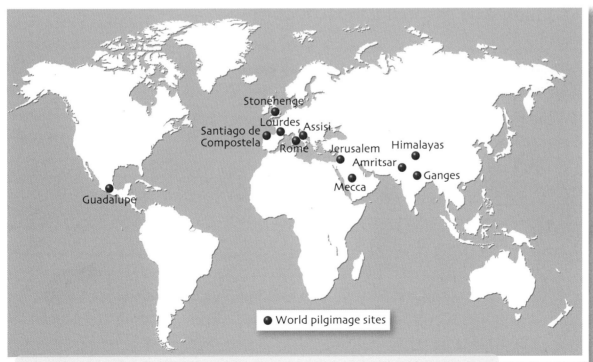

Choose one of these sites and find out more about it. Write a page on this pilgimage site, saying why it is significant and describing the rituals people go through when they go there.

Pilgrimage
A journey to a place of significance for a particular religion, carried out to show one's devotion.

People go on pilgrimages for lots of different reasons: to strengthen their faith, to help them through difficult times, to seek forgiveness, on a spiritual search, to show devotion to God or a religion. Some religions require followers to try to undertake a pilgrimage, while others don't. Most religions see the benefit of going on one.

There is more information on the pilgrimage to Mecca in Chapter 15.

Did you know?
The Camino de Santiago, or Way of St James, is the 1,000-year-old pilgrimage route to the Cathedral of Santiago de Compostela in Galicia in north western Spain, where legend has it that the remains of the apostle Saint James the Great are buried. Over 100,000 pilgrims travel to the city each year.

Pilgrimage in Ireland

In Ireland, many pilgrimage sites are connected to St Patrick. These include Downpatrick, Croagh Patrick and Lough Derg. Other sites include Knock, St Enda's Monastery, Glendalough and St Brigid's Well.

A pilgrimage site in Ireland: Lough Derg

Where is it? Lough Derg is about six kilometres north of the village of Pettigo in County Donegal. Station Island, the location of the pilgrimage, is often referred to as Saint Patrick's Purgatory.

When do people go? People can go there between April and September.

Why do people go there? The Lough Derg pilgrimage is said to be one of the most challenging in the world. People go for a variety of reasons. Some go for time out from daily life. A lot of people are seeking a quiet place to rest and reflect. For some, the challenge is an opportunity to prove you can overcome difficulty in life if your faith is strong. Others wish to strengthen their faith and some people like to meet up with other pilgrims.

What do people do there? Day retreats, workshops, faith-based seminars, family events and the traditional three-day pilgrimage. On a one-day retreat, people go through a guided day with traditional prayers, such as the rosary and the way of the cross. They may take part in the Sacrament of Reconciliation and attend Mass. However, most people go to Lough Derg in order to take part in the three-day pilgrimage. This involves fasting, an all-night vigil and prayers. Pilgrims usually do this pilgrimage barefoot.

The Fast Fasting is a common ascetic practice, enabling pilgrims to become more focused on their spiritual needs as opposed to material wants. From the midnight before arriving on Lough Derg, pilgrims fast completely (water and prescribed medication are allowed). The fast continues for three full days, during which one 'Lough Derg meal' a day is permitted. A Lough Derg meal consists of black tea or coffee, dry toast and oatcakes. The fast ends at midnight on the third day.

The Vigil This involves staying awake, completely and continuously, for 24 hours. It is the chief penitential exercise of the pilgrimage. It begins at 10.00 p.m. on the first day and ends after Benediction on the second day.

The Stations Three stations are completed before 9.20 p.m. on the first day. Doing a 'station' includes praying at mounds of stones known as 'beds', which are the remains of cells used by monks. Prayers are also said at two ancient crosses, in the church and at the water's edge. All the prayers of these stations are said silently. Pilgrims come together for the vigil during the night when prayers are said aloud in the basilica. Another station is made outside in the morning, after the Sacrament of Reconciliation, and a final one on the third day after Mass.

Looking into places of worship – churches

What do the following have in common?

- St Mary's Pro Cathedral, Marlborough Street, Dublin.
- The Mosque, Clonskeagh, Dublin.
- Christ Church Cathedral, Dublin.
- The Synagogue, Rathfarnham Road, Dublin.

They are, of course, all places of worship for some of the different religious communities in Ireland today. Religions tend to have places for worship, prayer or bringing the community together. Buildings like these are also places of significance.

Christian communities worship in a variety of buildings, usually referred to as churches. While creating sacred space, churches are designed to reflect the beliefs of the community and to show respect for God. In the Christian traditions, there are visible differences in the way churches are built, which reflect differences in opinion regarding interpretation of the Bible, the focus of worship and leadership.

Many church buildings are designed so that they are the *shape of a cross*. Many of them have a *spire*, which reaches up to the heavens. They often have a *bell tower* to call people to the way of God and many have stained glass windows, which often depict stories from the Bible.

It is typical to have the *baptismal font* near an entrance to the building or to the altar, to show that it is on entering the faith community that a person is baptised.

Since the Reformation, when the Western Church split into the Roman Catholic and Protestant Churches, there have been differences in the style of church building. To understand why there are so many different styles of churches within Christianity, we must look at the history of the Church and how the different branches developed.

What symbols are used at baptism?

How different branches of the Church developed

In the years following Jesus' death and resurrection, Christianity spread and developed. The early Christians, while retaining much from their Jewish background, started to allow non-Jews into this 'new' religion and to take on new customs and ideas. During these early years, Christians did not have churches to worship in. At this time of Roman persecution that would have been too dangerous and so, for the most part, they met in people's houses.

In the next three centuries, Christianity spread throughout the Roman world and beyond. When Emperor Constantine became Christian, it became a legal religion and Christians were no longer persecuted. Now Christianity spread even more rapidly and many churches were built.

Did you know?

Constantine first started to pray to the 'One God' before he went into a famous battle for the Milvian Bridge against his rival Maxentius in 312 CE. He believed he saw a sign in the sky, shaped like a cross in the form of the first two letters of the name 'Christ' in Greek. He ordered the sign to be put on the shields of his soldiers and he won the battle.

Two centres of Christianity emerged. The Christian communities that saw Rome as their centre were Latin-speaking, while those centred on Constantinople were Greek-speaking. The two existed side by side for a long time. During this period, a number of councils were held that agreed on some of the main beliefs of the Church, and outlined these beliefs in creeds (e.g. the Nicene Creed). These creeds contain the main doctrines or teachings shared by most Christians, including the doctrine of the *Incarnation* (that God was revealed in the human life of Jesus) and the *Trinity* (that God is Three-in-One, the Father, the Son and the Holy Spirit).

Why did the earliest Christians not build churches?

After years of existing together, the two centres of Christianity split in what is known as the 'Great Schism' of 1054. This split was between the *Orthodox Church* in the east headed by a *Patriarch* and the *Western Christian Church* in Rome headed by the *Pope*. The Eastern Orthodox Church has many branches, e.g. Greek, Russian, Armenian and Ethiopian. It is noted for its elaborate church buildings, rituals and icons.

Creed
An official statement of faith or belief.

Glossary

What features do you recognise?

The Western Church continued for a number of centuries as one branch of Christianity, but the power and wealth it enjoyed left it corrupt and slow to reform. Many became disillusioned with this and calls for reform became stronger. Eventually, reformers felt unable to remain in the Church and started many new Christian denominations. The reformers emphasised the Bible as the principal source of authority. They had a new understanding of the number and meaning of the sacraments, and they reduced the importance of the leadership and tradition of the Church. The period when the Western Christian Church split and these new 'reformed' Churches began is called the *Reformation*.

Did you know? In Orthodox churches, there is a feature called an *iconostasis*. This is a huge screen containing icons that separates the altar area from the rest of the church.

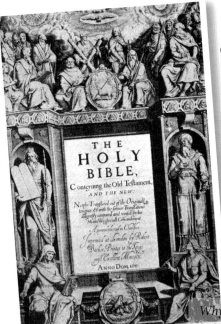

The word *Protestant* is an umbrella term for many different Churches that are considered to be 'Reformed' or that do not accept the Pope's authority. There are many branches of Protestantism in Ireland today, including the Church of Ireland, Methodists, Presbyterians, Baptists, Quakers and the Salvation Army.

After the Reformation, the Roman Catholic Church took steps to reform itself. It set up new orders and called the Council of Trent to deal with problems in the Church and to clarify its position on certain teachings, especially those that the Reformed Churches had questioned.

Why do you think the Reformed Churches were keen to translate the Bible into the spoken languages?

1. Name the first Roman emperor to become Christian.
2. Where did the first two major centres of Christianity emerge?
3. What language did the Church in Constantinople use?
4. Name one Christian creed.
5. What is the doctrine of the Incarnation?
6. When did the Great Schism occur? What was it?
7. Name two branches of the Orthodox Church.
8. Why did the Reformation take place?
9. What did the reformers emphasise?
10. What does the word Protestant refer to? Name three Protestant Churches.

Now that we understand something of the history of the different branches of Christianity, it is not surprising that there are many different styles of church building. The two main branches of Christianity in Ireland are the Roman Catholic Church and the Church of Ireland. We will examine these two different styles of church.

Features of a typical Roman Catholic church

A Roman Catholic church is designed to worship and glorify God. Members are encouraged to attend regularly and some days of the year are *days of holy obligation*. These are days when Catholics are expected to go to Mass. The focus of worship is the *altar*, which is especially holy and worthy of respect. The Catholic Church teaches that there are *seven sacraments* and that, in the Eucharist, the bread and wine is changed into the body and blood of Jesus. This is called *transubstantiation*. In this way, all partake in the sacrifice of Jesus. The following features all reflect important beliefs of this Church.

Tabernacle: The Church teaches that the bread and

What takes place at the altar during Mass?

wine is transubstantiated into Jesus' body and blood, so there is a cupboard or box where leftover wafers and/or wine are kept. A *light* (sanctuary lamp) will be placed nearby indicating that it is present.

Baptismal font: A stone basin where people are brought to be baptised, symbolising the washing away of sins and becoming members of the Church.

Confessional booth: One of the seven sacraments of the Roman Catholic Church is Reconciliation or the sacrament of forgiveness for wrongdoing. This booth is where the priest hears a person's confession on behalf of God.

Crucifix: A cross with Jesus on it. This reminds people of the sacrifice of Jesus on the cross.

Stations of the cross: Pictures of Jesus' journey carrying the cross to the hill of Calvary where he was crucified. Approaching Easter time, people pray along the stations as they remember this important moment in the story of God's love for all people.

Statues: Churches usually have statues as a focus for people to worship God. These may be of Jesus, Mary, an evangelist or another saint. These images may inspire people to have faith. Some believers pray to ask the saints to intercede on their behalf for help or forgiveness from God or to thank God.

Lectern/pulpit: Where ministers of the word read to the congregation. The place from where the priest delivers the sermon or homily.

Holy water font: On entering a church, Roman Catholics dip their fingers in the holy water font and bless themselves. This reminds them of their baptism as a Christian.

Candles: In Roman Catholic churches, it is usual to have candles that people can light. The lighted candle is a symbol of Jesus, who is 'the light of the world' for Christians. People who go into a church may light a candle and say a prayer for a loved one or themselves.

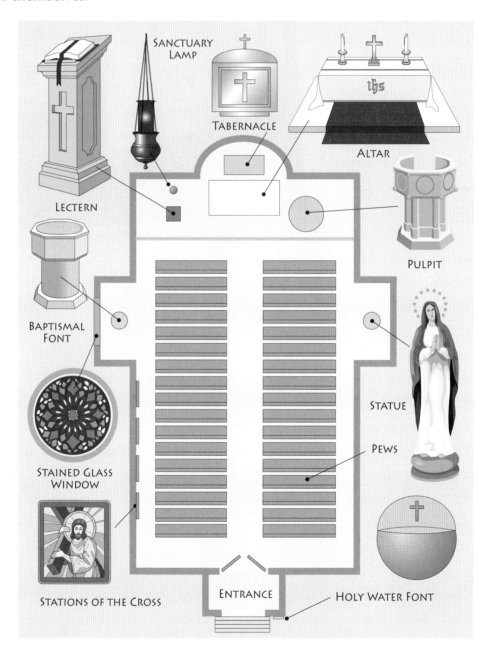

Features of some Protestant churches

Since there are many different Protestant Churches, it is important to note that there is a huge variety of styles of buildings used by Protestants for worship. From the beginning, the Reformed Churches emphasised the need for people to listen to the word of God in the Bible. As such, most Protestant churches are designed to create a space to do just that. Nevertheless, many Protestant denominations do carry out the two sacraments of Eucharist and baptism, so there are features that are used for those purposes. Of course, like all sacred buildings, Protestant churches are used by a community to worship God. The following example is closest to the type of church building used by the Church of Ireland, the biggest Protestant denomination in Ireland.

Lectern: Often placed in a central position, this usually has a Bible on it, emphasising the importance of hearing God's word. The lectern may be quite ornate and symbolic, for example with an eagle to represent the power of God's word. Readings from the Bible are made here during worship.

Pulpit: The place from where the clergyman or woman delivers the sermon; usually based on the Bible reading for that day.

No statues: The Bible refers to God's instruction to have no graven images, so Protestant churches, much like Jewish synagogues, avoid any carved images of people or God.

What is the focus here? Why do you think this is the case?

Baptismal font: A stone feature with a basin where people are baptised. It is often located near the entrance, showing how baptism symbolises entry into the community.

Altar: While not so much the focus of worship in many Protestant churches, there is an altar, or communion table, for the sacrament of the Eucharist, more commonly referred to as Holy Communion or the Lord's Supper. A chalice (cup) and paten (plate) may be placed on the communion table.

Plain cross: Many Protestant churches have a plain cross to remind worshippers of the death and resurrection of Jesus. The empty cross emphasises the belief that Jesus is risen from the dead.

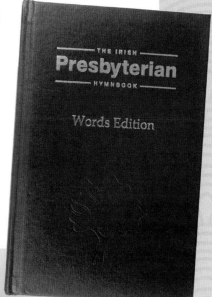

Hymn books and prayer books: Services of morning or evening prayer, as well as the Eucharist, are common forms of worship in the Church of Ireland. To take part in these services, the people use the order of service in the Book of Common Prayer. The whole congregation worships God through singing hymns together, so there is always a supply of hymn books.

Did you know?

A version of the Book of Common Prayer has been in use in the Church of Ireland since 1549.

Do you know the names of any hymns?

In most Protestant churches, you will not find the stations of the cross, a holy water font or a confessional booth.

Over to You

1. What is a baptismal font?
2. What is kept in a tabernacle?
3. What is a confessional booth used for?
4. What is the difference between a crucifix and a plain cross?
5. What are the stations of the cross?
6. What is the pulpit?
7. What is an iconostasis?
8. Do either a or b.
   a. Copy the drawing above of the Roman Catholic Church and fully label it.
   b. Write a page on the following: 'Churches reflect the beliefs and traditions of the community they belong to', comparing church buildings in Ireland today.

For information on the layout and features of a synagogue, see Chapter 12, or for a mosque, see Chapter 15.

Times and actions of significance

In life in general, some actions are quite significant: birthday celebrations, graduations, sports finals and marriages, to name just a few. Within the communities where people live, work and participate in, some times and actions are celebrated and acknowledged in a special way.

A time of significance in sport

Think about football and the cup final – this day is a special time in the sporting year. Marking it in a significant way involves all sorts of actions. The fans make the journey

How are the winners presented with their prize? What rituals take place around these sporting events?

to the game. The stadium and the pitch are set up for the match. The teams walk out onto the pitch and shake hands before kick-off. After the match, there are more significant actions: the build-up as the winning team do a lap of honour and thank the fans, the presentation of the cup and winners' medals, the captain holding the cup and waiting to raise it to the fans. The whole event is filled with special moments and with actions that are full of meaning and significance.

A significant day for one person

Why are these objects special for a person?

Birthdays are a special time for most people. Presents, candles, cards and, perhaps, a party are all part of the celebration that someone has reached another year in their life. For people, different traditions can grow up around birthdays, maybe a family meal, a trip to get a special present, a homemade cake or a visit to a special location. The action, however small, becomes significant for the individual that it means something to.

Actions of significance 〔Glossary〕
Events that are special or important for a person or for a group of people at a moment, time of the year or during a person's life. These actions have special meaning and purpose in marking an important time.

Religious times of significance

What is being celebrated? Is this a significant time for one person only or for a group?

For each of the major world religions, there are special times. Some are special for an individual, e.g. confirmation, while others are special for the whole community, e.g. Christmas. Some take place only once in a lifetime while others take place every year. Whatever the occasion, a time of religious significance will usually involve actions, gestures, words and ceremonies to mark it.

Times of significance for a whole community usually celebrate or mark a significant event in history, the birth or death of a founder, an important

Times of significance 〔Glossary〕
Special times for an individual or group may occur annually or once in a lifetime. The time set aside for a special purpose or to celebrate a special occasion.

time in the past or when an individual did something that has become a tradition in that community of faith.

For individuals, times of significance are often important stages in life which mark a passage from one stage in life to another. It may be a marriage, a coming of age ceremony or a ritual around birth or death. The individual times of significance are some of the most memorable in a person's life.

Is this a time of significance for an individual or a community?

Religious times of significance		
Religion	**Time of Significance**	
	1. **For the community**	2. **For the individual**
Christianity	Christmas	Confirmation
Islam	Ramadan	Birth
Hinduism	Diwali	sacred thread ceremony
Judaism	Passover	Bar or bat mitzvah
Buddhism	Wesak	Joining the Sangha

How can you tell Diwali is a time of significance for Hindus?

A time of significance for a whole community: Wesak

This festival, sometimes called 'Buddha Day', is when Buddhists celebrate the birth, enlightenment and death of the Buddha. A number of customs and traditions are associated with this day. One of the most common is the lighting of *Wesak* lanterns, hence the festival is sometimes celebrated as a festival of lights. In Japan, the focus is on the birth of the Buddha, while in Thailand, the main focus is on his enlightenment. In preparation for the festival, statues of the Buddha are cleaned and in some communities a Bodhi tree may be decorated with lanterns. People may visit the communities of monks called *Sanghas* and bring presents of flowers, incense and food. Sermons on the life and teachings of the Buddha are given and people have parties to celebrate the Buddha's enlightenment.

Did you know? The Bodhi tree is a symbol of enlightenment for Buddhists. It is the tree under which the Buddha sat meditating until he had reached enlightenment.

Do you know any other religious festivals that use light as an important symbol?

A time of significance for an individual: the sacred thread ceremony

In Hinduism, this special time takes place during adolescence and marks the beginning of the student stage in life. The ceremony is usually held at home. There is a ritual fire, readings from the sacred texts, offerings of oil and incense, and prayers

What do the threads represent?

are said. The sacred thread, which is made up of five strands of cotton, is then hung around the boy's chest as a symbol of his willingness to learn from the sacred scriptures. If the boy has his own guru or teacher to guide his spiritual life, the guru would traditionally perform this ceremony. There is a celebration after the ceremony, with food and presents, and new clothes are worn for the occasion.

In Hinduism, *Dharma* refers to 'sacred duty'. All Hindus, according to their age and stage in life, have certain responsibilities. The sacred thread ceremony marks the beginning of the stage known as *Brahma Charya*, when a person's duty is to concentrate on study. While their duties are to show respect to parents and teachers and to do their best in their studies, they have rights too: to receive education, shelter, food and clothing.

Times of significance in Christianity – the liturgical year

The liturgical year is the year of Christian rituals and festivals. It begins at Advent, the four-week period leading to Christmas. Advent is a time of preparation, when Christians light candles and start to make preparations for celebrating the season of

Christmas. It is about remembering the past but also a time to focus on what Jesus' birth means for the present.

Christmas is a very happy festival, a celebration. Christians give presents, go to church, send greetings of goodwill, visit family and friends and sing carols, which are songs about Christmas. Giving presents represents the gifts of the wise men to Jesus and also emphasises the Christian message of sharing and showing love to others.

First written in German by Josef Mohr, the song 'Silent Night' or 'Stille Nacht' was first performed in the Church of St Nicholas in Obendorff, Austria, on Christmas Day in 1818. The tune was composed by Franz Gruber.

Christmas means 'Christ's Mass' and most Christians attend their place of worship to pray and celebrate as a community. Many go to Mass on Christmas Eve to welcome in this special season. There are many different cultural ways of celebrating Christmas. Different countries have their own traditions, foods to eat and times for giving presents. In many places people put up a Christmas tree with a star or an angel on top, symbolising the star that led the wise men to Jesus or the angel that told the shepherds of his birth. Some people have a nativity scene or crib in their home. Schools hold nativity plays or carol services and people read the relevant passages of the Bible that tell the story of Jesus' birth.

In 1914, during World War I, at Christmas there was a truce when soldiers from the opposing armies stopped fighting and instead shook hands, exchanged presents and sang songs together.

For many charities, Christmas is a very important season. People give more to charity then than at any other time in the year. Perhaps the messages of 'love your neighbour as yourself' or 'peace and goodwill towards all' are most understood during this celebration of the birth of a poor boy in Bethlehem over 2,000 years ago.

The twelfth day of Christmas is known as Epiphany. This day celebrates recognising Jesus as God's son and the visit of the wise men. In Protestant churches the season of Epiphany lasts until Ash Wednesday.

Ash Wednesday marks the beginning of the next time of preparation, which is called Lent. Lent is a time to prepare for Easter and the focus is on repentance or saying sorry for wrongdoing. Many Christians take on a difficult task or give up luxuries during Lent. They remember the difficulties Jesus faced in the wilderness and reflect on his courage. Christians recall the death and resurrection of Jesus and what that means for the community. During Holy Week (the week leading up to Easter), many Roman Catholics go to Mass and move around the stations (artistic representations of Jesus carrying his cross to his crucifixion) and say prayers.

Holy Week leading up to Easter

Palm Sunday	– Remembering Jesus' arrival in Jerusalem.
Spy Wednesday	– Remembering Judas' betrayal of Jesus.
Maundy Thursday	– Remembering the Last Supper.
Good Friday	– Remembering the Crucifixion.

Easter Sunday is a celebration of Jesus' resurrection, when most Christians go to church, give Easter eggs and have a family meal. After Easter two important days take place. Forty days later is Ascension, when Jesus departed to heaven and fifty days later is Pentecost when the Holy Spirit descended on the early Christians, giving them the ability to spread the message.

Sacredness

Sacredness refers to something being set apart as special in a religious sense. It is something that is worthy of respect. Some places or times are sacred and special for a religious community. For example, many people see their place of worship, be it a mosque, church, synagogue or temple, as a place endowed with special sacredness. It is a place where someone is able to feel a spiritual presence or feel more connected with their God or Gods. In the Roman Catholic Church, the area around the altar is seen as a place of extra holiness or as being especially sacred. For Muslims, a mosque is so sacred that shoes are removed on entering it.

Why could this be considered to be a sacred object?

> **Glossary**
>
> **Sacredness**
> Something that is considered to have special religious significance or holiness and should be treated with respect.

Objects are also sometimes seen as sacred. For example, a copy of the Torah is kept in a special box in the synagogue, and taken out with great care and read from with special attention during communal worship in Judaism.

Some times are considered sacred too. Times when one is meditating, taking part in a sacrament, praying or going on a pilgrimage may be described as sacred moments for an individual.

Key Terms

places of significance, pilgrimage, creed, actions of significance, times of significance, sacredness

Chapter Questions

1. What does it mean to say a place is significant?
2. What are the names of the places of worship for Christians, Muslims and Jews?
3. Complete the following: When a person goes on a journey to a place of religious significance for their religion they are going on a _____.
4. Why is Bodh Gaya important to Buddhists?
5. Describe any action that is carried out in a religion and explain its significance.
6. What does it mean to say something is sacred?
7. What does Wesak celebrate? Who celebrates it?
8. What religion carries out the sacred thread ceremony?
9. What is Dharma?
10. In your opinion, what is the most significant time in a person's life? Why do you think this? How should it be celebrated?

Exam Practice

Higher Level 2009: Short question

In religious traditions the term 'sacred' means _____.

Higher Level 2009: Short question

In religious traditions the term 'creed' means _____.

Higher Level 2008: Short question

In religious traditions 'schism' means _____.

Higher Level 2007: Short question

Croagh Patrick is a place of religious importance in Ireland. Name another place of religious importance in Ireland _____.

Higher Level 2005: Short question

A temple is a place of worship in Islam: true or false.

Higher Level 2004: Short question

The River Ganges is sacred to which of the following world religions?
Christianity/Hinduism/Islam/Judaism

Higher Level 2004: Short question

An action that carries meaning for a person, and is of importance to him/her, can be said to have significance: true or false.

Higher Level and Ordinary Level 2009: Picture question

Pick **one** thing from this photograph that shows that these people are taking part in a pilgrimage.

Tick **one** of the following world religions and name a place of pilgrimage associated with it: Buddhism/Hinduism/Islam/Judaism

State **two** reasons why members of a world religion would take part in a pilgrimage.

Higher Level 2008: Section 4, question 5

Tick **one** of the following major world religions you have studied and name a time of year that has religious importance for its members: Buddhism/Christianity/Hinduism/Islam/Judaism.

Name of time of year: _____.

Describe **one** way in which members of a major world religion mark a time of year that has religious importance for them.

Outline the religious meaning of **one** ritual that marks an important time of year for members of a major world religion.

Mini-Project

Research religious places of significance in Ireland and draw a map showing the location of each. Write a brief description of each location.

The Experience of Worship

22

Key Concepts

ritual, worship, participation

There are many things in religion that are hard to express. It is not always easy to show what you believe or to show faith. To deal with this, most religions use rituals to allow people to be part of the religion and to let that religion put into *actions*, *words* and *gestures* what it is about. Rituals are, therefore, a way of expressing faith.

What is a ritual?

A ritual is an action or practice that has a deeper meaning and is usually carried out in the same way each time. A ritual will involve actions, words and gestures that are similar each time it is carried out. Rituals are often formal ceremonies. Some are carried out regularly while others are less frequent. Religions carry out daily, weekly, annual or once-in-a-lifetime rituals.

Glossary

Ritual
A set of patterned, formal, symbolic actions.

Why do you think it burns throughout the games?

Non-religious rituals

Do you know the ritual associated with the start of the Olympic Games? The Olympic opening ceremony always includes the lighting of the Olympic flame, a practice continued from the ancient Olympic Games. The Olympic flame represents a number of things, including purity and the endeavour for perfection.

Did you know?

The idea of an Olympic flame burning from the start to the close of the games was introduced during the 1928 Olympic Games in Amsterdam, where a fire was lit in the tower of the stadium, though no torch relay was undertaken.

Cutting the ribbon is the usual ritual for opening a new business enterprise.

Rituals with family and friends

Why are family celebrations important?

Maybe you or your family or friends have rituals you carry out at special times, such as a place you always visit on holidays, a present that is bought when someone in the family reaches a certain age, or a ritual for when you finish school or go to college. The actions are not important, but what they mean is. A special present or a family meal to celebrate someone leaving school is about showing the person what they mean, that they have achieved something important, that they are special. It is the same with most religious rituals. The actions and words are special because of what they mean.

Discuss

Can you think of any rituals associated with school or sport or that you carry out with your family and friends? Share ideas with your class.

Since rituals are used in many other parts of life, it is not surprising that they are used in religion.

How do people show others what their religion means to them?

- Going to church, synagogue, mosque or temple.
- Putting the teachings of their religion into practice.
- Praying or meditating.
- Taking part in *religious rituals*.

Such rituals involve symbolic actions, gestures and words.

What is worship?

Worship is about showing reverence or a deep respect for God. Worship takes many forms within the different religions practised

Why is Mecca the site of the annual pilgrimage?

in the world today. For Muslims, worship of God (Allah) is shown by praying five times a day in the direction of Mecca. It is also to try to go on the annual pilgrimage known as the *Hajj* and to fast during Ramadan. All these rituals are about worshipping or showing respect for God. Muslims believe that everything they do can be an act of worship of God; work, home life and school life should not be separated from worship.

In Judaism, worship can include prayer, observing Shabbat or wearing a *yarmulke*. To worship God reflects on everyday life, too. For a Jewish person, God is everywhere and central to life. The *mezuzah* (wooden box) on the door of a Jewish home contains the words of Deuteronomy 6:4–9.

Worship *(Glossary)*
Reverence to God or Gods which may involve prayer, rituals, singing or dancing.

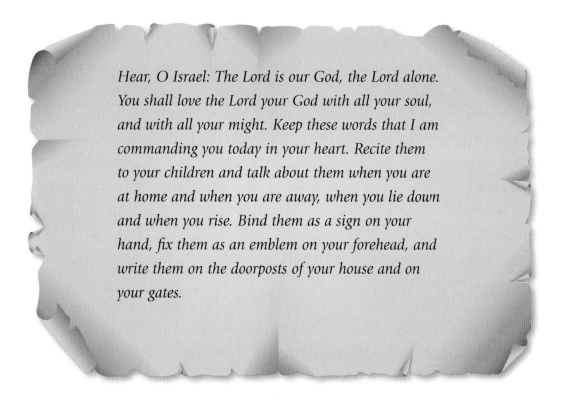

Hear, O Israel: The Lord is our God, the Lord alone. You shall love the Lord your God with all your soul, and with all your might. Keep these words that I am commanding you today in your heart. Recite them to your children and talk about them when you are at home and when you are away, when you lie down and when you rise. Bind them as a sign on your hand, fix them as an emblem on your forehead, and write them on the doorposts of your house and on your gates.

How is this object an expression of belief?

To worship God truly affects a person's whole life, not just one day a week. Communal worship of God is shown in prayer, song and symbolic actions. For a Christian, it takes place at weekly services held in the different churches, such as Morning Prayer, Mass, fellowship or a service of worship.

Christian worship goes back to the first Christians, whose worship is outlined in the book of Acts in the New Testament. There is a pattern of worship that still goes on today: teaching, prayer, fellowship and the 'breaking of bread'.

Symbolic actions involved in worship

How do you show respect for someone? First of all, you look at them while talking to them. It is a sign of disrespect to turn away from someone you are talking to. You use appropriate words, e.g. calling someone by their name and not using insulting or bad language, which would be disrespectful.

It shows respect to open a door for someone, to shake hands or to offer a seat. We have different ways of showing respect to people and it is the same in religion. Of course, for people who believe in God, no other person is worthy of quite the same level of respect and reverence. Therefore, the gestures and words used to worship God show the utmost level of respect. Take a look at the following examples:

When do people shake hands?

- Muslims entering a mosque take off their shoes, signifying the place of worship is sacred or holy ground.
- Jewish men wear a yarmulke while praying, to signify humility before God.
- A Christian entering a church may bow towards the altar, as this is a place endowed with sacredness.
- While praying, people bow their heads or close their eyes. These are ways of showing deep reverence to God and concentrating completely on communicating with God.
- Evangelical Christians raise their hands in the air when they worship God, as a sign of praise towards God.
- People get down on their knees to pray. Kneeling demonstrates humility and submission to God. For Muslims, this can be seen even more in the sequence of prayer that includes complete prostration.

- A Hindu carries out a daily *puja*, an act of worship at the family shrine, offers food to the God and invokes the God's presence.
- A person leaves a busy street to enter a church and light a candle as they pray to God. The candle is a symbol of the prayer.

What do these three pictures have in common?

The language of worship

Some phrases are used frequently in worship. There are words of significance that are familiar to members of a religion, though not necessarily easily recognised by others. Such phrases could include the Islamic '*Allahu akbar*' meaning 'God is greatest', the Christian 'Our Father, who art in heaven, hallowed be thy name' or 'Make a joyful noise to the Lord, all the earth' (Psalm 100). Music is also an important part of worship. Words put to sacred songs used during communal worship are called hymns.

Participating in Christian worship

Participating refers to taking part. In worship, it is to be actively involved, not just a passive spectator. People participate in different ways, e.g. by saying the prayers, singing the hymns, understanding the symbols, reading from the Bible, listening to the sermon and reflecting on it.

Participation
The action of taking part in something.

Glossary

Worship in a church today

The example below is a form of worship called Morning Prayer, carried out in the Church of Ireland, the largest Protestant denomination in Ireland today. This form of worship takes place regularly in churches throughout Ireland. The Church of Ireland also has regular Holy Communion (Eucharist) services, though not necessarily every day.

- Sentences of scripture.
- A general confession and absolution.
- The Lord's Prayer.
- A psalm from the biblical book of Psalms.
- Readings from the Old and New Testaments.
- Creed.
- A *collect*, a short prayer assigned to a particular day or season.
- Hymns may be sung.
- A sermon may be preached.
- Prayers.
- The Blessing.

Over to You

1. What is worship?
2. Explain three different ways in which people might worship God.
3. Where does Christian worship originate?
4. Why are symbols used in worship?
5. Give examples of three symbols used in worship and explain their meaning.
6. What is a hymn?
7. How can people participate in an act of worship?

The importance of religious rituals today

Taking part in religious rituals helps people to feel part of their religious community. The importance of participation in rituals for individuals can be seen in the hundreds of forms of religious ritual across the world and the millions of people who take part in them.

These rituals are an expression of the day-to-day concerns of the different communities of faith.

*How would you know
these are religious rituals?*

Rituals associated with five major world religions

Islam – Prayer five times a day

Christianity – Sacraments

Judaism – Shabbat

Hinduism – The Arti service

Buddhism – Meditation

Islam – prayer five times a day

Prayer five times a day, known as *Salat*, is one of the most important rituals in Islam. It is really important to a Muslim to communicate with God. Praying in Islam involves many rituals; washing, words, gestures and objects are all symbolically used in this act.

> '*O believers, when you stand up to pray, wash your faces, and your hands up to the elbows, and wipe your heads, and your feet up to the ankles.*'
> (The Qur'an, Surah 5:8)

*Do you think it helps
to have a focus while
you pray?*

The five prayers take place at the sames times every day. They all begin with the *wudu* or ritual washing. This can take place at home or in a mosque where there are washrooms. The ritual cleaning symbolises a break from the normal routine to concentrate on prayer. *Takbir* is entering into the state of prayer by glorifying God. A declaration of intention or *niyya* is required before praying. Muslims must then make sure they are facing in the direction of the Ka'ba, the 'House of God', in Mecca. Usually people use a prayer mat for praying.

To begin the act of prayer, they say '*Allahu Akbar*', raising their hands to the ears or shoulders. They also carry out a series of movements as they pray and set words are said. Each Salat is made up of cycles of prayer, called *rak'at*.

Time to pray

The prayers have set times: dawn (*fajr*), midday (*zuhr*), late afternoon (*asr*), sunset (*magrib*) and between sunset and midnight (*isha*). In this way, Muslim prayer is a ritual that gives a pattern to the day.

Are there any features that would indicate that this is a mosque?

Where to pray

While Muslims can pray anywhere, it is especially good to pray with others in a mosque. It reminds them of the equality of all before God.

Movements in prayer

The gestures used symbolise different things. When a Muslim places his or her forehead on the floor during prayer, he or she is symbolically submitting to Allah's will. Bowing shows reverence and respect for God, while kneeling shows humility before God. Standing upright shows alertness and placing hands to the ears represents pushing away all other distractions during prayer.

The importance for Muslims of this ritual

- While praying, Muslims believe they are in God's presence.
- Prayer at set times connects all Muslims around the world.
- It is a 1,400-year-old ritual.
- Muslims pray because they believe that God has told them to.

Discuss **Is carrying out rituals a good way of helping people to feel part of their religious community? What difficulties would a Muslim face trying to carry out the rituals of daily prayer in Ireland?**

1. What do Muslims have to do before they pray?
2. What is takbir?
3. Where do Muslims pray?
4. When do Muslims pray?
5. In your own words, write about the commitment needed to carry out this ritual.

Christianity – sacraments

Christianity is, of course, a very diverse religion and there are a lot of differences between the various branches of Christianity and their rituals. Sacraments are understood differently by different types of Christians. For Roman Catholics, sacraments are a fundamental part of their religion; there are seven sacraments that can be carried out. Among Protestant churches, there are differences in the number and importance of sacraments.

What is a sacrament?

Sacraments are very important Christian rituals. They involve symbolic actions, gestures, words and objects. A sacrament is a formal ritual or ceremony that is intended to bring an awareness of the presence of God to the person taking part in it. It has sometimes been defined as 'an outward and visible sign of an inward and spiritual grace'.

Sacraments are rituals that involve actions, words and gestures which express a belief in the presence of God. They are a way of people responding to the mystery of God.

In the Roman Catholic Church, there are seven sacraments:

1. Baptism
2. Eucharist
3. Confirmation
4. Marriage
5. Reconciliation
6. Holy orders
7. Anointing the sick or dying

The Orthodox Church also has seven major sacraments, often called 'mysteries'.

For most Protestant Churches, there are two main or fundamental sacraments. These are Eucharist (often referred to as Holy Communion or the Lord's Supper) and Baptism. Since the Reformation, Protestants have emphasised the authority of the

Bible and consider it the most important source of guidance. In the Bible, Jesus only carries out these two sacraments.

The importance of sacraments

- Sacraments are a way of building a sense of community.
- Sacraments can help people feel more involved, a way to participate.
- Sacraments are a way of dealing with the 'sacred'.

Did you know?

The Salvation Army, a Protestant Church, carries out no sacraments.

The Eucharist

While some rituals only take place once in a person's life, the Eucharist is a sacrament that can take place every day. It is a way for Christians to encounter God daily or weekly, and shows the importance of the central belief of Christianity: that Jesus died and was resurrected for them.

When did this take place?

What is this ritual about?

This ritual dates back to the very early Christian community. It originates with the Last Supper meal which Jesus shared with his disciples, when he gave them bread and wine, asking them: 'Do this in remembrance of me.'

What does this ritual involve?

The exact ritual varies in practice and understanding among different Churches. It involves receiving bread and wine as the body and blood of Jesus. In many Protestant Churches, the bread and wine are seen as symbols of the body and blood of Jesus, and the sacrament is not necessarily carried out at every service. In the Roman Catholic Church, the bread and wine are considered more than just symbols. By being consecrated or blessed by the priest, they become in substance Jesus' risen body and blood. This idea is known as *transubstantiation*.

What is the importance of this ritual?

Christians all over the world continue this tradition as a reminder of Jesus' sacrifice, death and resurrection. It is one of the most important teachings and practices in this religion.

Many Christians believe that they experience God's presence during the Eucharist in a way that strengthens their faith and helps them to live better lives as Christians.

Sharing the bread and wine also represents sharing a meal together as a Christian family.

Baptism

The majority of Christian denominations carry out this ritual once only. How it is carried out varies among the different Churches. It has been very important since the earliest days of the religion, since Jesus himself was baptised by John the Baptist.

What is this ritual about?

Jesus was baptised by John the Baptist in the River Jordan. John is described in the New Testament as baptising people to repent or say sorry for their sins, so they would be ready for the Messiah or chosen one. Christians from earliest times have been baptised as a sign of membership of the Christian Church.

When are most Christians baptised?

In the story of Jesus' baptism in Matthew's gospel, it says that Jesus 'saw the Spirit of God descending like a dove and alighting on him'. An ancient Jewish symbol, the dove has come to be a symbol of peace and of the Holy Spirit in Christianity.

What else is water used for?

What does this ritual involve?

Most Churches baptise babies or young children. The Baptist Church, however, believes in baptising adults only. The sacrament has a number of symbols. The most important of these is water.

Baptism can be performed by (i) full immersion – dipping a person's body completely under water, or (ii) pouring water on a person's head.

Baptism is a sacrament of initiation. This means that it represents becoming a full member of the Christian community. The word comes from the Greek word *baptizo*, which means 'to dip'. The main Churches all believe that baptism should be carried out once only.

Symbols used and their meaning	
Symbols used	**Meaning**
Water	Washing away sin; new life in God
Oil of Chrism	Strength as a member of God's family
White Clothes	Purity, a new life clothed in Christ
Candle	Light in darkness; Jesus is described as 'the light of the world'

What is the importance of this ritual?

For Christians, baptism represents a new beginning to life as a Christian, membership of the Church and the washing away of sin.

Judaism – the weekly ritual of Shabbat

For Jewish people, the day of rest is known as *Shabbat*. It begins at sunset on Friday and lasts until sunset on Saturday. The rituals of Shabbat vary among the different branches of Judaism (orthodox, reformed, hasidic etc.). In general, the following are the important traditions associated with this ritual:

- A family meal on Friday evening.
- Lighting candles.
- Prayers.
- Going to the synagogue.
- Day of rest.

 Monotheism refers to the belief in one God. Judaism, Christianity and Islam are all monotheistic faiths.

The meaning of the Sabbath

Shabbat is about taking seriously the commandment that says 'you shall keep the Sabbath day holy'. Traditionally in Judaism the Sabbath day is Saturday, but it begins as soon as darkness falls on Friday evening. It is a time for rest, contemplation of the holy books, family, and for worshipping and thanking God. All members of the family are expected to keep the Sabbath day holy, but in Orthodox Judaism the obligation to do certain things is different for the various members of the family. The Sabbath reminds Jewish people of the covenant or agreement with God. It is something to look forward to as a gift from God when people can take time out and rest.

Sabbath customs

No work must be carried out on the Sabbath, so everything is done beforehand, much like getting ready for a party. People have the cooking, cleaning and shopping done by Friday sunset to prepare for the Sabbath. People often dress in their best clothes. There is a lot of emphasis on the family being together to celebrate the Sabbath. Single people or those with no family around often gather together to celebrate it.

Some people visit the synagogue on Friday evening, but usually the whole family will go together on a Saturday.

Sabbath rituals

It is the tradition for the mother of a family to light the Sabbath candles before sunset on a Friday. Two candles are lit to represent the commandments to remember the Sabbath (*zachor*) and to observe the Sabbath (*shamor*). The greeting of '*Gut Shabbas*', 'Good Sabbath' or '*Shabbat Shalom*' is made by the members of the household to each other.

The father then blesses his children and recites the *kiddush* prayer to sanctify the Sabbath. A sweet wine is drunk from a kiddush cup or special glass. The sweetness represents joy and cheer.

Are candles used in any other religious tradition?

The blessing for daughters is that they should be like the four matriarchs in the book of Genesis in the Bible: Sarah, Rebecca, Rachel and Leah. The blessing for sons is that they should be like two brothers, also in the book of Genesis: Ephraim and Manasseh, who lived in harmony with each other.

What might people thank God for during Shabbat?

Sabbath bread is called *challah*. It is in the shape of a braid and should be eaten at the beginning of the meal. It is passed around to be blessed. Challah bread is eaten during festivals too, except for Passover when leavened or risen bread is not allowed.

The prayer recited before challah is eaten is: 'Baruch atah Adonai Eloheinu Melech ha'olam, hamotzi lechem min ha'aretz.' ('Blessed are you, Lord our God, King of the universe, who brings forth bread from the earth.')

Farewell to the Sabbath

The Sabbath ends when the first three stars are seen in the sky. The mother then says a prayer of farewell to the Sabbath: 'O God of Abraham, Isaac and Jacob, guard your people Israel for your praise.' A prayer for a good week is also said. A ceremony of separation signals the end of the joy of Sabbath as a day of rest and a return to weekday responsibilities.

Hinduism – the Arti service (worship of the sacred flame)

In Hinduism, an act of worship is known as a *puja*. While there are temples in Hinduism, many people carry out worship in their homes. In fact, in many Hindu homes the family has a shrine to their favourite God. The family shrine usually has an image or statue of the God in front of which the family place incense, a bell, a candle, a sacred lamp, food, flowers and milk.

Puja can be an elaborate ceremony or a simple offering of food to the God at a family shrine, accompanied by ringing a bell and saying prayers.

In a shrine room in a temple, the most popular form of worship is the *Arti* service or worship of the sacred flame. This is how it is carried out:

1. Before entering the shrine, people take off their shoes to show respect, reflecting the idea that they are entering sacred ground.
2. The person enters the shrine room and heads to the back, where a statue of the God is usually placed.
3. They approach the shrine, bow, pray and offer food and/or money in front of the image.
4. They then join other people for worship.
5. The service begins with singing hymns called *bhajans*, followed by prayers called *kirtan*. It also includes hand clapping.

Do you know the name of this Hindu God?

6. The priest prepares a tray with the following objects on it:
    a) A *diva* or oil lamp with five openings that represent fire, earth, light, air and water.
    b) A fan to wave in front of the image.
    c) A shell representing the elements.
    d) Offerings of food and water.
    e) Incense to sweeten the air.
    f) Flowers representing beauty.
    g) A small bell to alert the Gods to the intention to worship.

7. The priest approaches the image of the God or Goddess and performs worship – a puja. He will say verses from the holy books.

Does this remind you of any preparation during Christian worship?

8. The priest lifts the lamp to each God in a circular motion. This is the act of offering the sacred flame.
9. The bell is rung while people recite a hymn.
10. The priest faces the people and circles the lamp again.
11. Bells and drums may be used to create an atmosphere of worship.
12. The lamp will be taken around the people, who pass their hand over the flame and then over their face, hair and heart.
13. The *tilak*, or mark of worship, made from red powder, is placed on each person's forehead.
14. The service ends with the sharing of the *parshad* or food, which has been offered to the God and is, therefore, blessed.

The oil used in this lamp is from purified butter, which comes from cow's milk. Why do you think this type of oil is used in Hindu worship?

Buddhism – meditation

In Buddhism, one of the major steps in reaching the goal of personal enlightenment, called Nirvana, is to go through the eightfold path. One step of the path is right concentration or meditation.

Many Buddhists practise meditation quite a lot. It aims to cleanse the mind. There are two forms of meditation:

1. *Samatha*, or tranquillity meditation.
2. *Vipassana*, or insight meditation.

In what ways can meditation benefit a person?

'The avoidance of evil, the undertaking of good, the cleansing of one's mind; this is the teaching of the awakened ones.'

(Dhammapada, verse 42)

Samatha meditation involves clearing the mind of all distractions by focusing on an external object. Very often, the person sits with their back upright and they concentrate on their breath. If their mind wanders, they are able to bring it back to focus on the breath. They sometimes close their eyes, or they may sit in front of a statue of the Buddha. Other ways of clearing the mind include focusing on something like a *mandala*, a series of coloured concentric circles, or by repeating a simple prayer called a *mantra*, counting the times it is repeated using a prayer wheel. This type of meditation is said to bring about a refined state of spiritual and mental awareness.

Vipassana meditation is unique to Buddhism and is about realising that much of what we worry about is impermanent and can be overcome. The way this meditation works is to allow the person focus on everything – mind, body and spirit – that happens in that moment. Anything that arises in the mind or body is the object of meditation. It doesn't matter whether it is a pleasant or unpleasant thought, because when this works people see that everything passes, everything is constantly changing and impermanent. Through this meditation, Buddhists can overcome negative emotions, since they are replaced with a calm acceptance. It is written in one Buddhist text, 'Whatever harm an enemy may do to an enemy. ... an ill-directed mind inflicts greater harm on oneself.'

Try focusing on this for five minutes – does your mind wander?

Key Terms

ritual, worship, participation

Chapter Questions

1. What is a ritual?
2. How important are rituals in religious communities?
3. What does it mean to worship God?
4. How can people participate in worship?
5. Describe a ritual carried out by members of one major world religion.

Exam Practice

Higher Level 2010: Short question

Participation is one element in worship. Name **another** element of worship

_____.

Ordinary Level 2010: Short question

In religious traditions the term worship means _____.

Higher Level 2009: Short question

Worship involves activities in which God is honoured: true or false.

Ordinary Level 2009: Short question

Baptism is an example of a Christian sacrament. Name **one** other Christian sacrament.

Higher Level 2008: Short question

In religious traditions an example of a ritual is _____.

Higher Level 2007: Section 5, question 5

'Ritual can help people to express their faith.'

Discuss the importance of ritual for members of one of the following major world religions:

Buddhism/Christianity/Hinduism/Islam/Judaism.

Higher Level 2010: Picture question

Pick **one** thing from this photograph that suggests this person is performing a religious ritual.

State **two** reasons why people perform religious rituals.

Give **one** other example of a religious ritual.

Higher Level 2005: Section 4, question 5

In major world religions worship means _____

_____.

Briefly outline **one** act of worship you have observed or participated in.

Describe **one** religious symbol that is used during an act of worship.

Explain the meaning of this religious symbol.

Give **three** reasons why people pray during worship.

Mini-Project

Design a poster on rituals in one of the five major world religions. Use pictures, symbols and words to decorate it.

Test Yourself
eTest.ie

Worship as Response to Mystery

23

This is a higher level only section of the syllabus.

Key Concepts

reflection, encountering mystery, wonder, worship as a response to mystery or as an expression of ultimate concern, encounter with God, celebration, communication, worship

In many religions around the world, people believe in a God or Gods. Religion involves a way of looking at the world that includes, but also goes beyond, the world we can see, touch or hear. In the way that history discusses events that happened in the past and science attempts to show the physical laws that determine how things happen, religion is about the deeper meaning behind the world and people's lives. It does not deal with what or how things happen; religion tries to answer the *why* questions.

Over to You

Think of a number of questions that relate to the unknown aspects of life and write them out. Can you think of any answers to these questions that come from any religions?

Ways to reflect

Reflection, or thinking deeply about something, is done in different ways. Some people wish to be silent in order to reflect, while others may prefer to reflect while listening to music. Some people prefer stillness and some will reflect in movement.

Glossary

Reflection
To think deeply about something.

Where would you go to experience silence?

Silence

Sometimes, when thinking about God and about life, seeking a deeper understanding is carried out in silent reflection. Silence, for some people, is an opportunity to think, pray or worship and to allow an opportunity for communication with God.

Music

For some, music *transcends*. That means that it goes beyond words. As such, it allows a person to reflect deeply on something. It can make us feel things and understand things that we find difficult to put into words. Music has been described as 'the language of the soul'. In another chapter, we looked at how music can express a search for meaning. Some other forms of music express a sense of reflection and an encounter with mystery. Very often, this may be music without words. Sacred music is used to worship God in a way that words alone cannot always do.

Encountering mystery

Some questions remain a mystery, which even religious understanding can only go so far in answering. There are moments in life that are times of wonder and surprise, when we may feel 'lost for words' because we are experiencing something that seems completely outside of our ordinary experiences. These include events such as the birth of a child, the death of a loved one, falling in love or a breath-taking experience of nature. They can also be times that could be described as an encounter with mystery. Worship of God or some form of religious ritual is one way of responding to such an encounter. The following examples show how that can occur:

Encountering mystery Glossary
Experiencing a sense of something unknowable.

Wonder Glossary
A sense of amazement at something.

- Birth and death may bring about a feeling of an encounter with mystery and wonder. This may lead to a ritual or act of worship that aims to seek understanding of life.

What rituals take place at birth?

Worship as a response to mystery or as an expression of ultimate concern
To carry out worship as a way of showing what is really important in life, as an expression of having a meaningful place in the universe, when some things seem unknowable or amazing.

Why do such natural things give a sense of wonder to people?

- Natural phenomena, such as the northern lights, Niagara Falls or the Grand Canyon may lead to a sense of wonder. Worship is a way of responding to that feeling and giving thanks to God for them.
- The death of a loved one can lead to an act of worship or ritual, which is an expression of our sense of what is really important in life.
- A strong sense of the presence of God through a spiritual experience of prayer or meditation may lead people to focus more on God and to seek God through worship.

Encounter with God Glossary
Feeling an awareness or the presence of God.

What rituals take place at death?

Glossary

Celebration
A time to rejoice.

Glossary

Communication
A two-way process of imparting or exchanging information.

- Important times in life, when something wonderful happens or happened, such as the birth of a baby, the marriage of two people or an important achievement, may lead some people to worship God as a way to celebrate and to give thanks.
- A time when a person wants to communicate with God may lead to personal prayer. Some people pray to God when they are afraid, anxious or worried, e.g. when terrible acts of cruelty have occurred. Through prayer many people worship God.

What are the rituals associated with marriage? What does the ring symbolise?

Worship as a response to mystery

For the individual carrying out an act of worship, whether it is a Hindu performing a puja, a Muslim praying in the direction of Mecca, a Jewish person singing a hymn or a Christian lighting a candle, the act is important because of what it means.

Glossary

Worship
Reverence for God or Gods, which can involve prayer, rituals, silence, singing or dancing.

Worship is an expression of belief, showing that the person sees God and their religion as important, probably the most important thing in life. For some people, it is belief in God that makes sense of the world and gives a sense of meaning and value to their everyday lives. Worship helps to give people a sense that they are part of a truly meaningful world, and that they are participating in something that has great significance beyond their own lives and experiences.

Worship may bring a person closer to God

The following two extracts show an understanding that worship brings humans and God closer together.

The Bhagavad Gita, a Hindu sacred text: 'I am the same to all beings, and my love is ever the same; but those who worship me with devotion, they are in me and I am in them.'

The Gabriel hadith, in Islamic tradition: 'Worship God as though you see Him, for even if you don't, He sees you.'

Key Terms

reflection, encountering mystery, wonder, worship as a response to mystery or as an expression of ultimate concern, encounter with God, celebration, communication, worship

Chapter Questions

1. What does reflection mean? Describe ways in which people can reflect.
2. How may worship be a way of responding to mystery?
3. Write about two significant times that are celebrated in religion.
4. Can you think of any times when people might wish to communicate with God?
5. What is communication? How do people communicate with God?

Exam Practice

Higher Level 2005: Section 5, question 5

'I feel at home in a Hindu temple. I am aware of a presence, not personal... but something larger.' (Yann Martel)

Outline how places of worship help people to respond to the experience of mystery in life.

Mini-Project

Research an act of worship carried out by a religious community and find out if it reflects a sense of wonder or mystery.

Sign and Symbol

What is a symbol?

Symbol
An object, word, gesture or image that has many meanings.

A symbol is an image, picture, object, word or gesture that means something beyond itself. A symbol always means something more.

What does this picture make you think of?

Sign
An object, word, gesture or image that has only one meaning.

A sign is similar, but a sign only has one meaning, while a symbol has many. For example, a red traffic light is a sign for stop.

Is this a matter of interpretation? Why?

Complete the chart.

Signs				
Rail crossing	For Sale	Cork 24km	Euro	And

Symbols

Understanding symbols

As a symbol has many meanings, the same symbol can mean different things to different people. The meaning might be really positive for one person but negative for another. A symbol's meaning depends on a number of factors: *who is seeing it, where they are seeing it* and also *their past experience* of this symbol.

For example, think of a symbol associated with a football team. A supporter sees this and is happy, as it reminds them of the team that they like and support. They may have seen this symbol at matches or on the team jersey. It has very positive associations. A rival supporter sees the same symbol, but it reminds them of the opposition – a team that they don't like or support and want to beat. It has negative associations for this person. A person who is neither a supporter of this team nor an opposing fan sees the symbol and is not really affected by it at all. It has little meaning to someone like this.

Over to You

Think of a symbol that means something to you. Draw it in your copy and explain what makes it special for you. How could this symbol have a different meaning for other people?

The importance and use of symbols in religion

The use of symbols is hugely important in religions. Symbols put into expression many of the things religions are about. Indeed, much of what takes place in religious rituals is symbolic. Behind the actions and words of a ritual is a deeper meaning, pointing to things beyond the ritual itself. As with any symbols, which can mean different things to different people, there are commonly accepted interpretations of many religious symbols.

Major religious symbols

Hinduism Aum	Judaism Star of David	Buddhism Eight-Spoked Wheel	Christianity Cross	Islam Star and Crescent Moon

These are just some of the major symbols. All religions have many, many more symbols. Symbols need not be images like these. Symbols can be words: 'Peace be with you'. They can be gestures: taking off your shoes as you enter a mosque. They can be objects: a yarmulke or skull cap, worn in Judaism. In a way, we could say that *symbols are the language of religion.* Further examples of this are outlined below.

Who would own one of these?

When a Roman Catholic enters a church, they will normally bow towards the altar. What does this mean? They are showing respect and humility to God by this action. They are showing that they see the altar as significant and having a special place in the church, the part of the church that is particularly holy.

In Islam, a person performs ritual washing before praying towards the city of Mecca. Why? The washing shows that the person is preparing themselves for prayer, for an encounter with their God. Praying towards Mecca is showing their awareness of the special significance of the city of Mecca to their religion.

Did you know? The Qibla compass or Qibla indicator is a modified compass designed to show the direction for prayer in Islam.

The liturgy or official rituals of the Roman Catholic Church includes seven sacraments. These are Baptism, Confirmation, Eucharist, Marriage, Holy Orders, Reconciliation and Anointing the Sick or Dying. For other Christian Churches, there may be one or two important sacraments. The celebration of sacraments often involves the use of symbols, such as water in Baptism, the laying on of hands during Confirmation and the exchange of rings at a wedding. In the sacraments, an understanding of God and an opportunity to experience God's presence is developed through the use of symbols.

Since experiences like sacraments, prayer and other religious acts are difficult to communicate, symbols are useful ways of communicating them.

Discuss Why would people want to communicate a religious experience to others?

Symbols can also bring a sense of identity or belonging to people in a religious community. The identity of the community to which a person belongs is summed up in its symbol. A community may then be identified by its symbol. The symbol becomes the image by which the community is recognised.

Glossary

Sacrament
Something set apart as holy or sacred in which God is present. A sacrament is a formal ceremony that brings an awareness of the presence of God to the person taking part in it.

Glossary

Communicating experience
Putting an experience into words, images or gestures an a way others can understand.

Glossary

Identity
The characteristics that determine who a person or a group is.

How do these symbols represent the groups they are associated with?

Icons

Icons are Christian images or pictures, usually of Jesus, Mary, the Evangelists or saints, which are made of wood. They are extremely popular in the Orthodox tradition within Christianity. Many are famous as works of art. The word icon comes from the Greek word *eikon*, meaning 'likeness' or 'image'. Many different features of an icon may be used to teach things about Jesus. The way the figures are portrayed on icons is symbolic and requires interpretation.

Glossary

Icon
A devotional painting, usually made from wood, of Christ or another holy figure.

Candles

Many religions use candles. They are a symbol of light over darkness and good over evil. In Hinduism, candles are used during the festival of *Diwali*. In Christianity, they are used during Advent, Christmas, Baptism, Easter and at weddings. In Judaism, they are lit in a *menorah* during *Hanukkah*, the festival of lights. Throughout the world, candles have come to be a symbol of peace and the way to goodness.

Did you know?

Amnesty International has a candle surrounded by barbed wire as its symbol. The founder Peter Benenson once said, 'The candle burns not for us, but for all those whom we failed to rescue from prison, who were shot on the way to prison, who were tortured, who were kidnapped, who "disappeared". That is what the candle is for.'

Religious symbols and their meaning

Religion	Symbol	Meaning	
Hinduism	Sacred cow	The cow represents a gentle nature or an attitude of non-violence, known as *ahimsa*. It is also an animal that gives more than it takes.	
Christianity	Alpha and omega	The first and last letters of the Greek alphabet signify that God is the beginning and the end.	
Islam	The colour green	Believed to have been Mohammed's favourite colour and a symbol of vegetation or life. The Qur'an mentions that those in paradise will wear green silk.	

Key Terms

symbol, sign, sacrament, communicating experience, identity, icon

Chapter Questions

1. What is religion concerned with?
2. What is a ritual?
3. Why are rituals important in religion?
4. What is a symbol?
5. Why do symbols have more than one meaning?
6. Why are symbols important in religions?
7. Explain one religious symbol. Draw it.

Exam Practice

Short questions

Higher Level 2011: Short question

A symbol can have only one meaning: true or false.

Higher Level 2010: Short question

Confirmation is one example of a Christian sacrament. Name one other Christian sacrament.

Ordinary Level 2007: Short question

In religious traditions an 'icon' is _____.

Higher Level 2006: Short question

A sacrament is _____.

Higher Level 2003: Short question

Match the symbol with the religion with which it is associated:

Cross	Buddhism
Star of David	Christianity
Crescent Moon	Hinduism
Eight-spoked Wheel	Islam
Diva Lamp	Judaism

Higher Level 2009: Section 4, question 5

Tick **one** of the following world religions that you have studied:

Buddhism/Christianity/Hinduism/Islam/Judaism

Name **one** symbol associated with the world religion you have ticked above.

Describe the meaning of the symbol you have named for members of the world religion with which it is associated.

Explain **two** reasons why people use a symbol to express religious faith.

Ordinary Level 2010: Picture question four

Pick **one** thing from this photograph that suggests that this is a religious symbol.

With which one of the following world religions is this symbol most associated? Buddhism/Christianity/Hinduism/Islam/Judaism

State **one** reason why people use symbols when they are praying.

Mini-Project

Choose one religion and examine three symbols associated with it.

Key Concepts

communication with God, meditation, contemplation, petition, praise and thanksgiving, penitence, personal prayer, communal prayer

In most religions, there is belief in and worship of a God or Gods. When people believe in God, they want to communicate with God. One of the most common ways in which people communicate with God is through prayer. Prayer is varied and for many people it is a very personal expression of their faith, therefore it is hard to generalise about prayer. In the different world religions, there are certain traditions and understandings of prayer that should be examined.

Glossary

Communication with God
The way in which people try to understand and connect with God.

What is prayer?

Prayer can be ...

- Communication with a God or Gods.
- Worship.
- A request.
- Thanks.
- A confession.
- Public or private.
- With words.
- Without words.

Please help me.

I'm sorry.

Thank you.

There are many different types of prayer and many different ways and reasons to pray. People can pray alone or with others. They can pray anywhere and for any reason. People might pray for help with a problem or at a time of difficulty in life. They may want to ask God for help or support in dealing with sad times in life. People sometimes pray for others and sometimes pray for the wider community. People pray to seek forgiveness if they are burdened by guilt. Others pray when they are afraid. People pray for peace during wars or when disasters cause great damage or loss of life. Some people pray to thank God for good things in life or because they are amazed by the natural world. People may just want to talk to God, since they believe God is important to their life and they want to have a constant relationship with God.

Discuss   Is prayer important to people who want to have a relationship with God?

Why would people pray at a time like this?

The reasons and times people pray alone are personal, informal and varied. The ways people pray with others in a community tend to be more formal and have set words, gestures, symbols and purpose. As a result, there are set types of community prayer, such as prayers of thanksgiving, repentance, adoration and petition. There are symbols – words, gestures or objects – used in prayers. There are also very well-known prayers that different religions use, e.g. the Lord's Prayer or Our Father for Christians. There can be set times to pray. Communities also usually have places to pray, such as churches, mosques and synagogues. If we look at some of the well-known prayers of the major world religions it is clear they reflect the beliefs of the community and show what is important to members of that religion.

Prayers from different religious communities

Hindu prayer: The Gayatri mantra from the Vedas: 'We meditate on that most adorable Supreme Lord, may his light inspire and illuminate our intellect.'

The Vedas are the most ancient Hindu texts and in the four Vedas are thousands of hymns and mantras. The Rig Veda is the most important of the Vedas and includes the famous Gayatri mantra. This is a prayer said in worship during festivals and rituals.

Where do Hindus pray?

Jewish prayer: The Shema (Deuteronomy 6:4): 'Hear O Israel, the Lord our God is one. Love the Lord your God with all your heart and with all your soul and with all your strength.'

This sums up the central belief in Judaism that there is only one God. The prayer is placed in the *mezuzah*, a box fixed on the doorposts of Jewish homes, and in the *tefillin*, a symbol used during morning prayers.

What symbols is this person wearing?

Buddhist prayer/meditation: 'I go to the Buddha for refuge; I go to the Dhamma for refuge; I go to the Sangha for refuge.'

These are the three jewels of Buddhism and the only creed it has. Prayer is mostly in the form of meditation and there are also mantras that are used in other forms of worship. Some branches of Buddhism worship the Buddha.

What does Nirvana mean?

Christian prayer: One of the best known Christian prayers is the Our Father, which Jesus taught his followers. 'Our Father in heaven, hallowed be your name. Your kingdom come. Your will be done, on earth as it is in heaven. Give us this day our daily bread. Forgive us our trespasses as we forgive those who trespass against us. Lead us not into temptation, but deliver us from evil.'

It refers to the teachings Jesus outlined about God and the kingdom of God, where 'God's will is done'. It is a prayer that combines worship of God with requests for forgiveness and help from God. It holds within it the ultimate desire of Christianity for all people to work to bring about God's kingdom 'on earth as it is in heaven'. This prayer is said in many different Christian acts of worship, by people who gather for community activities and by people alone in prayer.

When praying, do Christians use any gestures?

Islamic prayer: The opening lines of the Qur'an: 'In the name of God, the Compassionate, the Merciful. Praise be to God, the Lord of Creation, the Compassionate, the Merciful, Master of the Day of Judgement. You alone do we worship and to you alone we pray for help. Guide us to the Straight Path, the path of those whom you have favoured, not of those who have incurred your wrath, nor of those who have gone astray.'

This is said at the five daily prayers known as *Salat*. It is also said in mosques and at festivals, rituals and rites of passage.

285

The call to prayer is made for the five daily prayers and whispered in a baby's ear shortly after birth:

God is most great

I bear witness that there is no God but God

I bear witness that Mohammad is the Messenger of God

Hurry to prayer

Hurry to success

God is most great

There is no God but God.

Are there any objects used by Muslims when praying?

Over to You

1. What is prayer?
2. What is the difference between formal and informal prayer?
3. Name a formal prayer used by a major world religion.
4. Where do people pray?
5. Mention two facts about prayer in Islam.

Many religions have a specific time for prayer. Most have a holy day once a week, during which people visit a place of worship and pray. Some have daily prayer. Muslims have prayers five times a day, while the Jewish tradition is three times a day. The *angelus* is a call to prayer for Roman Catholics. Other traditions encourage followers to pray in their own way at their own time. Many Hindus have a shrine in the home, where people can carry out a simple act of worship regularly.

Glossary

Types of prayer

Meditation: A type of prayer in which people aim to push out all thoughts and reach a relaxed state of mind, where they become open to a more spiritual state of existence.

Contemplation: To pray in a reflective way.

Petition: To pray for help in some way or to ask God for something.

Praise and thanksgiving: A prayer to worship and thank God, acknowledging God's blessings on the world and individual.

Penitence: To pray for forgiveness; the realisation that one needs to be reconciled with God.

Personal prayer: To pray alone; usually less formal.

Communal prayer: To pray as part of a community of faith, or with a group; usually more formal.

Places of prayer

Prayer is a part of worship. As we have seen, most
world religions have a special building set aside
for this purpose. The different buildings used for
worship include temples, churches, synagogues and
mosques. In each of these places of worship, there
are significant features and actions that demonstrate
that prayer is central to worship. In a Hindu temple,
there is a shrine to the God, which is the focus
of worship and to which prayers are directed. A
church may have kneelers (cushions to kneel on)
and many have prayer books to read from. In a synagogue,
for communal prayer to take place, there should be at least ten people present.
The *cantor* chants the prayers. In a mosque, one wall shows the direction of Mecca
and the floor is decorated with rectangles, which form individual prayer mats for
worshippers. The *imam* leads the community in prayer.

Why do you think there is a place to pray in a building such as this?

   Places for prayer can be found in other areas of life. Some shopping centres, airports,
hospitals and prisons have rooms set aside for prayer. Some people have a shrine at
home where prayers may be said.

   Many world religions have places set aside as particularly special for prayer. For Jews,
there is Jerusalem and especially the Wailing Wall. For Muslims, there is the Ka'ba in
Mecca. For Christians in Ireland, a place like Croagh Patrick, where St Patrick prayed
and reflected, has for centuries been considered a special place for prayer.

Symbolic objects used in prayer

Prayer wheel – Used in Buddhism; the outside of the
   wheel has prayers written on it.

What is it about wheels that makes them suitable for helping people pray?

When do some people receive their first set of rosary beads?

Beads – Used to keep
count of prayers that
are repeated. Beads
like these are used
in many religions. Roman
Catholics use them to count
the Rosary, which is a set of prayers and meditations.

Symbolic objects used in prayer *(contd.)*

Tefillin – A Jewish object used for morning prayer. It reminds Jews of their covenant with God. It has straps around the arm and head, and boxes close to the head and chest, inside which are biblical verses – keeping the covenant close to the heart and mind.

Incense – Used in prayer or worship to create a certain mood. The smoke represents prayers rising up to God.

Prayer mat – In Islam, a rectangular mat sometimes decorated with images of important mosques is placed on the floor for prayer.

Yarmulke (or kippah) – In Judaism, a man will cover his head when he prays, as a sign of humility before God.

Prayer shawl (or tallit) – Used in Judaism, it has four corners with tassels. This symbolises obedience to the Torah, the Jewish law.

Symbolic gestures used in prayer

Blessing oneself – People make the sign of the cross as a reminder of the sacrifice Jesus made on the cross. People may bless themselves with holy water and ask God to be with them.

Kneeling or bowing – Shows humility and respect before God.

Hands together – Sign of respect.

Amen – Means 'so be it'; used at the end of a prayer.

Silent prayer

For many people, praying may be a silent activity. Alone in silence, a person can pray from the heart. Some people believe this is the best way to allow God to communicate with them; it is about creating an opportunity for God to enter their hearts. Some religious traditions value silence more than others. The Society of Friends, known as the Quakers, is a Christian community that especially values silence. Their main form of worship is a meeting that is held in stillness and quiet, to allow room for people to be aware of God's presence. People can contribute a thought, Bible reading or prayer, but for much of the time, the meeting is held in silent reflection.

People of prayer

Most religions have historical figures who have influenced the way people pray, their understanding of prayer and many of the rituals around prayer. The following are some of the major figures who have influenced prayer in major world religions today.

Moses

Moses developed the religion of Judaism considerably, including the development of prayer. The ritual of three prayers a day comes from the three Patriarchs: Abraham, Isaac and Jacob. However, it is from Moses that the Jews have the words of the Shema, which is a prayer of worship and part of many Jewish rituals. The idea of a Sabbath day comes from the Ten Commandments, which Moses received on Mount Sinai. Shabbat is a day of rest and a time of prayer. Moses also brought the people out of slavery in Egypt and this event is celebrated every year during Passover. During this festival, many prayers are said and God is worshipped in synagogues and at home.

Buddha

Meditation, as a type of prayer, is part of the noble eightfold path of Buddhism: 'I take refuge in the Buddha, I take refuge in the Dhamma, I take refuge in the Sangha.' This means 'I take refuge in the enlightened one, in the truth and in the community'.

Jesus

Jesus taught his followers the Lord's Prayer or Our Father. In his Sermon on the Mount, he told people in prayer to ask in faith. In Matthew 6, he explains, '... for your Father knows what you need before you ask him'. Jesus told his followers that they should not pray to show off nor should they pray by repeating empty phrases.

Mohammad

Mohammad had a lot to say about prayer. He instituted prayer five times a day for Muslims and he instructed them to pray in the direction of the Ka'ba. For Mohammad, prayer was essential for Muslims to submit to the will of Allah.

Why do people pray? The benefits of prayer

There are many reasons why people pray. Individuals have their own reasons. People pray at night, in the morning, alone, together, at home or in a special building. People often pray in difficult times; prayer may bring comfort, strength and hope. Research suggests that people feel better after prayer, and that people are emotionally, spiritually and psychologically healthier because of prayer.

Most religions teach that prayer is not a wish list brought to God but rather it is communication with God. Through prayer, the lines of communication are open. In prayer, people make their thoughts known to God and they also seek to understand God's will for their lives. For many people, whether or not prayer works isn't something that can be proved, nor does it need to be. Prayers may help a person to understand more clearly and bring comfort in distress. They may feel someone is listening to them. It gives them a sense of connection with God, whom they believe to be in control of the universe. It is also a way for people to demonstrate that religion is important to them and they are showing, in prayer, that God is someone they wish to have a relationship with.

Discuss in groups when in life people often pray. Each group should present to the class a time in life when people might pray. Discuss whether prayer might help in this situation.

Difficulty in praying

Sometimes people may find it difficult to pray. There are many reasons why it is not always easy to pray. Some reasons can be caused by outside factors, while others may be inside a person. A person who belongs to a religious community and wants to pray will try to overcome such problems. Nevertheless, in a person's lifetime, there can be times when it is easy to pray, and times when it is very difficult, for example:

What role does prayer play in a place such as this?

- Not having the space, time or opportunity.
- Other people make it difficult to pray.
- Disturbances caused by outside noise or distraction.
- Not knowing how or not having the right words.
- Lacking faith.
- Anger with God.
- Feelings of guilt.
- Feelings of doubt about prayer.

Over to You

In your own words, write out three situations in which people may find it difficult to pray. Now suggest ways they might overcome these situations.

Key Terms

communication with God, meditation, contemplation, petition, praise and thanksgiving, penitence, personal prayer, communal prayer

Chapter Questions

1. Why do many religious communities encourage members to pray?
2. What do people pray for?
3. Where do people pray as a community?
4. What is meditation?
5. How many times a day do Muslims pray?
6. What are rosary beads used for?
7. What is considered the benefit of praying in silence?

Exam Practice

Higher Level 2006: Short question

A prayer of penitence is a prayer that expresses sorrow for sin: true or false.

Ordinary Level 2006: Short question

A prayer of petition is one that makes an appeal or request to God: true or false.

Ordinary Level 2006: Short question

Clearing the mind of all thoughts so as to have total awareness of God is a type of prayer known as contemplation: true or false.

Ordinary Level 2008: Short question

In a prayer of thanksgiving a person_____.

Ordinary Level 2009: Short question

In a prayer of praise a person is _____.

Higher Level 2011: Section 5, question 5

Profile the contribution made to the understanding of prayer by **one** person associated with the spiritual tradition of a major world religion that you have studied.

Higher Level 2007: Section 4, question 5

Give **one** example of a symbol people use when they are praying.

Explain why people use the symbol you have given above when they are praying.

Suggest **two** reasons why people can sometimes find it difficult to pray.

Tick **one** of the following types of prayer that you have studied: Meditation/Penitence.

Outline what is involved in the type of prayer you have ticked.

Outline **two** reasons why prayer is important for members of a world religion that you have studied.

Higher Level 2006: Section 5, question 5

'Communal prayer and worship show what a community believes and values.'

Discuss this statement referring to **one** community of faith you have studied.

Mini-Project

Research and describe a local place of prayer. Find out when and how it is used.

Useful Websites for Section E: The Celebration of Faith

For this section of the course, the aims are to show how ritual and worship have always been part of the human response to life and to the mystery of God, to identify how communities of faith express their day-to-day concerns in various forms of ritual and to explore an experience of worship. A further aim for higher level is to explore the link between patterns of worship and mystery or that which is of ultimate concern to individuals and communities.

To find out more about many of the topics from this part of the course the following may be useful:

Chapter 21

www.sacred-destinations.com
www.dochara.com/placestovisit/churches-holy-places
www.lourdes-france.com

Chapters 22–25

This portal has useful links for information on sacraments, icons and prayer:
www.scoilnet.ie

For information on rituals in Judaism, Hinduism, Islam and Buddhism:
www.bbc.co.uk/religion/religions

Information on religious communities and their rituals in Ireland:

www.hindu.ie

www.jewishireland.org

www.dublinbuddhistcentre.org

www.buddhism.ie

www.catholicireland.net

www.ireland.anglican.org

www.islamireland.ie

www.islaminireland.ie

Section

The Moral Challenge

This section of the syllabus aims:

- To explore the human need to order relationships at the personal, communal and global levels.
- To explore how this need can be expressed in a variety of ways.
- To identify how this need is expressed in civil and other legal codes.
- To show how religious belief is expressed in particular moral visions.
- To explore the moral visions of two major world religions, one of which should be Christianity.
- To analyse the impact of these visions on the lives of believers and non-believers in considering some current moral issues.

Higher Level only

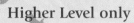

- To introduce students to some aspects of the relationship between religion, morality, and state law.

Introduction to Morality

26

Key Concepts

morality, influence, choice, freedom, relationships, consequences, society

What is morality?

Morality
Concerned with the principles of right and wrong behaviour.

Influence
The capacity to have an effect on the character, development or behaviour of someone or something.

The word morality refers to the idea of some things being right and other things being wrong. It is about good and bad, and whether certain actions and ideas can be considered to be either.

People sometimes say that something is not moral or is immoral. What do they mean? In general, they are expressing the view that something is not right or is fundamentally wrong. For example, many people would say that in the modern world it is wrong that millions of people are starving to death. It is immoral.

Many people see morality as somewhat personal. They accept that what one person considers right, another may not. Nevertheless, there are accepted standards of right and wrong within societies. These do change over time and they change from place to place, within different cultures, religions and political structures. Many of the ideas of right and wrong have been shaped by religion.

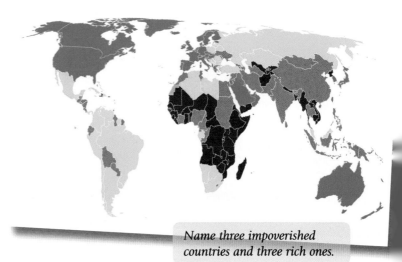

Name three impoverished countries and three rich ones.

What affects morality?

People have many different ideas of right and wrong, and it is not only religion that influences a person's thoughts about these.

Family

One of the first and biggest influences on a person's ideas of right and wrong is their family. This is the smallest community most people belong to. Through growing up and learning within a family, people are given ideas of what is the right thing to do in many situations. Values or a sense of what is important are passed on and this will make a difference to a person's morality too.

Friends

For most people, at different times in life, friends become a very important influence. They will also affect what a person sees as right or wrong. The influence of friends increases during adolescence. How friends act or behave in a variety of situations, what they think, say or wear sends out ideas of what is good or bad.

School

Believe it or not, schools play a part in shaping ideas of right and wrong for their students every day. The majority of schools have a code of conduct. Some schools even get students to write this out if they have somehow forgotten what it says! The behaviour expected of students in a school shows what is considered to be right or wrong by that school. This is not the only way schools influence ideas of morality. Other things that go on in schools suggest ideas of good or bad. For example, a school might hold fundraisers for people in need, have a green flag or sell fair trade products. All of these and more give students a moral compass, an indication of what is right.

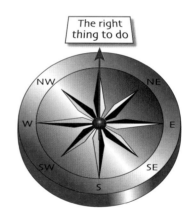

State

Through its laws, the state has a huge impact on what is allowed or not. This, in turn, influences what is seen to be right or wrong. For example, for the safety of all road users, it is not permissible to drive after drinking a lot of alcohol. This is the law and it also sends out a message about what is right behaviour. It is the law to ensure that your child receives an education. This suggests that it is good to educate children. Many laws send out ideas of what is moral or not. It is interesting to see how different countries around the world have different laws and that this can indicate different ideas of what is right and wrong. It is also interesting to see how laws have changed over time. What was once considered right and was backed up by the law may not be now.

Religion

Most religions are concerned with what is good or bad. The three monotheistic faiths – Judaism, Christianity and Islam – have versions of the Ten Commandments as a moral code or guide to suggest what is right or wrong. In Hinduism, the sacred writings such as the Mahabharata or Ramayana contain stories that teach what is right. Duty, love, loyalty and honesty are some of the values promoted in these stories. In Buddhism, the teachings of the Buddha, especially the noble eightfold path, has a moral vision for Buddhists to follow.

Media

The main means of mass communication – television, radio, newspapers, the internet, magazines etc. – communicate an almost continuous message of what is right and wrong. The way the media portrays people, either real or fictional, the way the media informs people, the opinions it expresses, the music it plays and the images it relays to people are a big influence on what people consider to be good or bad.

Which influences you the most?

What a person thinks is important or valuable will have an effect on their morality. For instance, if someone thinks the most important thing in life is money, they will think differently about some issues than a person who thinks people are the most important thing in life.

Everyone should write a list of the five most important things in their life. Discuss how what you value might influence what you think is right or wrong.

List three sources of morality in a person's life and assess how much of an influence each is.

Choices

Even though people are constantly being influenced by a variety of sources in their ideas of right and wrong, ultimately people have to develop their own morality. The individual always has a choice as to how they act in what they do or say. The choice is up to the person.

In the *Harry Potter* books by J.K. Rowling, when Harry is worried about the fact that the Sorting Hat had considered putting him into Slytherin house, he tells Dumbledore that it only put him in Gryffindor because he asked it to. Dumbledore tells Harry, 'It is our choices, Harry, that show what we truly are, far more than our abilities.'

What choice does Harry make?

In ideas of morality, or what is good and bad, people have many choices throughout their lifetime. Having as much information as possible when making a choice helps a person to make the right choice – it will inform their conscience.

Conscience is a person's ability to choose between right and wrong.

Choice Glossary
An act of making a decision when faced with two or more possibilities.

Freedom

To be free is to have control over your own choices and the right to live your life the way you wish. Freedom means living without fear of persecution or harassment. Ideally, the law is there to protect this right and has certain conditions concerning freedom in order to benefit everyone. With freedom comes great responsibility. To be able to act, speak and think freely has to be accompanied with an awareness of the freedom of others and consideration for the well-being of society.

Freedom Glossary
The power or right to act, speak or think as one wants.

'Freedom is indivisible, and when one man is enslaved, all are not free.'
American President John F. Kennedy, speaking in Berlin in 1963

Discuss why people who are free to act, think and speak the way they want have to consider the freedom of others.

The United Nations Universal Declaration of Human Rights ensures many freedoms and has a moral vision about what is right for human life. It therefore implies that the alternatives are wrong.

When World War II ended in 1945 the world had witnessed some of the worst human rights violations in history. The rights in the Declaration are an outcome of the horrors of that war and the realisation that a universal standard of human rights should exist. The Declaration of Human Rights – the work of the United Nations Commission on Human Rights – was adopted on 10 December 1948 at the United Nations General Assembly meeting in Paris.

The drafting committee that formulated the Declaration was made up of members from the following countries: the USA, USSR, UK, the Lebanon, France, Australia, Chile, Canada and China.

How much do you think recent history at that time influenced the ideas of the drafting committee?

Hernan Santa Cruz of Chile, a member of the drafting committee, wrote: 'I perceived clearly that I was participating in a truly significant historic event in which consensus had been reached as to the supreme value of the human person, a value that did not originate in the decision of a worldly power, but rather in the fact of existing – which gave rise to the inalienable right to live free from want and oppression and to fully develop one's own personality.'

There are thirty articles in the Declaration, which aim at a standard for all peoples and all nations to strive for.

For example, according to the Declaration of Human Rights, it is a right for people to have an adequate standard of living – adequate for the health and well-being of one's family, including food, clothing, housing, medical care and necessary social services. Thus, it is wrong when people do not have an adequate standard of living. Everyone has the right to freedom of thought, conscience and religion. There are countries where it is dangerous to be a member of an opposition political party or religious group. Under the Declaration, this is wrong.

Where is this building found?

Over to You

Describe what you consider to be an adequate standard of living. Do you know any organisation that campaigns for people to be allowed freedom of thought, conscience and religion? Research an organisation either in Ireland or elsewhere that works towards helping people have an adequate standard of living.

When does freedom have to be limited?

Should freedom ever be limited? On 15 September 1963, four young girls were murdered in an explosion in a church in Alabama, simply because they were African American. The organised attack was carried out by members of a branch of the Ku Klux Klan. People who have racist ideas and are willing to carry out such horrific crimes have the freedom to think the way they wish, but should they be allowed to act in such

a way? Of course not. Any act that impinges on the freedoms and rights of others cannot be allowed. Furthermore, people who incite hatred or encourage people to carry out acts that would be damaging to other individuals or groups have to be limited in their freedom of speech.

Which fundamental right was taken from these girls?

Can laws be wrong?

While in most cases, the law upholds what people generally accept as right, it can be the case that a law is wrong and may in fact be immoral. This has happened in the past and still happens in some parts of the world today. For example, in the past in Ireland, it was the law that a woman who worked in the public sector had to give up her job once she got married. Just because this was the law did not make it right.

Did you know? The removal of the marriage ban in the public service did not take place until 1973. This was a direct result of Ireland joining the European Community.

A park bench in Nazi Germany that says 'not for Jews'. Just because this was the law – was this moral?

In some states, laws have discriminated against individuals, ethnic groups, political groups and religious communities. The law was, of course, wrong and yet implied that such rules were correct and moral. In such cases, a person's own moral standard or view of what is right and wrong may well conflict with the state's morality.

In some parts of the world today, people are not allowed to practise their religion, as the law does not permit it. In others, women are not allowed to work in certain jobs, girls receive less education than boys and some people are not allowed to vote. While the laws of such countries support these situations, this is not necessarily right.

Personal morality versus state morality: topics for debate

1. **War**

   In wartime, it is very common for countries to call on individuals to fight. In the past, some countries have used conscription to get people into the army. For some people, war is never right. For others, a particular war may be morally wrong. In such cases, the individual has a conflict with state views of right and wrong. What should happen?

   What kinds of people seem to be against this war?

2. **Medical ethics**

   For some people, blood transfusions and some other forms of medical treatment are wrong. Is it always right for individuals to decide what treatments they should be given?

3. **Censorship**

   In the past, the state censored many books, films and even music. In Ireland today, a film certification office indicates the age that someone needs to be before they can watch a movie. The same applies to video games. Is it right to allow young people to watch movies or play video games when they are underage?

   Do you know any films that weren't allowed to be seen in Ireland?

Relationships

When it comes to making decisions about what is right and wrong, the choices people make frequently affect those around them.

Action and consequence

Imagine the following situation: you leave your house on Saturday night to go to a friend's house, promising that you will be home before midnight. On the way, you meet up with some friends who have bought alcohol from the local shop. They ask you if you want some and you drink some with them. When you arrive later than expected to your friend's house, they suggest watching a pirated DVD copy of the latest cinema release. You watch the movie. When you get home, it is one o'clock in the morning and your mother is waiting. You tell her that the bus never arrived and that you had to walk home.

> **Relationships** *Glossary*
> The connections people have with one another, as family, friends or members of the same community.

> **Consequences** *Glossary*
> Outcomes as a result of deciding to act in a certain way.

Over to You

1. What moral choices has the person in the scenario encountered?
2. What are the actions they have chosen?
3. What are the possible consequences of such choices?
4. Who has influenced their choices?

Society

People live in society with other people, sharing land, customs, laws and organisation. Living in society gives people rights but it also gives them responsibilities. Laws regulate society and affect how people live their lives. Thus, society has an influence on a person's opinion of what is right and wrong.

> **Society** *Glossary*
> An organisation of people living alongside each other.

When society needs to act in the best interest of its members

Road users have to accept the rules: driving on the right, stopping at traffic lights, not speeding etc. The law is simple. Drink driving is wrong and severe punishments can be given to those who break this law. Why? Quite clearly, to allow people to drink and drive endangers the lives of others in society. As people who have had too much alcohol to drink cannot control a car properly, and are not capable of reacting fast enough, the moral viewpoint of society as a whole is that it is wrong to drink and drive.

Discuss Can you think of other laws in society that are in place to protect everyone?

The death penalty – does it protect society?

In Ireland, the death penalty or capital punishment is no longer carried out. In the past, it was reserved for the most serious crimes, but, like many other countries throughout the world, Irish people decided in a referendum that it was not something they wanted. In some countries, and in many states of the United States of America, the death penalty is still used.

People argue that to protect others capital punishment is necessary. They say that a person who has committed murder, or other very serious crimes, no longer has the right to live in society. They believe that the only just punishment for such a criminal is to carry out the death sentence.

Is capital punishment necessary to rebalance the scales?

Others disagree. They believe that two wrongs do not make a right. They argue against the death penalty on the basis that it takes away a person's most valuable right – the right to life. It is evident, according to many studies, that societies where it is still used are no safer and have even been shown in many cases to be more violent places to live.

What do you think is the biggest influence on what Sr Helen thinks is right or wrong?

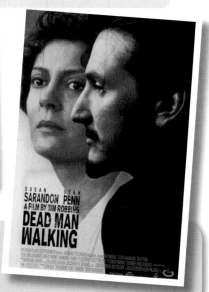

Classwork

Have a debate on the death penalty – three speaking in favour of Ireland re-introducing it and three against.

Key Terms

morality, influence, choice, freedom, relationships, consequences, society

Chapter Questions

1. What is morality?
2. What affects a person's morality? Mention at least three influences.
3. What is freedom?
4. What international code aims to ensure freedom for individuals?
5. Is there a relationship between state law and personal morality? Explain your answer.
6. Does a person's morality affect others around them? How?
7. Why do societies have laws?

Exam Practice

Higher Level 2010: Short question

A person's conscience helps him or her to_____.

Higher Level 2006:

To behave morally means _____.

Ordinary Level/Higher Level 2008: Picture question

Pick **one** thing from the photograph that shows these people are concerned about a moral issue.

Describe **one** other way in which people can show concern about a moral issue.

Give **one** reason why religion could influence a person's view of right and wrong on a moral issue.

State **two** things that can influence a person's view of what is right and wrong.

Describe **one** stage in the process a person goes through when deciding if something is right or wrong.

Ordinary Level 2006: Section 4, question 6

A person's understanding of right and wrong is influenced by many factors: Family/ Friends/School/State.

Tick **one** of the above and give an example of how it could have an effect on a person's understanding of right and wrong.

Higher Level 2003: Section 4, question 6

Imagine you are on a train with a woman and a man sitting opposite you. During the journey the woman leaves her seat without taking her bag. A moment later you see the man getting ready to leave the train with the woman's bag under his coat.

Describe **two** different ways of dealing with this situation.

Explain the consequences of **one** of the above ways of dealing with the situation for **each** of the following: the woman/the man/yourself.

Explain how a person's religious moral vision could influence their decision making in this situation.

Mini-Project

1. Do a research project on the Universal Declaration of Human Rights and present your findings to the class. The following should be researched:

    ● How it was formulated.
    ● What the thirty articles are about.
    ● Their role as a moral code.

    You can find the Universal Declaration of Human Rights on this website: *www. un.or/en/documents/udhr/*.

2. Research the work of Amnesty International and have an awareness week in your school community about the work that they do.

    You can find information about Amnesty International on their website: *www. amnesty.ie*.

Sources of Morality

27

Key Concepts

moral vision, laws, religious moral vision, authority, tradition

What is a moral vision?

A vision is a way of seeing how things could be and very often includes a view of how they should be. This includes a moral outlook, in other words a judgment of what is right and wrong.

A person with a strong moral vision will understand very clearly what they believe is right and wrong. They may wish to work towards eradicating what is wrong in the world, thereby helping to shape a better one. One such person in history was William Wilberforce.

> **Glossary**
>
> **Moral vision**
> A judgment of what is right and needs to be done to improve society.

William Wilberforce and the abolition of the slave trade

In the late eighteenth century, the slave trade was legal and thriving. Millions of people were treated as slaves and were shipped around the world to be sold as cargo. These people suffered greatly. William Wilberforce, a member of the British Parliament, believed that this was wrong and campaigned tirelessly to have the slave trade abolished in Britain. His moral viewpoint was that slavery was wrong. He had a moral vision, that is, a view of ending what was wrong and creating a better world. Due to Wilberforce's efforts, the slave trade was abolished in Britain in 1807. William Wilberforce was also involved in many other movements, including

What influenced Wilberforce's moral vision?

Is the treatment of animals an important moral issue for you?

trying to improve education for ordinary people and the conditions in prisons. He also helped to set up the Royal Society for the Prevention of Cruelty to Animals (RSPCA). He was very committed to the moral vision he had for the world.

Did you know?

The song 'Amazing Grace' was written by John Newton and is about his conversion to Christianity. 'I once was blind but now I see' refers to the fact that Newton had worked as captain of a slave ship and was blind to God or what was good. His conversion changed his life completely and he became a preacher. He was a friend of William Wilberforce and influenced him in fighting to end the slave trade.

JOHN NEWTON.

Listen to different versions of the song 'Amazing Grace'. Discuss the meaning of the song, and choose which version you prefer.

Sources of morality

A source of morality influences a person's idea of right and wrong. It can be looked to for guidance in making moral decisions.

The law

Laws are rules that regulate societies and how people can exist together. Rules like these are very important. After all, think of your favourite sport or game. Without rules to regulate how it is played, it would very soon become chaotic and no longer enjoyable. Some important rules that regulate society in Ireland are found in the Constitution – *Bunreacht na hÉireann*. The European Union also has laws that regulate member states and its citizens. Some people have challenged Irish laws by bringing them to the European courts for examination.

Find out when the constitution was first written.

> **Laws**
> Rules agreed upon by people and governments which regulate the behaviour of members of a society. If people break the law, they are punished.

The Golden Rule

One of the best known and most widespread religious codes for morality, or for doing what is right, is known as the 'Golden Rule'. A form of it is found in Judaism, Christianity, Islam, Hinduism, Buddhism and nearly every other spiritual path in the world. Put simply, it is the idea that you should treat others as you would like to be treated. So, if you don't want to be lied to, don't lie. If you don't want to be stolen from, don't steal. If you want to be treated with respect, treat others with respect. This can be described as a rule of reciprocity. The Golden Rule is expressed in the following traditions.

Religious expressions of the Golden Rule

Hinduism: Mahabharata 5:1517
'This is the sum of duty: do not do to others what would cause pain if done to you.'

Zoroastrianism: Shayast-na-Shayast 13:29
'Do not do unto others whatever is injurious to yourself.'

Judaism: Rabbi Hillel, Talmud, Shabbat 31a
'What is hateful to you, do not do to your neighbour. This is the whole Torah; all the rest is commentary.'

Confucianism: Confucius, Analects 15:23
'One word that sums up the basis of all good conduct ... loving kindness. Do not do to others what you do not want done to yourself.'

Buddhism: The Buddha
'Treat not others in ways that you yourself would find hurtful.'

Religious expressions of the Golden Rule *(continued)*

Sikhism: Guru Granth Sahib, p. 1299
'I am a stranger to no one; and no one is a stranger to me. Indeed I am a friend to all.'

Taoism: Lao Tzu, T'ai Shang Kan Ying Pien, 213–218
'Regard your neighbour's gain as your own gain, and your neighbour's loss as your own loss.'

Native Spirituality: Chief Dan George
'We are as much alive as we keep the earth alive.'

Jainism: Mahavira, Sutrakitanga
'One should treat all creatures in the world as one would like to be treated.'

Christianity: Jesus, Matthew 7:12
'In everything, do to others as you would have them do to you; for this is the law and the prophets.'

Islam: The Prophet Mohammad, Hadith
'Not one of you truly believes until you wish for others what you wish for yourself.'

Baha'i Faith: Baha'u'llah, Gleanings
'Lay not on any soul a load that you would not wish to be laid upon you, and desire not for anyone the things you would not desire for yourself.'

Unitarianism: Unitarian principle
'We affirm and promote respect for the interdependent web of all existence of which we are a part.'

Choose your favourite expression of the Golden Rule. Why did you prefer this one?

The Golden Rule could be described as a religious moral vision which crosses a number of religious traditions. Sometimes a religious moral vision is more unique to a particular religion.

The Ten Commandments as a moral code

For members of the three major monotheistic world religions – Judaism, Islam and Christianity – there is the guideline of the Ten Commandments to turn to. They are a set of rules to live by. Though not always easy, they are clear in relation to big issues such as stealing, lying and murder.

Examining the Ten Commandments

The two main traditions in Christianity have slightly different versions of the Ten Commandments.

The Protestant and Jewish versions are as follows:

1. Have no other Gods.
2. Do not worship false idols.
3. Do not take the Lord's name in vain.
4. Keep the Sabbath day holy.
5. Honour your father and mother.
6. Do not murder.
7. Do not commit adultery.
8. Do not steal.
9. Do not lie.
10. Do not covet (be jealous of) what others have.

The Roman Catholic version is as follows:

1. Have no other Gods.
2. Do not take the Lord's name in vain.
3. Keep the Sabbath day holy.
4. Honour your father and mother.
5. Do not murder.
6. Do not commit adultery.
7. Do not steal.
8. Do not lie.
9. Do not covet another's wife.
10. Do not covet (be jealous of) what others have.

Religious moral vision *Glossary*
The view of right and wrong put forward by a religion in its teachings or in the words and actions of its founder or an inspirational leader.

As you can see, the commandments can be divided into those which relate to people's relationship with God and those which relate to people's relationship with each other. They regulate the everyday, as well as religious matters. The Ten Commandments go all the way back to a thousand years before Jesus, to the time of Moses. They are found in the Jewish Tanakh, the Old Testament for Christians. The part of the Jewish sacred writings they are contained in is known as the Torah or Jewish law. They are the centrepiece of the Jewish law, which contains 613 instructions for life.

Looking into the Ten Commandments

Have no other Gods: Accepting that there is only one God is fundamental to the monotheistic religions. It is about acknowledging that God should take priority over any other competing demands for our attention. What things compete for our attention in today's world?

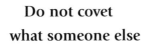

Do not worship false idols: In the past, this referred to putting up statues or worshipping false Gods. In today's world, what false idols do people worship?

Do not covet what someone else owns: If a person breaks this commandment, what other commandments could they break?

That new iPod looks good!

Do not lie: Are there situations when it might be acceptable to lie?

Do not steal: Can you think of three different types of stealing?

Do not murder: Murder seems like a straightforward case of right and wrong. Or is it? Some people consider euthanasia or 'assisted suicide' acceptable. Others think it is another way of killing. Some think abortion should be permitted in some circumstances while some people

see it as murder of the unborn. The death penalty is still practised in many other countries. Is this just a form of murder too?

Keep the Sabbath day holy: How can people keep one day a week special for their religion?

Honour your parents: In what ways do teenagers honour or dishonour their parents in today's world?

Do not commit adultery: This refers to having an affair with someone else's husband or wife. How many people could this affect? Who gets hurt?

Do not take the Lord's name in vain: For members of these religions, worshipping God alone and not taking the Lord's name in vain is about respecting God. It is an attitude of respect for God, oneself and the world. How can people respect the name of God?

The following headline appeared during the Rugby World Cup in 2011.

Devout Christian Euan Murray has questioned the need for Rugby World Cup matches to be played on Sundays

The Glasgow-born prop, 31, has chosen to prioritise his faith this weekend, meaning he will miss Scotland's Pool B clash with Argentina on Sunday. 'I don't see why there have to be games on Sundays,' said Murray. 'I hope things will change in future.'

Back in 2008, Murray did play on a Sunday when Scotland took on France in the Six Nations. But, after his faith deepened, he announced a year later that he would no longer be available for selection on Sundays.

At the time he said: 'It's basically all or nothing, following Jesus. I don't believe in pick 'n' mix Christianity. I believe the Bible is the word of God, so who am I to ignore something from it? I might as well tear out that page then keep tearing out pages as and when it suits me. If I started out like that there would soon be nothing left.'

Over to You

1. Why did Euan Murray not want to play in Scotland's match against Argentina?
2. When did he stop playing matches on a Sunday?
3. What does he mean when he says, 'I don't believe in pick 'n' mix Christianity'?
4. Do you think this was a difficult decision for him?

Other athletes who refused to play on a Sunday

- Eric Liddell felt compelled to pull out of the heats for the 100m at the 1924 Olympics.
- New Zealand rugby star Michael Jones was eventually omitted from the 1995 World Cup squad because he would have missed both the last eight and last four matches.

What was the difficult choice that these people had to make? What was the biggest influence on their decision?

Jesus' moral vision – the kingdom of God

Jesus' message about God's kingdom and how people need to live in order to bring it about is an important moral example for Christians. The attitudes and actions of Jesus towards others in the Gospels are used by Christians as a source of morality. What Jesus valued, what he considered important, is what Christians should also value. The moral vision of Jesus has inspired the work of many organisations in Ireland and the world today, e.g. Christian Aid, the St Vincent de Paul and Trocaire.

Mohammad – sunnah, the example of the prophet

Muslims, as well as following the Five Pillars, have the example of the prophet. Second only to the Qur'an as a source of authority in Islamic law, the *sunnah* refers to the words and actions of Mohammad. Therefore, Muslims look to the prophet's life as a source of guidance on the right way to live. *Hadith* is a word used to describe the traditions of Mohammad's words and actions, which are additional to the Qur'an. Since there are so many hadith traditions, Muslim lawyers have the job of deciding which hadith are more or less authentic.

Buddha – the noble eightfold path

For Buddhists, the moral guide is the Buddha, also known as the enlightened one. The Buddha outlined the noble eightfold path, which is made up of eight steps to the end of suffering and to help individual enlightenment.

They are as follows:

- Right view
- Right resolve
- Right speech
- Right action
- Right livelihood
- Right effort
- Right mindfulness
- Right concentration or meditation.

What does the wheel represent?

Over to You

Examine how each of the steps would benefit both the person carrying them out and others.

Buddhism also has five rules central to achieving 'the avoidance of evil, the undertaking of good', which is at the heart of Buddhist morality. These are:

1. Not to harm any living being.
2. Not to steal.
3. Not to engage in sexual misconduct.
4. Not to lie.
5. Not to use drugs or alcohol.

These beliefs are about cultivating a respect for love, kindness, dignity, honesty and integrity. For Buddhists, actions will produce goodness and, thus, are linked to morality. The law of Karma means that a moral action will produce a good consequence, while an immoral action will produce negative consequences.

Dharma – sacred duty: a guide to life in Hinduism

Dharma or sacred duty is an individual's role for a particular stage in life. The sacred duty comes with responsibility, but also comes with rights. For example, a young person has a sacred duty to study and do the best that they can to honour their parents and family. They have rights too, which are to have shelter and food, in other words to be taken care of. Dharma is, therefore, a source of the right way to behave for a

What responsibilities come with getting married?

Hindu. It is a way of life, rather than a set of rules. When people get married their Dharma will change. Now they have responsibilities around caring for their family. Later on, when children have grown up and left home, people's responsibility changes again. They should now concentrate on their spiritual well-being.

We all need someone to turn to for advice from time to time. In some situations, thinking about what is the right thing to do is not enough on our own. Perhaps we can turn to a parent, a friend, an older sister or brother, maybe a teacher or sports coach. Sometimes a source may not be a person at all but rather a special book or an important teaching.

Over to You

In pairs, discuss who you would turn to for advice on the right thing to do. Would it depend on the situation? What is it about that particular person that you feel would make them suitable to turn to for advice?

Sacred texts as authority

For Muslims, the source of authority is the Qur'an. This is the sacred text of Islam, believed by Muslims to have been revealed to the Prophet Mohammad by God.

Glossary

Authority
Something or someone whose role in providing leadership, information or guidance is accepted and respected in a community.

In Christianity, during the time of the Reformation, the reformers emphasised the Bible as the *only* source of authority that Christians needed to refer to. Thus, the Protestant churches became buildings designed to allow people to concentrate on the word of God in the Bible. The Protestant denominations vary in how they interpret some parts of the Bible, but they all look to it for guidance on moral issues, practices within the Church and personal faith.

How important is the Bible as a source of authority for Protestants?

The Seventh-day Adventist Church, like most Christian churches, puts the Bible at the centre of its faith. Adventists regard the Bible as literally true and its writers as inspired by God. They regard the Bible as an infallible guide to life (infallible means incapable of making mistakes or being wrong).

Personal health is specifically mentioned in Adventist doctrine (teaching), which tells its followers to regard their bodies as temples of the Holy Spirit. Adventists believe that what is good for the body is good for the soul and vice versa. One way Adventists keep healthy is by eating a healthy diet that follows the food rules laid down in Leviticus. A vegetarian diet is recommended but not insisted upon.

Did you know? Adventists were responsible for popularising breakfast cereal. The Adventist layman John Harvey Kellogg invented cornflakes as a replacement for eggs and bacon, to avoid cooking on the Sabbath.

For Roman Catholics, the Bible is an important source of authority. They also refer to the Church's teachings when looking for guidance on religious practices and moral issues. The Pope as spiritual leader and 'Christ's representative' is considered a very important source of authority. The Pope issues encyclicals on various matters – these are statements that Roman Catholics should consider when deciding on matters of faith and morality. The Catechism, a book of official church teaching, is another very important source of authority in the Roman Catholic Church.

Church teaching is part of the Roman Catholic Church's tradition. Tradition in this sense is not just something that is always done a certain way, but the idea that what has gone before, is important in helping inform people today about what is right or wrong.

How important is the Pope in helping members of the Roman Catholic Church to decide on moral issues?

When law and morality conflict

A person's own view on what is right or wrong is not always the same as the law's understanding of right and wrong. There are times when the two standards of morality may come into conflict.

In history, there are many such cases when the state's view of what was right did not coincide with what many people considered to be correct behaviour. For example, in the period when the Nazi

Glossary

Tradition
Teachings handed down through history that help to inform people today.

Party ruled Germany (1933–1945), it became law that Jewish people were not allowed to use swimming pools or park benches, go to cinemas, practise medicine, own newspapers, vote or even be considered citizens – simply because they were Jewish. This, of course, was totally wrong. There were some people who – because of their own strong moral viewpoint – could not agree with the new laws in Nazi Germany. Some of these people took a stand against the harsh regime, at a cost to their own lives. Three such people were Pastor Martin Niemöller, Sophie Scholl and Dietrich Bonhoeffer.

These three people faced a major personal moral choice: to go along with Nazism or to challenge it and face the consequences. Research the stories and choices of these people.

These three people could never agree to go along with the state. They not only had strong morals but also the courage to stand up for what they considered to be right, even when the propaganda machine said otherwise. Even in an extreme situation, personal choice still exists, though sometimes at a very high price.

Personal moral issues

Examining the following personal moral issues shows that when it comes to making a personal moral decision people will often affect others around them and may find opposition to their choice.

Dress

Many Muslim women consider how they dress to be a moral issue. Wearing the *burqa* is for some a personal moral choice. Many Muslim women choose not to wear a burqa, but others wish to. To complicate this issue, some women are forced to wear a burqa and so it is not their choice but the demand of others within their community. To wear something as an expression of religious devotion and which shows your moral outlook can be difficult in some societies and may conflict with the law. This can be a difficult personal moral choice.

Food

Some people do not wish to eat meat as a personal moral choice. This may be to do with animal welfare issues or for health reasons. For others, it is part of a religious tradition. In many religions, certain foods are forbidden, e.g. Muslims and Jews do not eat pork. Choices around food can be very important moral issues. We have choices whether or not to eat foods that have not been fairly traded, that have been shipped thousands of miles across the globe, that have been grown in countries where people are starving or by using methods that may be damaging the environment. These are big moral issues and show that a personal moral choice can have far-reaching consequences. They do not just affect the person making them, but may have an impact on other people who live thousands of miles away.

In France, the law does not allow people to cover their face in public. This, in effect, stops Muslim women wearing the burqa in public. Discuss whether people should be free to dress as they wish.

Did you think what you had for breakfast might be a moral issue?

War

For some people, war is never right. Pacifists are people who believe that it is always wrong to use violence as a way of settling problems. This personal moral viewpoint is not always shaped by religious belief. However, there are religious groups who hold pacifist beliefs, such as the Quakers (the Society of Friends). This moral choice is not always easy. In times of war, people in some countries are conscripted or told they must join the army. There are people who have been sent to prison or who have even been killed for being pacifists. Some countries allow people to be conscientious objectors in times of war. Some conscientious objectors, while not fighting, choose to help out in other ways, e.g. by joining the Red Cross teams that attend to the wounded in war.

What are the consequences of war?

Opposing moral viewpoints

Thankfully, for most of us extreme circumstances do not arise. Nevertheless, there are situations where a person's own morality may conflict with the state's laws or with the moral viewpoint of the majority of other people. People, of course, are expected to obey the law, but they can express their views on moral issues through debate, protest and choosing how to vote. For example, if the government decides to introduce a law that people think is morally wrong, they can lobby politicians, write letters and seek change. An individual can choose not to support a company that engages in immoral practices, e.g. a sportswear manufacturer that exploits people in the developing world by paying them very low wages or a food producer that damages the environment. Individuals are free to have a different moral outlook as long as it does not interfere with the freedom of others.

Key Terms

moral vision, laws, religious moral vision, authority, tradition

Chapter Questions

1. What is a moral vision?
2. Can people with a strong moral vision influence others? How?
3. How important is it for society to have laws?
4. What is the Golden Rule?
5. What is the most important moral vision for Muslims? Christians? Jews?
6. Does Buddhism have a moral vision? What is it?
7. In Hinduism, what is an important source for how to behave?
8. Name a religious founder and describe their moral vision.
9. What does it mean to describe something or someone as having authority?
10. How important is tradition as a source of authority?

Exam Practice

Higher Level 2005: Section 4, question 6

'Moral codes express the rights people are entitled to, as well as the responsibilities they have towards others.'

Name **one** moral code you have studied.

State **one** right it expresses.

State **one** responsibility it expresses.

Explain how the moral code you have named above could help a person in making a moral decision.

Outline a situation in which a person has to make a moral decision.

Explain how a person's religion could influence their moral decision making in the situation you have outlined above.

Higher Level 2007: Section 4, question 6

Outline what is involved in **two** stages of the process a person goes through in making a moral decision.

Give **one** example of a situation where there could be conflict between a country's law and a religion.

Higher Level 2009: Section 5, question 6

Analyse the ways in which a religious moral code expresses the beliefs of a world religion you have studied.

Mini-Project

Research the moral vision of the founder of one community of faith. Show how their vision influences members today.

Growing in Morality

28

Key Concepts

moral growth, moral maturity, conscience

Moral growth

Glossary

Moral growth
How a person's morality develops and takes shape as they grow.

Children's ideas of right and wrong are hugely dependent on the significant adults in their life. For most people, this means family members: parents, grandparents, aunts and uncles, brothers and sisters. Teachers, too, have some influence. At this stage, most children believe some things or actions are right and wrong because they have been told so. In general, children do the right thing because they don't want to get into trouble. The idea of right and wrong is only starting to develop within the child and is strongly influenced by others.

Two developmental psychologists, the Swiss Jean Piaget and the American Lawrence Kohlberg, showed that a child's ability to think morally depends on their general thinking abilities. They both constructed the stages at which children develop their moral thinking. For Kohlberg, the first stage is concerned with the self, both in terms of avoiding punishment and gaining reward. The second stage consists of comparing moral actions with

Who are children likely to listen to?

society's conventions on right and wrong. The third stage (known as post-conventional) is when people have their own perspectives on what is right and wrong, which may be called moral principles.

In adolescence, as people start to develop their own sense of morality, they think a lot about what other people do. For adolescents, friends play a big role in deciding what they consider to be moral or not.

While all people can develop morally, they don't all reach moral maturity at the same time. To have a sense of your own morality with an internal, justifiable view on moral issues is to become morally mature. A person will usually act on what is right and acceptable according to agreed standards of right and wrong. They may disagree with others when it comes to some moral issues (e.g. abortion, war, euthanasia etc.), but they will be able to explain their views logically and without becoming violent or aggressive towards others. A morally mature person has an informed conscience.

What, according to Piaget, affects a child's moral development?

Who are adolescents influenced by?

Moral maturity

When a person has a strong sense of right and wrong and is not overly concerned with what other people think. Such people have an informed conscience. They think of the consequences of their actions and do not only think of themselves.

Glossary

Over to You

1. What is the main concern for children when deciding if an action is right or wrong?
2. Describe the three stages of moral development outlined by Kohlberg. Show how someone at each of the three stages would respond to a particular moral decision.
3. What concerns adolescents when making a moral decision?
4. How does a morally mature person act when someone disagrees with their moral viewpoint?

323

Glossary

Conscience
The ability to judge right from wrong and act on what is right.

The role of conscience

Conscience is not a magic little switch in a person's head that tells them the right thing to do. It has to be informed. For example, if someone is considering where they stand on a moral issue, they must first have the facts of the issue. Only then can they consider the outcomes or consequences for everyone involved in acting in a certain way. If they need to, they can look for guidance to a source or sources of authority that they respect. All of this informs the individual's conscience and they are then in a position to listen to this internal moral viewpoint and reach a decision.

Informing conscience on a moral issue: to lie or tell the truth

First, the *facts* – if you lie to someone, you are robbing them of the truth. You are breaching their right to know the truth and this may be something important that they need to know.

Second, the possible *consequences* – the lie may hurt the person. The person who has been lied to may discover the lie and this may damage the relationship between the two people involved. The person who lies may have to invent more lies to cover up the first lie.

Third, looking to *sources of authority* on this issue – many will say not to lie. It is, for example, against the law to lie in a court. 'Do not lie' is one of the Ten Commandments. One of the Buddha's teachings is to respect the truth.

Now, armed with the facts, the possible outcomes and advice from sources of authority, a person's conscience that is informed in this way would most likely see that lying is wrong.

Discuss
There are times when lying may be considered acceptable to some people – can you think of such circumstances?

The term 'prisoner of conscience' is used to describe people who are jailed because of their political, religious or other conscientiously held beliefs. The organisation Amnesty International champions the rights of such people, monitoring the state of human rights in over 150 countries.

Did you know?
William Penn, founder of Pennsylvania and a member of the Society of Friends, wrote while in prison, 'My prison shall be my grave before I will budge a jot, for I owe my conscience to no mortal man.'

It is not always easy to decide what is right and what is wrong in any given situation. People's understanding of something can change and they may change their position with regard to a moral issue.

Ethical systems – deciding if something is good or bad

A variety of theories have developed that people use when trying to decide what is right or wrong.

Utilitarianism

This theory is based on trying to achieve 'the greatest happiness of the greatest number'. It was the idea of Jeremy Bentham (1748–1832) and later John Stuart Mill (1806–1873). Actions are right if they are useful or for the benefit of the majority. In this way, actions are evaluated on the basis of their consequences. For something to be good, it must be good for the majority.

Find out what Bentham and Mill campaigned for.

Hedonism

This teaching proposes that the aim in life is the pursuit of pleasure. It was the idea of an ancient Greek philosopher called Epicurus. He described pleasure as the greatest good. He saw pleasure as the avoidance of pain and the freedom of the mind from fear and anxiety. Modern definitions of hedonism have changed quite a bit from the ideas of Epicurus. Is it true that whatever is good is pleasant and whatever is pleasant is good?

Situation ethics

This ethical theory argues that right and wrong depend on the context or situation and universal moral rules don't apply. The right thing to do depends on the situation.

This theory of ethics was suggested by Joseph Fletcher in his book, *Situation Ethics*, published in 1966. Situation ethics means that people shouldn't rigidly follow a moral law but decide what action seems most loving in a given situation. It is about trying to achieve a good result, and can even go so far as doing something you may not consider always to be right if the right outcome will be achieved. Fletcher argued that the only thing that is good is love. As long as an action is decided on the basis of love, it is right and good. He was basing the idea of love on the Bible or, more specifically, Jesus' teaching of love for your neighbour.

Are there any problems with using any of the above theories as a basis for deciding whether something is good or bad? List the possible difficulties with each.

Key Terms

moral growth, moral maturity, conscience

Chapter Questions

1. How do most children develop a sense of right and wrong?
2. Define conscience.
3. What does 'prisoner of conscience' refer to?
4. Name an organisation that campaigns for human rights.
5. Who founded the state of Pennsylvania? What religious group did he belong to?
6. In utilitarianism, on what basis is an action judged to be good or bad?
7. What book did Joseph Fletcher publish in 1966?

Exam Practice

Ordinary Level 2007: Short question

A person uses their conscience to _____ .

Ordinary Level 2003: Short question

Morally mature people think only of themselves when making moral decisions: true or false.

Higher Level 2006: Section 4, question 6

What is moral maturity?

Family, friends, religion etc. can influence a person's idea of what is right and wrong. Outline how any **two** such influences can affect a person's idea of right and wrong.

In making a decision, how would a morally mature person deal with the many influences on their ideas of right and wrong?

Higher Level 2008: Section 4, question 6

Outline what the term 'conscience' means.

Explain how a person's religious faith could influence their conscience.

Apart from religious faith, explain how **one** other factor could influence a person's conscience.

Describe **one** way in which a person's conscience can develop as they grow older.

Higher Level 2010: Section 5, question 6

Profile the way in which a person's judgment of right and wrong can develop as they grow from moral immaturity to moral maturity.

Mini-Project

Research a famous person who was a prisoner of conscience and write their story – e.g. Aung San Suu Kyi, Nelson Mandela, Dietrich Bonhoeffer, Franz Jägerstätter, Aleksandr Solzhenitsyn, Thomas More.

Religious Morality in Action

29

Key Concepts

decision making, truth, integrity, justice, judgment, life, peace/ tranquillity, respect, forgiveness, reconciliation, sin, stewardship

Having knowledge of what is right and wrong is one thing, but putting those beliefs into action is another. In everyday life, people are continually faced with decisions that have a moral aspect to them. For example, what are the moral dilemmas in the following?

Decision making (Glossary)

Choosing between different actions or ideas in order to decide which to carry out or agree with.

- Should I buy local or imported food?
- Should I take the bus or walk to school?
- Will I finish all the chocolate ice cream before Mum gets home?
- Should I copy someone else's work and pretend it is my own?

What would you do?

The following are some steps involved in making decisions.

How to make a decision

- Having facts.
- Considering options.
- Considering consequences.
- Referring to a moral code.
- Considering others.
- Making a choice.

Is truth important?

What is true for one person is not necessarily true for another. So while people use the term 'true' as though it could not be argued against, it is not a straightforward idea at all. Think about the following three statements and decide which is most likely to be true:

1. There is an elephant in my pocket.
2. There is a ten euro note in my pocket.
3. There is a winning lotto ticket in my pocket.

Now the first statement seems impossible, the second quite likely and the third highly unlikely. If you were to ask people which statement they considered to be true, they would most likely go for the second. It would seem to have the most credibility. After all, how many people win the lotto? And elephants don't fit in pockets. Lots of people have a ten euro note and it is an object that would fit easily in a pocket.

In this case, the truth is actually the first statement, because the elephant is only a small toy elephant and it fits easily into a pocket. Perception is not always right and the truth is not always what it seems.

When it comes to the truth, people sometimes have clouded judgment and perceive things to be true that may not be. They don't always look for the hard evidence but make quick judgments, sometimes based on their own viewpoint, which may be biased or unfair.

> **Glossary**
>
> **Truth**
> The quality or state of being true; that which is true or in accordance with fact or reality; a fact or belief that is accepted as true.

Did you know?

In John's gospel, during Jesus' trial before Pontius Pilate, Pilate asks Jesus, 'What is truth?'

This picture is of an old woman or a beautiful young girl: which do you see? Who is right – which is it?

Is this designed to convey the truth?

'The first casualty of war is the truth'

On many occasions, this famous statement is all too true. In war, the enemy frequently becomes dehumanised, feared and hated. They can no longer be seen as they really are: human beings with hopes, fears, emotions, and the capacity to love and to be loved. In many cases during war, both sides want their people to believe things that may or may not be true: they are winning, they are right, they are acting fairly, they are using necessary force etc. War propaganda is used by all sides of conflict. It is justified as helping to boost morale, to achieve the desired outcome and to make people feel okay about killing.

But if both sides are sending out the same message, one must not be telling the truth, so where is the truth in such a situation?

Why truth matters

Does it really matter whether or not we tell the truth? Different people would, of course, have different opinions on this. For those who belong to the many different religious communities, the truth is really important. It is one of the Ten Commandments and it is one of the basic Buddhist precepts.

For others, lying is something that is wrong because it hurts people. Most people, whether members of a religion or not, would be very uncomfortable being friends with someone who tells lies all the time. Think about this – what sort of reputation would you have if people thought you were a persistent liar?

Why do people tell lies?

Glossary

Integrity
The quality of being honest and having strong moral principles.

Discuss How would a person of integrity behave?

Lies can also be a very dangerous source of conflict or unfair treatment. Some people spread rumours about other groups to encourage others to hate them. For example, people who are racist spread lies about a particular race. Others incite religious hatred with unfounded accusations about members of a particular religion. Of course, this is very damaging to individuals and also to society as a whole. This is sometimes viewed as a crime, though it can be difficult to prove.

What is the role of a judge? Who do they work for?

In some situations, lying is illegal. For example, in a court of law, a person is legally bound to tell the truth. If someone is found to have lied in court, that person can be in serious trouble, even in some cases imprisoned. Public figures, such as government ministers, politicians, judges, attorneys general etc. have a responsibility to tell the truth and may face investigation if they are suspected of lying in matters of national importance.

In some situations, since lies about someone can damage that person's reputation, career or personal life, there are laws about what can be said about someone. If you spread damaging lies about someone, you can be accused of *slander*. If you write something untrue, it is referred to as *libel*.

Glossary

Justice
Just behaviour or treatment. The quality of being fair and reasonable. Administration of the law in maintaining what is just, fair and reasonable.

Over to You

1. Why do governments not always tell the truth in wartime?
2. Name a religious code that encourages people not to lie.
3. Do you think it is important for public figures, such as politicians, to tell the truth? Why?
4. When is it illegal to lie?
5. Write a debate supporting the motion: 'For a person to be moral, telling the truth is essential.'

Is that fair?

One of the biggest human dilemmas is the suffering of innocent people. For some people, God's lack of interference when people suffer is at best infuriating and at worst cruel. Others do not believe that God should intervene, as humans are intended to have free will and make moral choices. Many believe that innocent suffering is caused by humans, even if those who cause the suffering are not those affected by it.

Discuss

Does innocent suffering question God's justice?

In the Bible, the story of Job is about the suffering of an innocent person. It was written at a time when it was believed that a person suffered if they had done something wrong. Since Job was a good person, this story showed that anyone can suffer and that there are many things humans do not understand. Job is angry and rages at God in this book. In the end, however, he responds to God in an act of worship and he is ultimately rewarded for his faith.

Over to You

Read the story of Job found in the Old Testament. Describe the character of Job. What image of God is there in this story?

Glossary

Judgment
A decision, opinion or conclusion about someone, something or a set of circumstances.

Many people believe that every individual will experience justice at the end of their life and that God will judge a person's deeds, as carried out in life. People will receive justice at this point, a kind of ultimate justice that affects their afterlife. Many religions teach this idea. In Islam, final judgment awaits a person straight after death. In Christianity, the Nicene Creed, a very old statement of basic Christian beliefs, says: 'He shall judge the living and the dead.' In Hinduism, people are reincarnated, depending on how they lived their life.

Sanctity of life

While most people recognise that life is valuable and acknowledge a person's right to life, most religions emphasise that life is sacred. It is special and given by God. Life, as a God-given gift, should be protected and prized. This affects how people view many aspects of life. For many people of faith, the belief that life is sacred means it has a dignity and purpose that makes it

Glossary

Life
The condition that distinguishes animals and plants from inorganic matter, including the capacity for growth, reproduction, functional activity, and continual change preceding death.

What do these pictures say about respect for human life?

more meaningful. In Hinduism, all life comes from the one divine and unknowable source – Brahman. The universal soul is part of all that lives, therefore all life is sacred. In Christianity, all people are made in the image of God. They are unique and loved by God and, therefore, each human life is sacred.

Did you know?

When the first atomic bomb was dropped by parachute on Hiroshima on 6 August 1945, from an American B-29 bomber known as Enola Gay, the blast destroyed more than ten square kilometres of the city. The fires that broke out lasted for three days. Between 60,000 and 80,000 people were killed instantly. Many more died as a result of the long-term effects of radiation sickness. A second bomb, weighing 4,000 kg, was dropped on Nagasaki on 9 August.

War ...

One of the Ten Commandments is the law, 'You shall not kill'. This also demonstrates the importance of life. One situation when life is threatened is war. There have been many wars in history and war seems to be an ever-present problem in the world. There are many causes of war, but the outcomes are always similar: loss of life, destruction, economic problems and homelessness. While some people view war as always wrong, others believe it to be necessary in some situations. One of the best known moral theories on war is the Just War theory, which was developed by St Augustine and later by St Thomas Aquinas. This theory outlines very limited circumstances when a war may be just, while recognising that war is never desirable. This theory outlines the conditions when the use of military force is justified and how to conduct war ethically.

Glossary

Peace
A period when there is no war.
Tranquillity
Freedom from disturbance, which provides the opportunity for people and society to flourish.

Discuss

Is peace simply the absence of war or something more?

'Blessed are the peacemakers, for they will be called the children of God.'

(Matthew 5:9)

... and peace

The Zen Buddhist leader and pacifist Thich Nhat Hanh has plenty to say on the subject of peace. He himself experienced the Vietnam War and was not removed from the suffering of the people. In the 1960s in Saigon, he set up the School for Social Youth Services to rebuild bombed towns, and to set up schools and medical centres. It was founded on Buddhist principles of non-violence and compassionate action. Thich Nhat Hanh was not allowed back to Vietnam in 1966 after he went to France and the USA on a peace mission. Since 1982 he has lived in Plum Village, a Buddhist community in France.

> 'To work for peace is to uproot war from ourselves and from the hearts of men and women. To prepare for war ... is to plant millions of seeds of violence, anger, frustration, and fear that will be passed on for generations to come.'
>
> Thich Nhat Hanh

What work does UNICEF do?

Respect Glossary

A feeling of deep admiration for someone or something; regard for the feelings, wishes or rights of others.

Many problems need to be addressed to bring about peace in the world and to create circumstances in which harmony can exist. This was recognised when the United Nations was set up. The United Nations was established following World War II to try to prevent future wars and to provide a way to deal with conflict through politics and discussion. The United Nations also set up many agencies that try to bring about peace by dealing with issues to improve the lives of many people around the world, such as the World Health Organisation, UNICEF and UNESCO.

When people are not respected, they are often treated unfairly and may not be given the same rights as others. When we respect someone, we treat

How could people show respect for the elderly?

them well. We don't lie to them or hurt them. We consider their feelings in how we talk to them and behave towards them.

One group of people that is not always shown respect is the elderly. Some elderly people are treated as a nuisance, as if they have nothing to contribute to society and they should not be allowed to do certain things. Their feelings are sometimes disregarded and their wishes often ignored. Treatment like this can become a form of age discrimination.

1. What do most religions say about life?
2. What are the results of war?
3. What does the Just War theory outline?
4. Can you think of people in Irish society who are not always treated with respect? How are they treated?
5. Write out three things people could do in a school community to show respect to other members of that community.

Forgiveness and reconciliation

One of the most difficult challenges for many people is to forgive someone else for something. It isn't difficult to accept a 'sorry' for some small thing, but when it comes to feeling really hurt, it is a very hard thing to hear and truly appreciate. In Christianity, teaching about forgiveness is included in the Our Father: '... and forgive us our trespasses as we forgive those who trespass against us.'

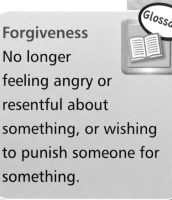

Forgiveness
No longer feeling angry or resentful about something, or wishing to punish someone for something.

What are the benefits of forgiveness? To forgive means to repair a broken relationship. When a person truly forgives someone, they are acknowledging the hurt and accepting the apology. In doing so, they are allowing a way to a better understanding and relationship between themselves and the person whom they have forgiven. Forgiveness also allows a person to move on from a past hurt and not allow it to dictate their life.

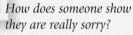
How does someone show they are really sorry?

335

Christianity and forgiveness

In Christianity, there is a sacrament known as Reconciliation. It is one of the seven fundamental sacraments of the Roman Catholic Church, which teaches that through the sacraments people experience the risen Christ. This sacrament is about repairing a person's relationship with God. The sacrament is commonly referred to as confession and it involves a person seeking God's forgiveness for wrongdoing. In this way, the person is acknowledging that they have acted against God's will and have consequently damaged their relationship with God. To reconcile themselves with God, they believe they need to seek God's forgiveness.

Since the main ethic or principle of Christianity is to show love of God through love of other people, how people treat others is really important. The word used to describe an action against God's law, which damages a person's relationship with God, is sin.

> **Glossary**
>
> **Reconciliation**
> The restoration of a relationship, making one view compatible with another.

> **Glossary**
>
> **Sin**
> An act considered to be immoral and against God's law; an act that damages a person's relationship with others and with God.

Judaism and forgiveness

Yom Kippur or the Day of Atonement is an important holy day in Judaism. It is concerned with forgiveness and becoming closer to God through prayer and fasting. In the ten days before Yom Kippur people are encouraged to seek out those they may have offended and to ask them for forgiveness. On the day of Yom Kippur many prayers are said and songs are sung to seek God's forgiveness. The book of Jonah is read to show that God will forgive those who repent. The emphasis, on this day, is on spiritual renewal of both the individual and the community.

Over to You

1. What Christian prayer asks God for forgiveness?
2. What sacrament is concerned with repairing a person's relationship with God?
3. An action that damages a person's relationship with God is known as a _____.
4. In Judaism, which day is concerned with seeking forgiveness from God?

Morality in action – responsibility for the earth

One of the biggest problems facing the modern world is the damage that has been done and is being done to the earth. For most people, whether or not they are members of a religious community, this is a serious concern. Members of many communities of faith believe that the earth is a gift from God and that humans have a responsibility to take care of it. The major world religions are being encouraged by people, including their members and other groups (e.g. the Alliance of Religions and Conservation), to develop environmental programmes based on their core beliefs.

> **Did you know?** The Alliance of Religions and Conservation (ARC) was started in 1986 when the president of the World Wildlife Fund (WWF) invited leaders of the five major world religions to come to a meeting to discuss how they could help save the natural world.

Stewardship, in religious communities, refers to the responsibility that members have to maintain and use wisely the gifts they believe they have been given by God. In the Bible, it says, 'the earth is the Lord's and everything in it' (Psalm 24:1). For many religious people, managing what God has given is about honouring God. The opposite is to dishonour God and everything that people are blessed with.

> **Glossary**
>
> **Stewardship**
> To manage or look after. It has come to refer to humankind's responsibility to take care of nature or the world.

Christian stewardship in Ireland

Eco Congregation Ireland is a project of the main Irish churches. It encourages all Irish churches to take an approach to worship that shows their responsibility to care for the earth:

> Our vision is to see churches of all denominations throughout Ireland celebrate the gift of God's creation, recognise the inter-dependence of all creation and care for it in their life and mission and through members' personal lifestyles.
>
> We ask Christians everywhere to reflect on the beauty of God's world and to consider what practical steps can be taken to prevent further damage to the environment. Also, to pray for our wounded planet, for people in the developing world already affected by climate change and for future generations.

www.ecocongregationireland.com

Respect for the earth in Hinduism

In Hinduism, the world is full of God (Brahman), who lives in everything. Many Hindus see the earth as mother, taking care of people, providing them with food, shelter and clothing. In order to respect the earth people must take care of it. The following Hindu prayer, found in one of its most important sacred texts, shows the importance of nature in Hinduism: 'Supreme Lord, let there be peace in the sky and in the atmosphere. Let there be peace in the plant world and in the forests. Let the cosmic powers be peaceful. Let the Brahman, the true essence and source of life, be peaceful. Let there be undiluted and fulfilling peace everywhere' (Atharva Veda).

1. What problems does the natural world face?
2. Why do many members of religious communities feel they have a duty to look after the earth?
3. What is the ARC and when was it founded?
4. What is the vision of Eco Congregation Ireland?
5. How do Hindus view the earth?

Moral choices in relation to the environment

The issues that face the planet include climate change, species extinction, pollution, the use of finite resources such as oil and coal, the debate over nuclear power and the supply and distribution of food and water. When it comes to individuals and governments, there are moral choices in dealing with many of these issues. Should people invest money and time in developing renewable energy sources? Should governments support measures to help the environment? Should people act in an environmentally friendly way with regard to what they buy and eat or how they travel? Is there a desire to help people in countries affected by natural disasters or who are suffering the effects of climate change?

Sometimes people feel that there are difficulties in helping others or in dealing with a global issue like climate change and that these difficulties are not easy to overcome. Consider, however, the words of Peter Scott, founder of the WWF, who said, 'We shall not save all we should like to, but we shall save a great deal more than if we had never tried.'

What does this organisation try to do?

Why would people wish to use these forms of energy?

Did you know?

Peter Scott was the son of the famous Antarctic explorer Captain Robert Falcon Scott, who wrote to his wife Kathleen Bruce in his last letter, 'make the boy [Peter] interested in natural history if you can'.

Did you know?

The first 'fair trade town' in Ireland was Clonakilty, in County Cork. A fair trade town is one that has met six goals, showing that it has made a commitment to supporting fair trade. Clonakilty was given this status in 2003 and many more towns have followed since then. Do you know if your town is a 'fair trade' one?

Morality in Action – Fair trade

Another moral issue facing the modern world is the question of fair trade. In the world today, there are huge multinational companies that have more wealth than some small countries. Some people who work for such companies live below the poverty line. Some of those who work to produce crops like coffee beans, bananas or cocoa beans never receive a fair price for their efforts. Some products, however, are referred to as 'fair trade', which means they are purchased for a fair price from the farmers or other workers who produced them. The way the world's resources are controlled is a huge problem. The current statistic is that 80 per cent of the world's resources are controlled by 20 per cent of the population. This kind of inequity leads to poverty, injustice and unrest.

One faith-based organisation that has campaigned on the issue of fair trade is the charity Christian Aid. Its vision is to end poverty. It works globally to get rid of the

Have you ever seen or bought products with the Fairtrade logo?

causes of poverty and to try to achieve equality, dignity and freedom for all, regardless of faith or nationality.

Ultimately, in most major world religions, morality comes down to showing respect for God by respecting others. The Golden Rule, which is found in all major faiths, is fundamental. It states that people should treat other people in a way that they would wish to be treated themselves. This shows that people, whether Hindu, Muslim, Jewish, Buddhist or Christian, need to consider their actions in terms of consequences.

Key Terms

decision making, truth, integrity, justice, judgment, life, peace/tranquillity, respect, forgiveness, reconciliation, sin, stewardship

Chapter Questions

1. Explain the term justice.
2. Is preventing people from telling lies about others a form of justice?
3. Explain peace. What factors contribute to the issue of peace?
4. What are the benefits of being able to forgive someone?
5. How do the Ten Commandments show respect for human life?
6. What does stewardship refer to?
7. Write about any moral issue in terms of actions and consequences.

Exam Practice

Ordinary Level 2010: Short question

Considering the alternatives is one stage in the process of moral decision making. State **another** stage in the process of moral decision making.

Ordinary Level 2009: Short question

In religious traditions the term 'sin' means _____.

Ordinary Level 2008: Short question

In religious traditions to act with 'integrity' means behaving in a way that is in keeping with your beliefs: true or false.

Higher Level 2012: Short question

In religious traditions the term 'reconciliation' refers to_____.

Higher Level 2005: Short question

Major world religions view stewardship as an important part of living a good life. One example of stewardship is _____.

Higher Level 2011: Picture question

Pick **one** thing from this poster that suggests it is designed to encourage people to work for peace.

Give **one** example of a way in which members of a community of faith work for peace.

State **two** reasons why the members of a community of faith work for peace.

Higher Level 2011: Document question

I recently visited a farm run by a religious order. It was a great experience. We were shown all the animals on the farm and how crops are being grown without using chemicals. After the tour of the farm we went to a meeting room where the people who work on the farm talked with us about how they enjoyed living close to nature. They spoke about the way Jesus treated everyone with care and respect and the duty we all have to care for the plant, animal and human life around us. They welcome visitors to their farm so as to encourage people to live in a way that respects all the forms of life that exist in the world today. They also showed us pictures about how the earth is being polluted and people are dying of hunger. I was shocked to see how much damage can be done when people do not take care of the earth that has been given to us. From what we were shown on the farm you could clearly see how the behaviour of each person has an effect on others. Before we left the farm we talked about how each of us could use our own talents in a way that respects all forms of life and makes the earth a better place for everyone i.e. planting trees, giving to charity etc.

Outline how the connection between *either* actions and consequences *or* rights and responsibilities can be seen in the above extract.

In religious traditions the term 'stewardship' involves _____.

Describe **two** examples of how people practising stewardship can be seen in the above extract.

Outline **two** ways in which a person's religious faith could encourage stewardship.

Higher Level 2012: Document question

On the first Sunday in November 1987 people gathered in Enniskillen, Northern Ireland, to remember those killed in past wars. As people gathered at the war memorial a bomb exploded showering the area with debris. Gordon Wilson and his 20 year old daughter Marie, a student nurse, were buried several feet under the rubble. In the dark and chaos, father and daughter just managed to reach out and hold hands. Gordon asked his daughter 'Are you all right Marie?' Marie squeezed her father's hand saying 'Daddy I love you very much.' These were her last words. The bomb killed eleven people including Marie, who later died in hospital. Gordon Wilson, her heart-broken father, was injured in the explosion but amazed reporters who interviewed him that evening when he said 'I bear no ill will …. I bear no grudge' towards the bombers as it is 'not going to bring her back to life.' He said that because his daughter's last words were words of love, he would pray for the people responsible for the bombing and be thankful for the strength of God's never-ending love. Throughout the rest of his life Gordon Wilson was often called upon to speak about this experience. Through the meetings he attended, the interviews he gave and his writing, Gordon Wilson worked hard to bring about peace and overcome bitterness between people.

(Source: Adapted from *Revolutionary Christians Who Live the Gospel* by C. Richards)

Describe **one** way in which forgiveness can be seen in the above extract.

Explain how *either* integrity *or* religious faith can be seen in the above extract.

In religious traditions the term 'sin' refers to _____.

Outline **one** example of the teaching of forgiveness found in a major world religion you have studied.

Profile how members of a major world religion express their need for forgiveness in an act of worship.

Higher Level 2005: Section 5, question 6

Show how a community of faith can help its members to respond to a situation in which truth *or* peace may be threatened in today's world.

Mini-Project

Research the story of Sasaki Sadako, a child from Hiroshima at the time of the atomic bombing of the city. Or: research the work of a global or national organisation that helps the environment.

Law and Morality

30

This is a higher level only section of the syllabus.

> **Key Concepts**
>
> civil law, Constitution, religious fundamentalism, libertarianism, pluralism

Law

The law is one of the sources of morality for people. Each country or state has its own laws and in Ireland, as part of the European Union, we are also required to follow European law. Laws are passed by the government, which is elected by the people to have responsibility for running the country, including making whatever laws are necessary. As such, laws usually reflect the views of the majority of the population. They may, however, become out of date and may need to be changed or reviewed. The most fundamental laws in Ireland, on which other laws are based, are in the Constitution.

> **Glossary**
>
> **Civil law**
> Laws that govern the running of society.

Civil law covers laws about society and how people should behave to live their everyday lives in their communities. This includes laws about driving, trade, paying taxes, education, employment and social welfare. The many laws regarding these issues reflect the moral decisions that are made about issues like these. They reflect a general view on what is right and wrong in such everyday situations. For example, a consumer law that protects the consumer from being overcharged indicates that it is considered wrong to overcharge people. An employment law that states that people are entitled to be paid when they are ill shows that it is considered right to look after people in this situation.

The Constitution

The Irish Constitution was written in 1937. It is often referred to as 'de Valera's constitution' as he was the leader at that time and largely responsible for it. The Constitution was passed by a referendum on 1 July 1937 and came into force on 29 December the same year. The Constitution protects citizens' rights and outlines how Ireland is governed. It includes basic laws about governance, international relations, courts, rights and about how the Constitution may be changed. Any civil laws that are passed by the Oireachtas must be in agreement with the basic principles in the Irish Constitution. Sometimes governments have to introduce changes to laws due to legal rulings by the Supreme Court if it finds that a particular law is not in keeping with the Constitution.

The Constitution cannot be changed without a referendum, when Irish citizens have the opportunity to vote on whether or not the change should be approved. People have to register to vote and be over eighteen. Unfortunately, many people don't bother voting, which leads to fewer people making decisions that affect everyone. A change to the Constitution is called an amendment. It is very interesting to look at the different amendments over the years as they very often reflect changes in the moral outlook of the people.

Glossary

Constitution
The basic law of Ireland; any laws passed by the Oireachtas must agree with the principles in the Constitution.

When was this written? Was Ireland very different then?

Did you know?

The vote to adopt the Constitution was passed in 1937 by a majority of 158,160. The votes in favour were 685,105 and against were 526,945.

Amendments to the Irish Constitution

Many of the changes to the Constitution had to take place because of Ireland's relationship with the European Union. The first of these was enacted on 8 June 1972 and allowed the State to become a member of the European Economic Community.

Examples of other amendments include:

- The 5th Amendment, 5 January 1973: removed the special position of the Roman Catholic Church and recognition of other named religious denominations.

Does being part of the EU influence ideas of morality? Why?

345

- The 15th Amendment, 17 June 1996: provided for the dissolution of marriage in certain specified circumstances.
- The 21st Amendment, 27 March 2002: prohibited the death penalty.

Over to You

1. How important is the Constitution for protecting citizen's rights?
2. Does the Constitution influence people's ideas of right and wrong?
3. How can the Constitution be changed?
4. List three changes made to the Constitution and say when they occurred.
5. Why do you think the changes you listed were made to the Irish Constitution?

Religious understandings – fundamentalism

To say something is fundamental is to view it as being of the utmost importance. Of course, religion is fundamental for many people. It is a source of guidance, morality, meaning and value in life. It gives people a sense of community, belonging and purpose. Having the view that something is fundamental to your own life is perfectly acceptable, and not everyone who considers their religious beliefs to be of fundamental importance is necessarily a religious fundamentalist.

Glossary

Religious fundamentalism
A form of religion that upholds belief in the strict and literal interpretation of scripture or tradition, and sees this interpretation as the only valid one.

Religious fundamentalism involves a very strict following of one's own religion. It usually only allows a very narrow interpretation of the sacred writings of that religion. The difficulty that arises with religious fundamentalism is how people see viewpoints or beliefs other than their own. With most religious fundamentalism, there is little or no scope for seeing truth or value in religious perspectives other than one's own. As religious fundamentalists believe that their viewpoint is the only valid one; they believe it should apply to everyone. Sometimes this takes the form of wanting their beliefs to be applied by the laws of the state they live in. In some countries, religious fundamentalist groups may be quite large and influential. Below are two types of religious fundamentalism.

Modern Christian fundamentalism: This type of fundamentalism began in America in the nineteenth century. In many ways, it was a reaction to liberalism, which was seen to reject many traditional beliefs and to promote individual freedom.

Fundamentalist Christian Churches teach that creation took place in seven days and argue that no other version of the beginning of the world is valid.

Islamic fundamentalism: First appearing in the eighteenth and nineteenth centuries, it asserts that Islam is central to both state and society, and advocates strict following of the Qur'an and of Islamic law (*sharia*). Islamic fundamentalists believe that women must never be seen in public with their face uncovered. They would wish to apply this rule to all women who live in the state, regardless of a woman's own wishes or beliefs.

Sharia law is a body of law for the Muslim community that is derived from the Qur'an and the *sunnah* (the example of the Prophet Mohammad). It is regarded as divinely authoritative. Some Islamic fundamentalists would want this to be the law applied to the state and to impose it on all who live in it.

Discuss What problems might arise from having sharia law as state law?

> **Libertarianism** *Glossary*
> The belief that people should be free to do what they like, as long as it doesn't affect other people's freedom.

The idea of *libertarianism* is, in many ways, a reaction to strict religious practice or fundamentalist belief systems. Most people, including many members of religious communities, value freedom, but they do not express it in libertarian terms. After all, with freedom comes responsibility and even the libertarian viewpoint acknowledges the need to respect another person's freedom. The idea that one is free to do what one likes in relation to any moral issue comes back to the consideration of choice and consequence. Making moral decisions will be shaped by many factors and the libertarian position is another viewpoint to consider.

Religious understandings – pluralism

> **Pluralism** *Glossary*
> The belief that truth or truths may be found in more than one religious or non-religious viewpoint. A pluralist recognises that there is a place for more than one outlook in society.

In many ways, pluralism is about tolerance and inclusion. Pluralism rejects the idea that one absolute belief, outlook or opinion is right and, therefore, others are wrong. Pluralists can accept that there is value in traditions other than their own. While their own beliefs may be important and strongly held, they do not negate the importance of other belief systems and may look to see what can be learned from them. Pluralism often involves trying to understand different religious traditions and world views.

Pluralism is about how individuals and their communities interpret the beliefs they hold and the relationships they have with others in society. A person can be a pluralist and be a Catholic, a Protestant, a Jew, a Muslim, a Buddhist or a Hindu. At the same time, of course, not all people in the many different religions are pluralists.

Over to You

1. What is religious fundamentalism? Give examples.
2. What is the source of morality for sharia law?
3. What does it mean to say something is infallible?
4. Describe pluralism.
5. Contrast a pluralist with a fundamentalist outlook on religious beliefs.

If you go back to the beginning of this textbook, it was noted that worldwide there are hundreds of religions. The biggest ones are Christianity, Islam, Judaism, Hinduism and Buddhism. Within each of these, there are also many branches, denominations or groups. There are many others, including Sikhism, Baha'i, Zoroastrianism, Candomblé, Unitarianism, Jainism, Taoism, Confucianism and Shinto, to name but a few.

Over the course of this book, you will have seen how religion is about many different things and means different things to different people. Hopefully, by studying Junior Certificate Religion, you will have gained a greater understanding of one of the biggest phenomena in the world and an appreciation of different cultures and world views. All that is required to benefit from this study is an open mind and an inquisitive nature.

Key Terms

civil law, Constitution, religious fundamentalism, libertarianism, pluralism

Chapter Questions

1. What does civil law refer to?
2. When was the Irish Constitution enacted?
3. How does a pluralist view other religious beliefs?
4. What does religious fundamentalism mean?
5. Define libertarianism.
6. Write about law as a source of morality.

Exam Practice

Higher Level 2011: Section 5, question 6
Compare how the relationship between a country's law and religion is seen from **each** of the following points of view:
Libertarianism/Religious fundamentalism

Higher Level 2007: Section 4, question 6
Tick **one** of the following and outline how it sees the relationship between a country's law and a religion:
Pluralism/Religious Fundamentalism

Mini-Project

Research the Irish Constitution, finding out what it says on matters of personal rights, education and religion. Investigate how many amendments have been made to it. Find out what the most recent amendment was about.

Useful Websites for Section F: The Moral Challenge

For this section of the course, the aims are to explore the human need to order relationships at the personal, communal and global levels, to explore how this need can be expressed in a variety of ways and to identify how this need is expressed in civil and other legal codes, to show how religious belief is expressed in particular moral visions, to explore the moral visions of two major world religions, one of which should be Christianity, and to analyse the impact of these visions on the lives of believers and non-believers in considering some current moral issues.

A further aim for Higher Level is to introduce students to some aspects of the relationship between religion, morality and state law.

To find out more about many of the topics looked at in this section of the course the following may be useful:

www.scoilnet.ie – this portal has useful links for information on morality.

Chapter 26

www.amnesty.ie
www.un.org/en/

Chapter 27

To find out more about the moral vision of founders of the major world religions and to see a religion's views on a range of ethical or moral issues go to:

www.bbc.co.uk/religion/religions/

Organisations inspired by a moral vision for the world:

www.svp.ie
www.trocaire.org
www.islamicaid.com

Chapter 28

To research more on the following prisoners of conscience:

Aung San Suu Kyi – *www.burmacampaign.org.uk*

Nelson Mandela – *www.nobelprize.org*

Dietrich Bonhoeffer – *www.ushmm.org/museum/exhibit/online/bonhoeffer*

Chapter 29

www.christianaid.ie

www.ecocongregationireland.com

www.arcworld.org

www.plumvillage.org

Chapter 30

www.constitution.ie

The suggested DVDs below are worth looking at for the following topics:

Sophie Scholl: The Final Days is extremely interesting for a discussion on when state law and personality conflict. It is also useful for talking about choice and moral maturity.

The Grave of the Fireflies, a Japanese animated movie, is a very moving film about the consequences of war for ordinary people and how innocent people suffer in wars.

Amazing Grace, the story of William Wilberforce, is an excellent film, dealing with the campaign to end slavery in Britain. It is also good as a starting point for talking about a moral vision and the influence of belief on behaviour.

The Journal Work: Tips and Pitfalls

31

The Junior Certificate exam in Religion requires all students to write a journal.

The journal is like a project and students are asked either to do it on their own or as part of a group. Your teacher will usually have the list of titles during the second year of the Junior Certificate course. The titles may be given as something to be worked on for a period of time, perhaps a term or maybe a year.

The aim of the journal work is:

- To facilitate a variety of teaching and learning methods.
- To promote the development of skills in research, analysis, drawing conclusions, presentation etc.
- To afford the students the opportunity to encounter religion as part of life and facilitate the exploration of an area of personal interest or concern to the student.

> **Marks for the exam and journal work**
>
> Final written examination: 75% Ordinary Level or 80% Higher Level
>
> Journal: 25% Ordinary Level or 20% Higher Level

The twelve titles cover the six sections of the syllabus. There are two titles for each section. The following are general points that may be useful when doing the journal.

Section A, Communities of Faith: The two titles are generally, but not always, more about local than international communities. The title may be something like: 'Write about the work done by a community of faith in Ireland today' or 'Find out what inspires the work of a community'. Talking to a member of the community of faith you are studying would be useful when doing this.

Section B, Foundations of Religion – Christianity: The titles will be about Christianity. The journal is often about researching the Bible and an aspect of Jesus' teaching or life. When doing journal work, students should be careful that sources are reliable. Check information against more than one source to be sure. It is usually a good idea to read the Bible yourself and not just rely on books that tell you what it says or is about.

Section C, Foundations of Religion – Major World Religions: The journal work title will be on one of the major world religions, i.e. Hinduism, Judaism, Buddhism or Islam. Make sure not to work on Christianity or any other religion for this study. The title may be about the founder, a place of worship, a ritual etc. Check whether it is asking you to look at one or more of something. The title is usually specific about this. For example, 'Research *one* ritual associated with' indicates the study is on *one* only. While other rituals may be used for background information, they should not be the focus of the study.

Section D, The Question of Faith: The journal work may involve research carried out through a survey or interview. It may be on attitudes to faith or questions of belief and meaning. It can involve differences between ages, e.g. the image of God people of mature faith have compared with the image of God that young people have. When doing a survey you should remember that the most important thing is to ask the right questions. Spend time on constructing questions that will give you useful information.

Section E, The Celebration of Faith: The title will cover all major religions. including Christianity. The title may ask you to research a time of significance, symbols or practices in any one of the many communities of faith. As in Section C, be careful to check whether you need to examine more than one thing. For example, a title like 'Research the meaning of two symbols used in Baptism' is asking for two symbols, therefore *two* must be examined and explained. Other symbols can be studied but should not be the focus of your journal.

Section F, The Moral Challenge: The title may well involve students reflecting on their own thoughts and considering what influences behaviour and attitudes. This may again involve a survey or interview. When your interview or survey is complete, it is important not just to record the results but also to write up your conclusions based on this information.

Important points when preparing your journal work

- Be very careful to understand everything that the title is asking.
- If working as a group or with another person, divide up tasks evenly.
- Keep a list of sources used as you use them.

- Write out any thoughts as you have them.
- Go back to the title to check you are keeping to what it asks.

Important points when writing up the journal work booklet

- Don't include names of people, your own included, on your journal.
- You can draw pictures or diagrams on your booklet but you cannot attach things to it, as they may fall out.
- Be careful to write your Junior Certificate exam number on the front.
- Indicate whether you did the work alone or in a group.

When doing the journal work, you will use and develop different skills and when writing out your journal work booklet, you will be asked about two of the skills you have used. Here is what is involved in using the skills listed:

Enquiry skills: Enquiring about things, people and organisations.

Observational skills: Observing something and interpreting, expressing and recording what you see.

Problem-solving skills: Seeing the problems when undertaking tasks or activities and deciding on solutions to the problems.

Research skills: Finding, recording, analysing and using appropriate research material.

Reflective skills: Reflecting on (thinking about) findings or observations.

Organisational skills: Organising your time and skills, and planning, managing and completing tasks.

Evaluation skills: Being able to decide the usefulness of information, examining and judging carefully what is researched.

Writing up the journal work booklet

The booklet is sent to schools to be filled out by all students before the exam. A date for submission is given and students must meet this deadline.

The booklet has five sections and each section has a list of questions along the side to help you when writing it up. Not all these questions have to be answered, but they are useful as a guide to what the section is asking you to write about.

Section 1, Introduction: The first page asks for the title you have chosen. Put in the full title from the list here. Then you must write in your own title. Don't just repeat the title from the list. Put in your own words what the title is about. Next you are asked about why you chose this title – what was it that made you choose to do this instead of one of the others.

Section 2, Getting started: In this section you outline how you went about planning and organising the work involved. It can include plans to visit the library, research on the internet, speak to people, visit a place of worship, interview someone, write a survey or how you set about dividing tasks. Detail what you planned to do. Sometimes students find some things they plan to do are not feasible. For example, it may not be possible to speak to a Buddhist monk or visit a mosque, but you can still say that you planned to and later on you will have the opportunity to mention that this was a problem and how you managed to overcome it.

Section 3, Work: Here you write about what you actually did when doing your journal work. This section can outline all the tasks you did. If you were working in a group, explain what each person did. Write out sources you used, places you went to, how you obtained any information, what you observed, what you researched etc. Explain why you chose to do the journal in this way, and why your particular title suited the approach you took. You are also asked to detail one thing you did or included and say why. Choose an activity or something you included in the journal work that was of particular importance and relevance to what you were trying to do and explain it in detail. You are also asked to give your reaction to what you did or found out. If you are working with others you can explain how your reactions were similar or different. Don't worry, your reactions don't have to be amazing, but they should be relevant to the title.

Section 4, Discoveries: This is the section where students have the opportunity to detail findings. There isn't a huge amount of space for putting down what you found out, so keep to very important details and especially to what is relevant to the title. For example, if you are writing about the historical origins of Buddhism, during the course of doing the journal you may have found out much more than the origins. When writing up the journal, however, it is best to keep the information to what was asked.

In this section, you are asked for reflection, to give a reaction to what you discovered. Did it surprise you? Was it interesting? Would you say you understand something better? Your thoughts and understanding may not be much different from before and that is okay. Simply say what you think about what you discovered. Not everyone has the same reaction. Your own is as important as anyone else's. By doing the journal, you should hopefully have learnt something and you should say so.

This section also asks about skills you used doing the journal. Choose two and explain how you used them. Most people will have used research skills, looking up information in books or the internet, or going to the library. You will also have had to organise yourself, your time, what you found out and how to do the journal. There may be a problem you had to deal with. For example, if there was a lack of information on something or the information didn't agree, explain what the problem was and show how you overcame it.

This section also asks you to show how your journal relates to themes on the Junior Certificate course in general. The important thing to remember is that it has to relate to the RE course, not to other subjects like history or geography, although they may well relate to what you studied. The course has a wide range of topics and themes so it shouldn't be too hard to find at least two that you can relate it to. It can be something really obvious or something much more subtle. As long as you explain the relationship, it doesn't matter whether or not it is obvious.

Section 5, Advice: When you have completed the journal, you have already achieved something. Now you have the opportunity to reflect on what you did and to highlight your journal work's strengths and possible weaknesses. Here you can mention how some things you may have planned to do couldn't happen or how you overcame difficulties along the way. You have had the experience of finishing the journal and so you can advise others on what went well or not so well and how things could have been improved. Again be careful to refer back to the title and explain whether your final journal fulfilled what the title asked.

Using the internet

One of the most useful sources of information today is the internet. However, it is very important to be careful when using it. You can very easily come across websites that are inaccurate or ones that deliberately want to give false information. People have very strongly held beliefs about religion and they sometimes base information about their own community of faith or other religions not on facts but on their own opinions. You should always try to obtain information from several sources so that you can be more certain that it is accurate. If you can, find out who is responsible for the website and what it is set up to do. This may help you decide if it is trustworthy.

Finally ...

The journal is aimed at giving students the opportunity to realise that religion is a part of life and to explore an area of personal interest. It aims to develop skills and to give an opportunity for reflection. The journal is not just about finding out lots of information, so when you are completing it try to write more on what you think than just about what you find out. Always put in something of your own thoughts and not only the facts.

Best of luck with the journal work and just try to make the most of the opportunity to learn more about something!